Leadership Alchemy:
The Magic of the Leader Coach

The Leaders Coaching Leaders Series

Leadership Alchemy:
The Magic of The Leader Coach

Susan Wright and Carol MacKinnon

TCP Publications
A Division of The Coaching Project Inc.

Toronto   Phoenix   Vancouver

The Coaching Project Publications
Toronto, Phoenix, Vancouver

www.thecoachingproject.com
1-800-350-5536

ISBN 0-9733260-0-X

National Library of Canada Cataloguing in Publication

Wright, Susan, 1946-
    Leadership alchemy : the magic of the leader coach/
Susan Wright, Carol MacKinnon.

ISBN 0-9733260-0-X

    1. Leadership. I. MacKinnon, Carol, 1951- II. Title.

HD57.7.W74 2003   658.4   C2003-903229-9

Editing	Sue Ritchie, Bowen Island
Cover design	Merkley Designs, Toronto
Indexing	Lari Langford, Toronto

Printed in the United States of America
West Group Publishing, Egan MN

Contents

Preface

We are aware, as we invite you to join us on this journey, that this book is different. It is a textbook based on rigorous research and validated ideas. It is also a workbook for skill development. And it is more. It is a place in which you can track your own development as you explore with us the concepts we present. It is a place where you can learn new processes and immediately practice them in your own context. It contains ideas that are in the incubation stage and require your involvement and engagement to help them hatch. And this book is different in that it has the active presence of the authors, as people, running throughout the book. We talk with you rather than at you and invite you into a dialogue with us both in the book and beyond it.

We bring to the book our more than twenty years each of experience as business leaders. We have worked in and with a wide variety of companies in different industries as executives ourselves and as advisors to them. We have also been students, teachers, coaches and presidents of our own companies. We are currently faculty members in an innovative MBA program where we work with these ideas with committed and curious adult learners. And we are searchers for some new ways of being both in the work world and the broader community. We bring all of these considerations to the writing of this book. And rather than hide discretely behind the anonymous 'we', we have chosen to tell you more about ourselves than you might find on the back of the book jacket.

We also know that, despite a century of advancement, it is less common for women to teach in a business school, for women to be authors of a book on leadership or coaching, and for women to be leaders in organizations. While there are sectors where women predominate, there is still emerging the sense of a feminized style of leadership. We believe that this alchemic mixture of leadership and coaching is reflective of that style. So we are women writing about and practicing leadership coaching.

We have written this book together because we share a passion for growing leaders for the hyperturbulence of the twenty first century. We share a common philosophy and point of view that a new kind of leader is needed and that there is a way to develop these leaders. We also come to the question from different perspectives and different backgrounds and we have added some of our individual reflections and moments of awareness as well. So this is our story. It is a culmination of two women leaders' lifetimes of experience. And we therefore need to present ourselves to you.

We first worked together almost twenty years ago in a large Canadian insurance company. Susan was in Organization Development and Carol was in Compensation, both functions within a large and advanced human resource division. We connected there and have worked together in a variety of contexts since. Most recently, we have developed and delivered business school programs in leadership and coaching and inaugurated a three-month leadership coaching development program in partnership with the Niagara Institute/Conference Board in Canada. In the intervening two decades, though, we've had dramatically different lives despite the common themes.

Susan is essentially a designer – of everything from clothes to interiors to lifestyles and organizations. She has spent her career as a change agent, challenging the system, seeking design strategies for more democratic forms of organization. She studied and worked with Eric Trist in the early '80s and has since applied his socio-ecological ideas both as an internal executive in large corporations and as an external consultant on social and organizational change. He described her as having a "great capacity for joy". Having worked for fifteen years on large scale strategic change projects, Susan shifted gears six years ago to work with individuals and teams as an executive coach, to support the design of their meaningful work and leisure lives. She began The Coaching Project with two colleagues. This coincided with her shift to working and living part time in Phoenix with her new life partner, designing a unique cross-border lifestyle.

Susan is a middle child, a rebel from a very early age, with a persistent drive to do things another way…to change the status quo. She has often found herself breaking new ground – as a young working mother, as the first woman in teams of men, as a part-time executive balancing work and leisure, as an adult learner wanting non-traditional education. This gritty determination may stem from watching her artist mother struggle to find life purpose when the work world was denied her, and her railroader father find joy and satisfaction in keeping the trains on the tracks and on time. It was easy to see which life she was destined for, and which she would prefer.

Susan has always been a teacher and a learner. She began teaching art classes with her mother as a teen, became a professional designer and taught design while she was in graduate school, became an organization development specialist and taught management programs while completing her doctorate in leadership. She has been a Program Director for five years at The Hudson Institute, a premier coach education school in the US, where she completed her own professional coach education. Susan's calling is to engage others in purposeful play to stimulate their, and her, learning and growth.

Carol is passionately interested in and committed to the possibility of adults exercising choice in their lives, to find their unique paths and callings. This is likely due to two major drivers: her experience growing up in a family where work was no source of joy, but rather a source of anguish and anomie. The other was her own work life, and particularly her battle with the power of that legitimate addiction, work-aholism. Having consulted and led consulting teams in an unhealthy way, she is now very aware of how much richer life is, when it is lived in a balanced and integrated way. This healthy way serves the organization, the community and her clients as much as herself.

Her life today is back full circle, to the West Coast, to much of the day spent in nature, to a life full of music-making and singing, and the joys of discovery. Her forays into the business and academic worlds are enriched by this counterpoint of working and living fully in the moment.

Whether working through coaching relationships, teaching MBA students, consulting to leadership teams, or holding workshops for women interested in transformation, Carol works with the intent to provide the container for transformation. She has experienced the power of transformation in her own life, and is conscious of the opportunity and responsibility to be a role model for a different way of being. Her stories focus on her dawning awareness of how this leadership alchemy needs to be embodied, and how a coaching approach transforms the managerial and leadership role.

So, that's who we are, and why we've written this book. We are more IN this book than on it, more in conversation with you than in a monologue. We are curious about your responses to these ideas, and are serious in stating that the book is incomplete without you. You will change these ideas by your interaction with them, and your embodiment of them.

Susan Wright
Carol MacKinnon

Dedication

This book is dedicated to the contributions of our students and teachers, our families and friends, our colleagues and clients, both those we know and those we have yet to meet.

List of Illustrations

Prologue

A Fable

> "In the crescent moon furnace, jade flowers grow;
> in the cinnabar crucible, quicksilver is level.
> Only after harmonization by means of great strength
> can you plant the yellow sprout, which gradually develops."

Whatever did that mean, she wondered. It was found in the old library of the great manor house in which her ancestor Isaac Newton had practiced alchemy experiments. Even the explanation that followed seemed mysterious: "encouragement for the practice whereby one places great effort into cultivating a still mind so that real knowledge, the awareness of things as they really are, can arise in the mind of Tao ('the real mind'). One nurtures this process with sincere intent."[1]

She had been surprised and delighted to discover she was a direct descendant of Isaac Newton, and even more delighted to be the one to discover his writings, hidden away in the library of an English country house, for more than two hundred years. It seemed a tremendous responsibility to honor his memory and contribution, to be not the 'keeper of his secrets' but to share his writings on Alchemy. Isaac Newton was a perfect representative of the Renaissance Man, both a scientist/mathematician and an alchemist. Alchemists strove to transform base metals into gold and silver and in melting down the gold, to create an elixir of eternal life. Newton, the founder of modern science, was also one of the greatest spiritual alchemists of all time, though this knowledge of him had been suppressed for centuries.

What was Alchemy, anyway? Images of stars on pointy sorcerers' hats, of cauldrons bubbling with potions, of searchers desperately seeking the key to eternal life and immense wealth…

The Greeks held the alchemic belief that all things are composed of air, earth, fire and water. Alchemy traces its roots to the Hellenistic period of Egypt and particularly Alexandria[2]. From Alexandria was it – or another case of spontaneous discovery - Alchemy was developing in China, and perhaps became the source for the Taoist writings she'd found in Newton's diary. In Arabia's School of Pharmacy, the oldest book on Chemistry, the "Summit of Perfection", was published. For alchemists believed the Aristotelian doctrine that all things reach perfection with the application of both skill and diligence. Indeed, they imagined there was an element more perfect than gold, the Philosopher's Stone, the universal medicine, the source element. While alchemists experimented and sought the means to transmute one thing into another, in their "blind gropings" they discovered many useful processes. So alchemists were experimenters, in the laboratory, mixing different elements, continually striving, persisting, believing in the potential, the possibility of creating gold. They were seekers, searchers, explorers, learners and teachers. They were seen as sages, as spiritual guides, as mystics, as dealers in destiny, symbols and dreams.

And yet, from the beginning, what had started as the art of transformation, base metals into gold, mortal into eternal life, quickly became associated with a darker, more dangerous side. It seems that there was the potential for abuse of power in Alchemy. What had fired the imagination seemed to be stoked by avarice. What had started as a science and an art had, by the fourth century, been labeled astrology, ritual and magic. The Greeks banned books on Alchemy. It was suppressed and the alchemists marginalized and vilified. And now, with the alchemic writings of Newton rediscovered, there was a chance to recast Alchemy, to alchemize…to create a new blend, a mixture tested in the fire.[3]

What were the lessons from this ancestor of hers? What could she carry forth into the twenty-first century? What lessons did her alchemical relative teach? And how could she, herself, transmute those teachings to apply to a world so different from that of a Renaissance Man? Surprisingly, the lessons of alchemy are powerfully appropriate for leading in the twenty-first century.

The first was probably to acknowledge and celebrate that she **was** a woman and that leading as a woman might mean some new and different things. She was happy in the notion of inclusion, of the mixing together of elements and attributes that might create something new and precious. She was keen to explore the idea of searching for something magical, something which would require diligence, commitment, a pure intent. Alchemy is about an art you practice, and a science with which you experiment. Its goal is ultimate meaning, happiness, pursuing the purpose of creation. It's about a journey of discovery, sometimes uncovering not what we set out to do or see but what we unearth along the way…

She was ready to begin.

EndNotes:

[1] See Chang, Po-tuan. "Understanding Reality", in *The Taoist Classics.* Tr. Thomas Cleary. Shambala. 1999.

[2] That same city where Lawrence Durrell would present the Alexandria Quartet view of four people: Justine, Cleo, Mountolive and Balthazar, four people's perspective on one story, two thousand years later.

3 See F.E. Manuel. *The Religion of Isaac Newton.* Oxford University Press, 1974.

Introduction

To be an effective leader, one must be an effective coach. That is the foundation of the book. It sounds simple and obvious but has profound implications. For the way we work, the way we behave, the priorities we set, the results we get, the way we relate to others.

Our case for stating that they are interdependent processes comes from our work as coaches and our experience as leaders. For example, in a recent client assignment where Susan[1] was asked to compare a global corporation's standards of leadership competency to those required for coaching, the needed skills were more than 75 percent the same. This is typical of our findings in our leadership development practice – to be an effective leader, one must be an effective coach.

Leadership Coaching is therefore "*both/and*" – both leadership and coaching. And the book is about the need, concepts and applications of *both/and* principles in organizations today. It is about *being* a leadership coach.

And it is also more. We believe these principles have magic in them. Magic to transform the way we see ourselves as leaders and the way we then lead with others. This is the alchemy. Taking both leadership and coaching into the alchemic chamber and transforming them from concepts in everyday use, like the base metals of the ancient chemists, into something more complete, more valuable, like the mysterious emergence of gold. A leadership alchemy.

And we consciously choose the metaphor of alchemy – the elusive quest to transform the ordinary into the precious – because we know we describe here an ideal, a magical formula that we may aspire to, sometimes sense we have a partial grasp of...but which we suspect may be as difficult to achieve and sustain as discovering how to make gold. Rather, we are in a constant state of learning, of experimenting, of searching for the magic mix that will be ME, leader and coach, here and now.

Why Now?

Coaching has become a leadership style. It is no longer only for psychologists, trainers or organizational development professionals who come in from the outside - coaching is now something that is done by managers at all levels. Coaching is being recognized as a significant part of leadership, demanding a range of skills that managers have to develop. Companies are developing "coaching cultures" where leaders are responsible for coaching their teams, their colleagues, even their bosses. Coaching is the way leaders lead for high performance.

Coaching is fundamental to change leadership. Organizations are hungry for concepts and applications to help them with continuous change and its impact on people and productivity. Coaching is a profession born of change, embracing change and providing skills for dealing with change effectively.

Current leadership literature is recognizing the need for growing the leader from the inside out - building character, self-awareness, courage. These competencies are critical for the leader in change and central to the self-understanding that is the essence of a good coach. Leaders need to know who they are before they can successfully lead others.

There is a need for books on the integration of these two topics – leadership and coaching. How does coaching fit into leadership? How do leaders apply coaching in their role? There are many books on *either* leadership *or* coaching. The need is for "both/and" – *both* a theoretical underpinning *and* its application – so that leaders understand the basis for integrating the ideas, and can apply the concepts in their everyday leadership in organizational settings.

There are many basic coaching books for managers – how to's, skills development, step by step procedures. However, there is a need for a more advanced treatment of leadership coaching, one that appeals to leaders who want to grow personally and organizationally, one that provokes deeper thought and challenges assumptions about the leadership role in turbulent times.

The current ethical crisis in business and particularly in leadership means that a values-based definition and practice of leadership is especially important for practitioners and students of leadership now.

Intentions

With this book, our intention is to challenge you. We have challenged ourselves in thinking about what leadership really means in today's realities. We have stretched our thinking and played with it. And we would like to invite you to join us in this process.

We have approached the book a bit differently as a result. For example, it is a hybrid, a blend of a more academic treatment with a popular style - we use theories, models, history and references to underpin our ideas, and we also write in a conversational tone, avoiding the passive objective stance. We are ourselves both academics and business leaders and practitioners.

Another related example is our goal of incorporating ourselves into the book, as well as our perspectives and ideas – we tell our own stories, in our own voices, so you can get to know us as individuals as part of our principle of modeling our espoused values. We write from who we are. A third example is that we have tried to extend beyond the mind, the usual thinking dimension, to include other aspects of the self – body, heart and spirit – because we believe the ideas are richer, the learning deeper, if we encounter ourselves in all our complexity. We have therefore included poetry, fables, metaphors and stories.

So we will explore *both/and* models to structure your thinking about leadership coaching. For example:
-   Both theory and its application
-   Both personal and organizational levels
-   Both your understanding and your ongoing development.

Think of a kaleidoscope. When we are describing the application of a theory at the organizational level, for instance, a pattern emerges, a sense of the parts that comprise the whole. When we then tell a story as an example, you have a new perspective, the new pattern establishes itself, comprising the same elements but with a different twist! So this is part of our invitation to you, to create your own alchemy. It's in part about the juxtaposition, the interplay between and among the parts. And words or any representation in two dimensions may be flat and less evocative than your own imagination. So twist the kaleidoscope, see the pieces re-assemble themselves in new ways, new pictures…what do they teach you, offer you about leadership coaching?

We also want to journey farther afield to imagine what magic there is in combining leadership and coaching in an alchemic way. How do we transmute the base metals into gold?[2] How do we transform the basic competencies into highly effective leadership? We have used this metaphor to expand our own thinking and want to share this with you. Of course, there is a shadow side to this metaphor, a negative use for the magic. We see this in the world around us – when the principles are the same but they are used for destructive purposes. We make the journey, then, in the need to join with others who seek ways to bring enlightened leadership to balance the shadows.

This is just a beginning. It should be considered a work in progress, a draft, an experiment… It is not neat or easy but it is, like we are, in a process of changing and growing and learning. We are different as authors at the book's completion than we were when we began – we have in a sense been transformed by the writing of it. Our invitation to you is to journey along with us, to join in the co-creative process. We offer several means for you to participate in extending and transforming the ideas with interested others into a more complete picture than we can hope to offer here.

The Framework of the Book

The book is laid out in four parts. **Part One** is the conceptual material where we present the ideas we will be working with. We look back in order to look forward, taking an evolutionary approach to leadership and coaching and bringing us to our concept of *both/and* leadership and its relevance today. We then ask the stretch questions about where this blending of concepts could take us if we put the magic of alchemy to work.

Chapter 1 considers the evolution of leadership ideas. How has the thinking about leadership changed over the years? We introduce four competency clusters we believe represent current leadership requirements. Our view is that our mental models are still based on outmoded views of leadership that must change to cope with the turbulent contexts in which we function. One of these outmoded models is the either/or way of thinking that seeks right or wrong, yes or no, answers in a world much too complex for these simple distinctions. We make the case for *both/and* thinking as the mental framework we must adopt to be successful now and tomorrow.

Chapter 2 looks at the evolution of coaching in organizational settings, taking the position that coaching is essentially applied leadership. It is the way effective leaders lead. There has been exponential growth in the coaching field in the last decade and we will outline some of the themes emerging from a number of influential authors. One of the central themes is the realization that in order to build trust in the coaching relationship, we need to understand ourselves and be authentic in our expression of who we are. We coach from who we are. We can't hide for long behind our personas without giving ourselves away. This is of course true for leadership as well. Understanding the self is the prerequisite for understanding, and leading, others.

Chapter 3 reaches the heart of the matter. It takes both leadership and coaching, adds heat, and transforms our leadership thinking one step further. What will have to happen for organizational leadership to be effective in dealing with hyper-turbulence? We revisit our four competency clusters from Chapter 1 and present a transmutation of each, alchemic outcomes suitable to possible futures. We suggest that we co-create visions of desired futures that we then carry as "code" to know when it is our right and responsibility to lead and help others to find meaning. In so doing, we find meaning ourselves. We call this alchemic outcome the Leader Coach. We consider this just a beginning – it needs input, refinement and diverse perspectives. Meaning can only truly come from relationships with you, the reader.

In **Part Two**, we move from concepts to contexts, the domains in which the Leadership Coach practices. The first is the inside-out context of the inner self, the place where the learning journey of the Leadership Coach begins. Who am I as a leader? How do I express my self as a leader? How can I get in my own way as a leader? The second is the outside-in context of meeting the change needs of others as they seek our leadership. Where can I best practice my leadership? What circumstances require my leadership attention? How can I serve?

Chapter 4 discusses what Leadership Coaches need to be successful and particularly explores the inner terrain of the self. Our position is that many leaders have significantly underdeveloped senses of self, and that this causes immeasurable damage in organizational life. When we think of context, we tend to think outside ourselves, but perhaps the most complex and interesting context is the inner domain of the self. We believe the biggest change needed in leadership development is refocusing on this neglected inner context.

Chapter 5 explores the shadow side of these competencies, which if unexplored and ignored can block our growth and contribution as Leader Coaches. If understood and incorporated, the shadow can increase our self-awareness and compassion for both others and ourselves. The shadow can be the block or the bridge to insight for the Leader Coach.

Chapter 6 moves to the more traditional leadership contexts, looking at the practice of the Leader Coach in organizational settings. Both leadership and coaching are born of change and change is the basis for their practice. We present a map of leadership at varying scales – the individual, the team, and the organization as a whole. We also look at the depth of Leader Coach relationships at each of these scales – from transactional to transformational. We provide examples of each of these contexts and the particular competencies that are required to practice them successfully.

In **Part Three** we discuss leadership coaching as a process, outlining the stages in the relationship and highlighting the roles and responsibilities of the Leadership Coach in each stage. Because major change is so much a part of our lives as leaders, we include a chapter on the role of the Leadership Coach in major change and give examples of how the role plays out.

Chapter 7 introduces the stages in the leadership coaching process as an example of the application of the holographic metaphor presented in Chapter 3. We believe there are three fairly distinct phases in any coaching relationship, that is, the overall view of what the process will look like and what the requirements are for it to be successful. Within each of the stages, too, we believe these same three distinctions can also be made. And again, within each meeting or interaction, the same is true. So the whole process is replicated in each of the stages of the relationship to give it a constancy, a robustness that contributes to transformational change.

Chapter 8 describes a case of major change – an acquisition, change of CEO, and market re-alignment - and outlines the role of an evolving Leader Coach in generating positive outcomes. Organizations have become so fluid with regard to whole-scale change that any leadership concept must address this fact of organizational life. The chapter uses this case to provide a fuller analysis of the concepts, contexts and processes presented in the book and how they might be adopted as an effective change leadership framework.

Finally, in **Part Four** we close the book with an invitation to you to join our community by participating in a variety of ways in the ongoing development of the ideas and practices, in the co-creative process.

How to Use the Book

In the earlier chapters we have presented the concepts and the applications follow. Depending on your interests, you can dig in anywhere. One of our alchemic principles is the hologram, a form of photography where the whole picture can be reproduced by shining light onto any of its parts. So each of the chapters in the book has the core of our message in it - wherever you shine the light, you will get the sense of the whole.

To balance the conceptual thinking, each chapter has:
- At least one personal story
- A model, framework or drawing to graphically demonstrate ideas
- A personal reflection for you
- An exercise you do with someone else
- An exercise you do with your team or work group
- A self assessment tool

When you've finished, our intention is that you will have some new understanding of yourself in relation to leadership coaching and some new skills that you can continue to develop as you practice. You may also want to use parts of the book in your own leadership coaching. It is full of useful tools, questions, quotes and stories to enhance your practice of leadership coaching with your clients[3], your teams and your organizations.

It is our hope that you may want to join the community of those who are interested in further developing the ideas, co-creating something of greater value to us all.

The Role of the Four Box Model

We will use a number of four-box models throughout the book. The reason is that they are a wonderful way to look at "*both/and*" alternatives to our usual "either/or" way of thinking. We are all guilty of imagining things are either one way or another – true or false, right or wrong. This is not surprising given the way most of us have been raised and educated. But it is a dangerous way of being in a world that is complex, chaotic, and multi-dimensional.

Others

Coach Leader[3] Practice	Team Building
Personal Reflection	Feedback

Self

Self   **Others**

Figure 1: A Model Relating Self and Other

So we are suggesting that we change our frame of reference to thinking in *both/and* terms. Here is a simple example using **Self** and **Other** as the two concepts, set out along each axis in the model. In addition to looking at self and other, we want to highlight the both/and dimension of the relationships *between* self and other. Let's use this model as a way of describing some of the options available for building your competencies through practice.

If we look at the bottom left box, we see the **Self in relation to the Self**. Here, the development opportunity is to use the book as a catalyst to spark self reflection. What questions come to mind as you read? What insights does the book kindle in you? What are you curious about? How does this fit with your own experience? These are the kinds of questions we will be asking at the end of each chapter to provoke your self reflective learning.

If we look at the top left box, we see the **Self in relation to Others**. Here, the opportunity is to take what you have learned and practice it with someone else. You may have coaching clients[4] that you can work with, a number of individuals who report to you as their Leader Coach. We will give you an exercise in each chapter to practice with someone else. However, we hope that you will extend your practice to all those areas in your life where you are or can be a Coach Leader.

If we now look at the top right box, we see **Others in relation to Others**. Here, you will be facilitating Leader Coach interactions between members of your work group or team. The practice, this time, is at the group level. How can you help others to become Leader Coaches in their interactions? The situation might involve a group of peers, of which you are a member, exploring a problem or setting a strategy. It might be your own direct report team brainstorming ways to improve productivity. It might be the team members coaching each other about specific work-related developmental challenges and opportunities. Each chapter will include an exercise you can do with your team or work group. Ultimately, we hope you will practice in all your group contexts.

Finally, if we look at the bottom right box, we see **Others in relation to the Self.** Here, the opportunity is to hear what others have to say and to incorporate it into your ongoing self-development. Feedback is one of the best ways to learn about yourself. Most of us don't get enough of it. We need to practice asking for it, hearing it without defensiveness, and taking what makes sense and acting on it to improve. We will include in each chapter an assessment you can use with others, and on your own, to compare your own perception of your competencies with those of others who see you in action.

This is the first of several models we will use to describe our *both/and* concepts – in this case, both the self and others in relation to practice opportunities. One of the benefits of these models is that they stretch our thinking to include new perspectives and relationships. We hope that as you move through the book, you may add a few of these models of your own that offer you new insights into your own leadership coaching.

We invite you to create a development plan for yourself, adding elements from the exercises at the end of each chapter, so that when you are finished, you have a plan for developing as an "alchemic leader" yourself. We offer in Appendix I a good development plan template you can use if you wish. The discipline of having a written plan with objectives, activities and timelines adds significantly to your motivation to honor your commitments. However, it is just as important that you find your own developmental style. People often write in a journal about their reflections and use the themes that emerge as development edges to be further explored. Stories and quotes that resonate personally are a great way to collect more information about your development interests. Whatever suits your learning style, this developmental perspective is central to leadership in change.

---

[1] We will tell numerous stories from our own experience through the book. Although we write as a team, using "we", we will identify the storyteller in each case so you, the reader, know whose experience you are reading about and get to know us as individuals as well.

[2] We know that there is a limit to the usefulness of *all* metaphors, and we don't mean to suggest that there is a value judgment of 'baseness' associated either with you or with those you lead – rather we mean base as in the untransformed state.

[3] The term 'client' is often used to describe the person being coached, and that is how we will use the term. The client may be a peer, a direct report, a team, even a boss. The coach may be the team leader, the accountable manager, the peer, etc

Part One – Concepts

The Invitation

We begin with concepts, the ideas that have shaped our understanding of both leadership and coaching. Leadership has had a long and rich history in the world of ideas. Thousands of studies provide a wide variety of perspectives on leadership, including its meaning and philosophy, its themes and elements, its competencies and their application, and its development. Coaching, on the other hand, is new on the scene in the business context, and has been primarily viewed as a skill set enhancing the managerial ability to generate performance. Coaching has also been seen mostly as something delivered by professionals from the outside in, as a "fix-it" for problem cases, or as an adjunct to other leadership development initiatives rather than a significant part of the leadership role. Because of this skill orientation, coaching has not had as much conceptual emphasis. Coaching perspectives, by contrast with those of leadership, have primarily centered on the process, the tools, the required skills, and the different settings in which coaching is practiced.

So our purpose in this first part of the book is to introduce our own perspectives on the evolution of leadership and coaching, and to highlight in particular the important themes in both domains that pertain to our current world of turbulent change. We believe that the central themes in both leadership and coaching are converging as these roles become critically important in responding to the dramatic increase in the pace and scope of organizational change. We focus on competency themes or clusters that are similar in both and discuss why we believe this is so. Beyond the integration of leadership and coaching, we also propose that there is transformative potential in seeing coaching as a way of applying leadership that sparks new ideas about what constitutes effective leading in today's organizations. We have used the metaphor of alchemy to help us stretch and blend and extend the concepts, which we then explore in more detail in the chapters that follow.

Chapter 1 presents a high level overview of the history of leadership ideas and a set of four competency themes that have emerged as a result of the leadership context of turbulent change. We also note the more recent emergence of self-leadership, the need for authentic presence, character and integrity. Chapter 2 surveys five recent works on coaching and draws out their competency themes to provide a conceptual basis for the comparison of coaching and leadership.

In Chapter 3, we bring the two together, with coaching acting as an alchemic catalyst that transforms traditional notions of leadership into something new and desperately needed in the 21st century. We offer four alchemic competency themes that encompass both domains and describe leadership coaching as a way of building results and relationships equal to our current organizational challenges. It is the addition of a coaching perspective to the notion of leadership - bringing together the longer, more conceptual frame of leadership with the newer, more practical frame of coaching – that gives us a different kind of transformative potential to explore in the rest of the book.

The ingredients of our alchemy are therefore the common competency themes, the chalice or container is the organizational context, the fire is hyper-turbulent change, and our quest is to discover the magic emanating from the history of this brew into the dawn of the new century. We recognize the limitations of this metaphor, indeed of any metaphor, but we also understand that we must reach beyond the rational, the logical, the comfortable, the known, if we are to confront the complexity and uncertainty ahead. So at the outset we ask for your indulgence, in some senses to play along, with our imperfect language and metaphors, in the faith that when we are finished, we will have created a worthwhile outcome.

We invite you to join us on this conceptual journey, perhaps into some new territory… to suspend your disbelief temporarily and approach our ideas and your own reactions to them with the curiosity of a learner's mind. Chris Argyris[1] developed a model that is worth recalling here. For each of us, there is a realm of understanding and behavior that is beyond our current competence and that we are unconscious of. We are at the level of "unconscious incompetence" - in other words, we don't know what we don't know. When we are presented with new information, we move from unconscious to "conscious incompetence" – we now know that we don't know.

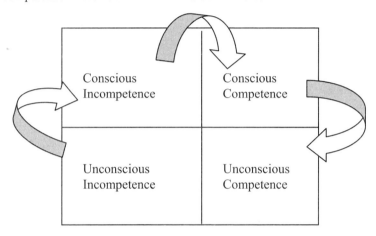

Figure 2: A Model Relating Conscious and Unconscious Competence

Think of learning to ski as an adult. It looks like fun and easy enough, as you watch others gracefully gliding down the hill… until you actually strap on your skis and face the slippery downhill slope. It's awkward, uncomfortable, and much harder than it looks. The same is true of encountering a new idea, or old ideas in a new perspective… and will also be true when you begin to try out your ideas in practice.

As you progress as a learner, you follow the steps carefully, you are fully aware of your performance, or lack of it, and trying to improve. You have reached the level of "conscious competence" – you can get down the slope but you have to remember how to make the turns, talking to yourself, remembering each of the lessons you've learned. Finally, after a period of time, you don't have to think about it so much, you can let go and just let it happen, be in the flow – you have reached the level of "unconscious competence", like the skiers who are effortlessly and rhythmically dancing with the contours of the mountain.

And so it is with the learning journey we hope you are embarking on with us here. There will be some ideas so familiar, you will practice them unconsciously and competently. There may be others that are less familiar and will require you to become aware for a time of how you practice and how competent you actually are. And we hope there will also be some brand new ideas that you haven't thought about before, or thought about in this way, that bring a new consciousness to your thinking about leadership and coaching, and perhaps a desire to build new competency in your role as a Leader Coach in your organization.

---

[1] Argyris, C. and Schon, D. *Organizational Learning: A Theory of Action Perspective.* Addison-Wesley, 1978.

Chapter 1
The Evolution of *Both / And* Leadership

Perhaps the first and most important thing to acknowledge, as we begin to examine the evolution of the concept of leadership, is that there is no consensus, no clear and unequivocal understanding of the critical aspects that distinguish leaders from non-leaders. And indeed, in one sense we will ask you to consider whether *everyone* in the organization is, or has the potential to be, a leader. The debate continues to rage as it has for more than a century – perhaps since the time of Aristotle – as to what makes a leader[1].

While there were some more focused studies in the twentieth century as to what makes a leader, they were mostly fragmented and partial studies that asked as many questions as provided answers. What we present here is a very brief synopsis of the key historical milestones that address the concept of leadership. The review is of course only our subjective assessment of the highlights and we may have omitted a writer or theory that has influenced your own understanding of how concepts of leadership have evolved. The point is to try to paint a picture in broad brush strokes, to provide the foundation for what we are portraying as a different definition of leadership,

A Quick Retrospective

Essentially there are three different theories of leadership and, if you remember nothing else, remember: Fate, Trait, State ...three variants of the "nature versus nurture" debate that has occupied the last century. Fate - that "some are born great"; Trait - that there are certain personalities and behaviors that predetermine your likelihood to be a leader; and State - that the circumstances within which you are placed determine both whether you are a leader and also what kind of leadership is appropriate and successful. These are not mutually exclusive; they all still exist and inform our leadership thinking to some extent. We'll explore each of these in a little more detail.

Fate:

The earliest Western writers suggested that leaders were born, not made….that such "uncontrollables" as birth family and social class preordained that some would be leaders and many others not. This view held sway for much of modern history, through the Reformation, the Victorian era, the First World War, and into the 1930s. Sir Winston Churchill in his autobiography attempts to understand his parents and grandparents in his own search for what made him a leader. Even today, corporate biographies fill bookstore shelves with the lives and times of "great" leaders like Jack Welch of GE.

Trait:

As the shock of the Great Depression seemed to suggest that what had traditionally been sufficient in terms of leadership might not be enough, the research began to examine what common traits might distinguish 'great men'. The "Great Man" theory of history was able to trace large-scale changes back to the whims and decisions of a single, powerful man such as Alexander, Columbus or Napoleon. The research between the 1930s and the 1950s focused on personal and behavioral variables which defined leadership and what made one leader more effective than another. In this era, the research often focused on a list of traits or attributes that were found in leaders. These might include:
– A strong drive for responsibility
– Originality in problem solving
– Self-confidence and a strong sense of personal identity
– Persistence in pursuing goals
– Initiative
– A willingness to accept consequences
– A strong technical knowledge, greater than that of the followers.

From the list of attributes, one might deduce at least two things: if you were an individual seeking to become a leader, or to develop one, these were traits to cultivate. Secondly, if you didn't have these traits, or didn't observe them in someone aspiring to be a leader, the chances of success were greatly reduced.

As you might expect, many examples occurring in the popular press and in one's personal experience would contradict, expand on, and supplant this or any other list of leadership attributes or traits. So, despite another twenty years of exploration of the topic, there was still no clear pattern of the characteristics of effective leadership. In addition, during this period, the definition of success was beginning to change. The events of the Second World War cast the leaders of previous decades into a different light.

In the 1950s and 1960s, the writing tended to shift towards an examination of leadership behavior and leadership style. The search was still on for the best traits but researchers were concerned with how behaviors might be grouped to form a "style". Well-known examples are Blake and Mouton[2] who proposed a "managerial grid", McGregor[3] who developed the explanations of different leadership styles as "Theory X and Theory Y", and Likert[4] who presented his "System 4" approach. These authors tended to focus on the relationship between task and people (Figure 3). They and many others were still bent on discovering the one best way to lead. As you might expect, while this line of research led to some interesting discussions, it proved inconclusive. Fate and Trait are really just a combination of "Nature and Nurture" and the great debate continues.

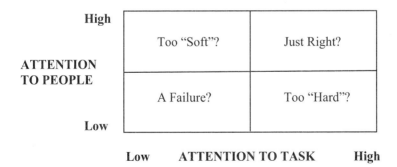

Figure 3: A Model Relating Task and People

State:

Overlapping with this interest in leadership style, was the beginning, with Tannenbaum and Schmidt[5], of an examination of the importance of situation or context. Writers began to consider the "state" or condition of things apart from the leader, to include the immediate context within which leaders lead, thinking about external contingencies that would affect the leader's behavior. Fiedler[6] explored the relationship between leadership style and situational control and in particular looked at task complexity, leader-member relations and the notion of leader position power. And Hersey and Blanchard[7] popularized the idea of situational leadership, using the maturity of the group being led as the variable, to determine the extent to which the leader would be directive or supportive of group members.

In the 1980s and 1990s, as business became increasingly complex, contradictory and global in scope, leadership writing and research tended to focus on leader-environment relations, extending the focus from the state of the leader's immediate situation to conditions beyond her local purview and into the external world. The role of this "contextual" leadership was now to look to the outside and to the future, to set a course of action and gain the willing cooperation of others to achieve common goals - and to do all this under conditions of escalating change.

As we reach the present day, what we see is that the single contingency of leading in continuous change has pervaded leadership research over the past twenty or so years. It is the predominant, almost overwhelming, challenge of our current work lives and therefore of our leaders. This condition has become widely known as "turbulence", coined by Eric Trist and Fred Emery, because it is made up of circumstances in which rapid change, high complexity and interdependent relations lead to levels of uncertainty never experienced before.[8] It is not that change is new. It is that change is continuous, not an event with a beginning and end. The current environment is so complex that single minds, no matter how skilled, cannot hold all the needed information. And change is pervasive rather than local, so there is no escape. Turbulence implies surprises. It is characterized by unpredictable and uncontrollable paradoxes where decisions must be made with incomplete and often conflicting perspectives, and where problems are "wicked", so solving one creates many others, and so on.

In the mid '70s, Henry Mintzberg[9] shone a light on this new reality with his study of what leaders actually do with their time. He found that they work at a frenetic pace with little control over their activities, that only about half their time is spent with direct reports, and that their work is characterized by brevity, variety and fragmentation. This work has been followed by volumes of leadership writing and research focused on coping, even thriving, on change. Rosabeth Moss Kanter[10] talks about "giants learning to dance", the Drucker Foundation[11] has published extensively on the leader of the future, and in 2001, the Harvard Business Review[12] published its first-ever special edition, dedicated to leadership.

The External Context

We want to step back for a moment here to consider this dramatic shift in leadership thinking. It has happened only in the last 15 to 20 years and has challenged all our previous beliefs and assumptions. We feel this is critical to note because its impact on leadership effectiveness has been so profound. Many of us who are leaders today operate out of a history, an education and an experience that has been swallowed up in change. And although we can adapt on the surface to cope with our new circumstances, underneath we often still hold tight to some outmoded concepts.

How, then, has this external environmental influence changed our thinking about leadership?

Leadership Dimensions	Stable Environment	Competitive Environment	Turbulent Environment
Focus	Internal: local maintenance tactics	Transactional: industry marketing strategies	Contextual: global strategic anticipation
Approach	Short-term: procedures and routines	Medium–term: planning and control	Long-term: vision and values
Style	Regulating others: autocratic	Consulting others: participative	Empowering others: self-managing
Criterion	Status quo: efficiency	Periodic adjustment: effectiveness	Continuous rapid change and learning: survival

Chart 1: A Framework of Environmental Contexts

The framework above uses Trist and Emery's environmental distinctions between Stable, Competitive and Turbulent environments as a starting point for considering leadership challenges. What, then, are the corresponding distinctions in the leadership role in turbulent environments and how is this different from earlier times? How can we apply a contingent or "state" approach to examining leadership under these different conditions?

In stable environments:
- The focus of the leader is on internal relationships, concentrating on achieving efficiencies at the local level on a short-term basis.
- Because change is slow, procedures and routines can be set out and followed systematically; there is little need for innovation.
- The most appropriate style of leadership may be autocratic, the leader having access to the information required to make decisions and to regulate the work of others, usually through a functional structure with control centralized at the top.
- The criterion for success is to efficiently maintain the status quo.

This is the classic assembly line plant, the family farm, the corner "Mom and Pop" store, Pleasantville, and it was the working model for organizations until the last twenty years or so. It is difficult to find stable conditions in any organizations today, although parts of some businesses attempt to, using the larger structure to protect the islands of stability from change. Most of us, at times, still yearn for things to slow down, be less complicated and more predictable.

In competitive environments:
- The leadership focus shifts from internal to transactional relationships, dealing with the multiple and often competing interests of customers, suppliers and competitors; managing these relationships requires the leader to take a strategic view of the industry so that the organization can be positioned effectively in relation to its markets.
- In addition to efficient short-term operations, the leader is also responsible for medium-term plans and the coordination and control of the financial and human resources needed to fulfill the organization's strategies.
- A participative leadership style may be the most appropriate because the leader no longer has all the information needed for decision-making and must consult with functional specialists and those who have front-line intelligence; the structure is often decentralized to position the business close to its markets.

–   The criterion for success is the capacity for periodic adjustment to market changes in order to remain effective in the industry.

This is the world many of us grew up in and are most familiar with - the telephone companies, the railways, the banks, the oil companies. And it is the world many of us behave as if we were still in. In so doing, by competing for industry advantage through growth and control, we in fact add to the complexity and uncertainty.

In turbulent environments:
–   Where the entire planet is the enterprise's potential market, the leadership focus again shifts from transactional to contextual relationships, dealing with the interdependence of the business with local and international governments, banks, investors, and a multitude of interest groups, as well as uncontrollable shocks of terror, war and fraud; the leader must not only understand strategic relationships but must also be able to anticipate the potential impact of these global events and manage within the uncertainty of constant change.
–   The leader must develop a longer-term vision based on shared organizational values that can act as a compass and guide to others making decisions.
–   The leader must empower others through this common frame of reference to be self-regulating so that needed change and innovation are initiated as required; responsibility and control are often widely dispersed through a complex structure of diverse businesses located around the world.
–   The criterion for success in turbulent environments and survival in the global arena is the capacity for continuous change and learning at all levels in the organization.

To summarize, our thesis is that a changing external context changes the requirements of leadership – the focus of attention, the planning horizon, relationships with others, and what makes for success. And although we may delude ourselves that we are jostling for position in a game that can be won by competing more effectively than others like us, the fact is that there is no way today to predict or control who will be in the game, how they will play, or what hurdles will be thrown up along the way.

A planner named Dror explained the dimensions of this game – one he called 'fuzzy gambling'.

"In a fuzzy gamble the very rules of the game are unknown and in part unknowable and have a propensity to change, sometimes greatly, during gambling and pay-off producing processes...The game may change in the middle from poker to bridge without the players noting it; the casino is in an earthquake zone; some crazy players move around who in the past sometimes distributed diamonds and sometimes shot players but are known never to repeat themselves, and so on... The metaphor can be translated into a model of decision making...When decisions must be made under conditions of true uncertainty, surprise propensities and ignorance, then the decision involves a deliberate choice between in part unknowable but often very significant consequences. This is a 'fuzzy gamble'. "[13]

The Internal Context

But what about the leader herself? We have discussed the impact of turbulent times on the leadership role but continuous change also presents challenges to the leader as a person. What is the internal impact of all this chaos? We examine here not the external context we have been discussing but the internal context of the person. We believe that this inner context, although less familiar territory, is as critical, perhaps more so, in shaping leadership during turbulence.

First, it is important to note that our chaotic world is not just a concept, as it might have been 35 years ago. It is right in our faces, in our everyday experience. In stable and competitive times, our social institutions – our families, governments, corporations, our religious values - buffer change and provide safe harbors. In turbulent times, there is no protection or escape. The middle ground has disappeared and it is up to us as individuals to recreate it for ourselves and others. The boundary between the leader and her turbulent world is right at her skin. This means we have to draw strength from within, rather than without.

We believe it is from this need for inner as well as outer wisdom in change that an interesting body of thought has recently begun to emerge...an increasing awareness of and interest in leadership *from the inside out*. Robert Greenleaf[14] articulated the notion of Servant Leadership in 1983, turning the traditional notion of leader as a director others on its end. Suddenly in the early 1990s, there appeared a spate of books, articles, conferences and conversations which cemented the realization that all that had been explored so far, with its concentration on externals, was not enough.

Some of the writers we see as having had a larger impact here are:
- Peter Block's challenging and eloquent exploration of leadership in Stewardship: Choosing Service over Self-interest[15] (1993), following on from Greenleaf's work..."Accountability without control or compliance".
- Peter Senge's The Fifth Discipline: The Art and Practice of the Learning Organization[16] (1994) whose startling contribution may have been to suggest that all organization members can be, and indeed need to be, both leaders and learners.
- David Whyte's lyrical The Heart Aroused: Poetry and the Preservation of the Soul in Corporate America[17] (1994), using the legends of Beowulf, for instance, to explore leadership in metaphors and poetry - such a departure from the prescriptive essays of earlier generations. Whyte encourages leaders to use poetry as a vehicle both to get in touch with their own souls and to encourage dialogue and conversation in corporate settings. This revelation of authenticity, he states, would model a new way of having conversations in the workplace.
- Robert Quinn's Deep Change: Discovering the Leader Within[18] (1996), which proposes that corporate renewal begins with how to use the depths of your personal reality in the outer work of your life.
- Daniel Goleman's Emotional Intelligence[19] popularized the notion of "EQ" as distinct from "IQ" as a parallel and essential competence of leaders, based on brain research showing that our emotions, not our intellect, control our behavior. His more recent work Primal Leadership[20] builds on this notion, demonstrating that emotions are contagious and that the leader's mood sets the tone for the whole organization.
- Kevin Cashman's Leadership from the Inside Out: Seven Pathways to Mastery [21] (2000), defines leadership as originating in the essence of the person and radiating outwards to be in service to others, going beyond competencies and skill-building to character and personal development.
- Jim Collins' Good to Great: Why Some Companies Make the Leap and Others Don't (2001) describes 'Level 5 Leadership' as the highest level of skill and contribution a leader can make, building enduring greatness in the organization through a paradoxical blend of personal humility and professional will. [22]
- John Kotter's The Heart of Change[23] (2002) builds on his earlier change model for leaders found in Leading Change (1996) and emphasizes the role of feelings and the emotions in successful change strategies.

And suddenly, so many others…Deal and Bolman talking about Leading with Soul[24], conferences about Spirituality and Business, conversations and speeches about the role of spirit in the workplace…there were suddenly thousands of people sharing this different perspective.

You likely have your own favorites from this period, the books and speeches that resonated with your sense that there was something deeply missing, that there was an entire inner context, a whole continent, unexplored, perhaps even unacknowledged. What precipitated this sudden avalanche of a different perspective? Perhaps the impending millennium change had an impact, the dawning of the Age of Aquarius….perhaps as the first of the Baby Boomers reached that period of adult development where interior explorations become more important, they began to explore this realm….perhaps the depression of the early 1990s sent out ripple waves about the impermanence of 'the old employer/employee deal'….perhaps the collapse of organizations apparently 'built to last' led to questions about what leadership really was.

Whatever their personal change journey, as the century drew to a close, many writers were examining what was not working, what was not enough, to navigate in the complexity of permanent white water. Certainly many factors had an influence. Our proposal is that the underlying theme is contextual turbulence – both within and without. Two interdependent and potentially contradictory themes might be said to be emerging from the research and thinking that accompanied the new millennium….BOTH an increasing awareness of the importance of understanding the external context and learning how to lead in true turbulence…AND an increasing awareness of the importance of leading from the inside out, from who you are, from the values and principles which can generate the resilience required to lead in turbulent times.

The Emergence of *Both/And* Leadership

Earlier we mentioned Trist and Emery's conception of turbulence. Susan was fortunate to know Eric Trist and provides this reflection on *Both/And* Leadership.

When I returned to school in the late 70s to do a graduate degree, I was fortunate to be able to first study and then work and teach as a colleague with Eric Trist, one of the forefathers of organizational change and community development. Eric was semi-retired but teaching as a Professor Emeritus at York University in Canada because he still had such fire for his vision of a "social architecture for a human future".

Eric had begun his career in the war office in London, studying leaders and what made them effective under battle conditions. The Second World War was decimating the population of leaders and more were needed, in a hurry. He had gone on to discover innovative approaches to work and community all over the world. From his work with the coalminers of Northern England, he had coined the term "socio-technical" to describe the kind of organization where social and technical systems would be balanced for the benefit of all. He saw leaders as "social architects" who orchestrate the development of a community of people who willingly devote themselves to the work of their organizations because they have a stake and a say in things.

There was a broader agenda. Eric was not convinced that the way of life and work in Western societies was sustainable in a global environment of exponential change. In 1965, he and his friend Fred Emery came up with the term "turbulent" to describe environments characterized by rapid change, high levels of complexity and interdependence, which resulted in global uncertainty. He feared that our current North American organizational forms, with command and control leadership based on assumptions of stability, would not be able to withstand the onslaught of turbulence. At the time, it was a concept, a presumption based on an insightful examination of global conditions.

We have seen in the last 20 years some of the consequences he predicted – more bankruptcies than ever before, more stock market volatility, more global strife, more corporate power and growth, and lately more terrorism as a reflection of the hatred of our way of life and the emptiness of those who give their lives to destroy others.

And how have we, as leaders, responded? From an organizational systems point of view, Eric often decried the work of organizational experts who laid out 'wiring diagram' plans and implementation steps in order to bring about change, ignoring the very people on whom the change depended for its success. When I worked with Eric in the early 80s, the quality movement was gaining ground and it, too, talked of "re-engineering" the organization as if it was a machine part rather than a collection of social networks. And on a global scale, our parochial interests and wasteful lifestyles have teased and tempted but ultimately excluded most of the world's people.

This "either/or thinking", as Eric called it, was the scourge of change literature at every scale. He longed for the day when both the personal and the organizational, the human and the machine, the social and the technical, the local and the global, would be jointly optimized rather than maximizing one at the expense of the other.

Well, it is 20 years later and I think there are some signs on the horizon that Eric's hope may become a reality. In the organizational and leadership fields, there has in the last few years been a move to take a more inclusive look at what is required to make organizations and their leaders adaptive to change. A new blending of the elements that have been separated since the Industrial Revolution is emerging, resulting in the possibility of a "both/and" rather than an "either/or" way of both "thinking" and "being" for success in the 21st century.

One clear example of *both/and* is the growing need to live with contradictions in every facet of society, with our own abilities to hold paradoxes in our minds and lives….**both** an increasing use of seatbelts **and** an increasing interest in extreme sports, **both** increasing disdain for drinking and driving, with lower consumption of hard liquor, **and** increasingly lower levels of fitness in our society, **both** the increasing sense of isolation **and** the speed of global communication, **both** increasing recycling **and** increasing packaging of consumer goods. These paradoxes constantly call us to live with ambiguity and uncertainty – classic conditions in turbulence. Our only anchor is a sense of values and purpose, of what is important to us…a way to balance paradox, to guide our choices, to keep us on course.

What, then, does this *both/and* leadership consist of? Where do the two streams of leadership research we have been reviewing – the "outside in" and the "inside out" - lead us? Here's a list of some paradoxes…some apparent opposites that *both/and* leadership requires us to hold in mind and act from, all the time, at the same time. We've already mentioned most of these. We'll explore the first one here, and you might want to journal or reflect on the rest or others, as the list prompts your imagination.

Both	And
Self	Other
Inside Out	Outside In
Individual	Community
Change	Continuity
Vision	Implementation
Purpose	Paradox
Leading	Learning
Process	Structure

Chart 2: A Framework of *Both/And* Thinking

Both Self and Other:

It used to be that we had to leave our "selves" at the organization's door, to be one-dimensional - the "man in the grey flannel suit" - without individual distinctiveness, inner desires or human frailties. Leaders were expected to be entirely "other" directed. The self, that inner domain of passion, longing and spirit, was locked down, denied, avoided at all costs. What a waste! For it is from the self that our best imaginings and creations come. Of course, if the goal is to be fixed in terms of "inputs" and "outputs" and variables of any kind are seen as negative, then the "organizational man" makes some sense. But that is not our world, not any more.

Today's world is characterized by diversities of every kind and leaders are challenged to encompass the complexity and variety, not only in gender and ethnicity but also in thought, opinion and perspective, that is needed for decision-making. It is through expansion of self-awareness, knowing oneself intimately for better and worse, that the leader can then appreciate others in all their good and bad aspects as well.

Leaders are looked to for their passion, their ability to inspire others to accompany them into uncertain futures and their ability to care and show concern for the inevitable setbacks that occur along the way. These are the elements of the self, of the whole person, that are the hallmarks of leadership now.

What is important to take away from this *both/and* discussion is that it is not necessary to resolve apparent contradictions as much as to live within them, to reframe them, to hold more than one possibility at the same time and be comfortable with that. It is much like a figure/ground reversal. You are no doubt familiar with the puzzles that, when looked at one way show one picture but when looked at differently, show another – the old and young women, the vase and the profiles. In case you aren't familiar with these *both/and* pictures, there is one below. At first glance, it is simply a few abstract shapes on the page, but when the figure and ground are reversed, that is, when you look at the white spaces rather than the black shapes, you see a word. You can go back and forth, figure and ground, neither taking precedence, just existing simultaneously depending on where you focus your attention. This is the experience of *both/and*.

Figure 4: A Model of Figure and Ground

At the end of the chapter is a reflective exercise which might help you to explore your own thinking about this list. And in the next section, we will examine these apparent paradoxes in a discussion of the competencies required of leaders in turbulent times. But first, having covered the basic evolutionary ground, we can introduce our definition of leadership before we get too far. It is important that you, the reader, understand what we mean when we say "leader" or "leadership". Although the words have tremendous power these days, they are rarely well defined – we just assume we all mean the same thing.

Our Definition of Leadership

Leadership is the process of getting to know both the self and other(s) and establishing a relationship of mutual trust and awareness for the purpose of working together to reach a common goal.

Leadership is a process. Although, as we have discussed, we tend to endow our leaders with personal qualities that leave the impression leading is an innate capability or a set of personality traits, these tell us little about the process of leading itself – where the action actually happens. Here is Jaques'[25] explanation of this phenomenon:

> "Under circumstances where we have a person exercising great competence in a role with leadership accountability, the effect is to bind people together; the binding together touches the deep recesses of our values for social cohesion, and we are suffused by warm feelings that we tend to associate, incorrectly, with personal qualities in our leaders rather than with effective competence."

Leadership is part of a role. Leadership isn't something we can simply go out and do. It always involves a relationship. We lead in relation to others. So leadership is embedded in roles we play in social contexts. The leadership role can be part of an organizational role – manager and direct report; a parental role – mother and child; a community role – volunteer board member and staff; a political role – elected official and constituents; but it is always part of some role in relation to some "other". This is an important point because leadership is often confused with the role itself. It is not the role – the role is manager, parent, volunteer, official. Leadership is the process used to carry out the role in relationships with others. There will be aspects of the role that are not leadership, such as doing administrative work, buying groceries, and so on.

Leadership happens in context. The nature of leadership changes dramatically depending on context. Leading a team of direct reports to improve its working relationships is very different from leading them out of a burning building. Context is everything. Leading an organization in the post war boom of the '50s was different from leading an organization today. Today, leadership is all about change. Leaders who are effective in one context are often ineffective in another. Steve Jobs was a very effective leader of the innovative Apple computer company in its start-up days but was not effective once it became a major corporation. Conditions change; roles change. The process that is successful becomes the reason for failure. It is characteristic of our times that we must consider context and be adaptable to changing roles and relationships in our exercise of leadership.

Leadership Starts with the Self. With all this talk of processes, role relationships and contexts, it would be easy to assume that leadership is all "out there". It is not the case. One of the great paradoxes of leadership, and the missing ingredient in many would-be leaders, is that it starts with who you are, how you show up, what you bring to the role and process. There is a transparency about leading that we have all experienced. We can see whether or not the leader is congruent with who she is and how she acts. There are numerous adages that express this transparency: walk the talk, the audio matching the video, and so on. These are all expressions of the need for leaders to be authentic in bringing themselves to the role and the relationships with others. Without this self-awareness and sensitivity, leaders appear arrogant and disconnected from the role they play.

There are essential and fundamental aspects of leadership which we use in our definition – that leadership is a process, part of a role, happening in context, and that it starts with the self.

With this common understanding, let us now move to the competencies required for exercising this leadership in turbulent times. These competencies were first introduced early in this chapter (Chart 1) in the comparison of different organizational contexts.

The Four Leadership Competencies for Turbulent Times

Our proposal to you is that turbulent conditions need a new kind of leadership, one that includes the ability to hold many disparate and apparently contradictory thoughts in your mind at the same time, and still act, achieving great results. And it is our contention that this kind of leadership requires certain competencies that can be learned and measured. The notion of a competency - that success or performance could be described by the behaviors, traits, skills, knowledge and attributes of the performer, in addition to the results achieved - was actually an early[26] 'both/and' reality. The idea of a competency held within it the notion that performance included both *what* was accomplished and *how*.

The twenty-first century notion of a competency differs in a key aspect, however. Traditionally, competencies have been defined in terms of performance of a particular job or role and define or detail how to be effective in that role. They have also been structured to ensure that there is no overlap or possible confusion between two different competencies. This was intended to ensure validity and simplicity of observation and measurement and reduce the possibility of double counting, and perhaps double paying, for a particular competency.

Now, in permanent white water, the definition of a competency cluster for complex contexts **requires** the interdependence of the competencies. There can be no strategic anticipation without learning, no vision can be realized without empowering others. This will no doubt make both the acquisition and the measurement of these competencies more complex but will also reflect more appropriately the reality of turbulence. In fact, it is in the interconnections that real generative learning can occur. What we are presenting here are four clusters of competencies that we believe combine and interrelate to promote a leader's success in turbulent times.

Strategic Anticipation  **Empowering Others**

Vision and Values

Learning and Change

Figure 5: A Model of Leadership Competencies

Strategic Anticipation:

It seems almost silly to say that when times are turbulent leaders must keep their heads up, constantly scanning the horizon for changes that will affect the business. But it is amazing how many leaders fail to carry out this most critical leadership role. Change becomes overwhelming; analysis leads to paralysis; it is impossible to make the "right" decision, so no decision is made at all. These are characteristic responses to information overload.

Leaders today and into the foreseeable future will concentrate their efforts on understanding strategic relationships and interdependencies – what has an impact on what? How are things tied together? Who needs to be connected to whom? And not just at the level of the organization as a whole, but at the regional, national and global level, where all organizations interact in social and political environments that are in constant flux. Leaders must anticipate possible business and social impacts and manage within them, using networking and alliances to be "in the know" about relevant impending changes.

It is not possible to predict or control events but it is imperative to understand through multiple connections what is probable or possible. Leaders are constantly asking questions about what you know, why you think so, what you would do. They are continuous learners with an insatiable curiosity about anything that might have an effect on their business. They get out in front of trends and cast a broad net in their hunt to see what patterns may exist. And they make their decisions based on the best information they can get, knowing it is insufficient.

When, as a leader, you are responsible for the livelihood of sometimes thousands of people, when the direction you set may not be the optimal one but your gut tells you it's the best you can do with the intelligence you have and you must start now, when you seem to be setting off into a wilderness no one else sees or understands but you are asking others to follow you anyway, that is when you are exercising strategic anticipation. It takes courage, stamina, confidence and vision. It takes a person who has a strong sense of self, who has moved beyond ego and is able to draw on an inner conviction, a person who is congruent in expressing their vision and acts consistently to achieve it.

So there is both an outside-in aspect to this competency theme – the sifting and sorting of information from many sources in relation to the organization and its strategies – and an inside-out aspect – the ability and the courage to set a direction based on the information gathered and inspire others to follow on a course that will, almost by definition, be incorrect and require people to change in ways that are uncomfortable and unfamiliar. Leaders must be willing to admit they don't know all the answers, to proclaim that they are learners along the path with everyone else, to be authentic in their fears and doubts rather than falsely omnipotent.

In demonstrating behaviors of mastery in Strategic Anticipation, the leader:
– Scans the wide environment, forecasts probable and possible circumstances, keeps abreast of future trends and innovations, uses scenario planning to anticipate outcomes across a range of circumstances, identifies "fracture

lines"[27] in current assumptions and theories and creates plausible alternatives.

- Is a master at managing many challenges at once, including the multiple stakeholders involved in the organization's future, and at providing direction and constancy within change so that confidence in the future is maintained.
- Is proactive in seeking information and making sense of it in terms of the business strategies needed for success.
- Is open to repositioning strategies in light of new circumstances, relating changes to the values and longer-term directions of the organization.
- Has the political skills to resolve the inevitable conflicts that arise in social complexity.
- Values diversity of opinion and input as a source of innovative information.
- Sees interdependencies and works to make their advantages explicit to others.
- Builds bridges and alliances within and across normal channels. Reframes competitive postures to demonstrate the value of mutual consideration. Is socially responsible in making decisions affecting others.
- Takes a global view of issues and recognizes their impacts at the national, regional and local levels.

Vision and Values:

The leader manifests the organization's vision and values – in every decision, in every presentation, in every interaction. The leader creates, refines, articulates and constantly reconfirms the vision, making it act as a common frame of reference. The leader creates mechanisms to ensure that all stakeholders have a shared sense of what is important, that they share a set of values that act as guides for decision–making. The values provide a frame within which action and decisions are made, enabling the leader to ensure that meaning is managed and organizational reality shaped.

The leader creates mental and verbal pictures of desired future states and scenarios, sharing and creating a new reality with others in and associated with the organization. The leader is a constant model of values congruence, of 'walking the talk' and is alert to the need for vigilance to ensure there is no 'say/do disconnect' between the stated and operant values of the organization. By her decisions, actions, behaviors and words, the leader guides, motivates and gives meaning and purpose to people, both as individuals and as members of an organization.

In her inside-out work, the leader has spent enough time in personal reflection to be certain of the core values which are essential to her own life of purpose and meaning. She can state with passion and conviction that the organization's values are in alignment with her own. The leader's life, in all aspects, both inside and outside the organization - in the community, in the family, in interactions with strangers - manifests this commitment to living a life of meaning and purpose based on those core values. The leader invites scrutiny to ensure that she is living a life of integrity and ethical leadership. She will model and mentor that approach to living and leading in all her relationships. She will be the first to admit that she is not perfect, to admit when she has not always lived up to her values, and to explore the reasons why. She will tell the truth, admitting that there is an incomplete picture on which to make decisions. She will assess the incomplete and potentially conflicting information …and will make decisions anyway. She will treat her various 'publics' – her peers, direct reports, bosses, customers, and other stakeholders - as adults, and will act as an adult herself.

This competency reinforces the connection with Strategic Anticipation, in requiring the leader to be a values-driven visionary. It also requires the "Empowering Others" competency in listening to, synthesizing, articulating, responding to and recrafting the appropriate vision for the future, with the major stakeholders of the organization.

In demonstrating behaviors of mastery in Vision and Values, the leader:
– Has the ability to hold up the vision as a guiding star that draws the organization forward, through the turbulence and apparent ambiguity.
– Routinely spends time with employees, customers, and other major stakeholders describing and iteratively responding to challenges to the vision of the future for the organization, and how the shared set of values inform that vision.
– Actively seeks out feedback from employees, customers and major stakeholders about the degree of congruence between her personal behaviors, language, decisions, actions and inactions, and the values of the organization.
– Facilitates communication processes to ensure that major stakeholder groups are represented in the crafting of the organization's possible future organization and marketing/product development redesign, to harness the best contributions of all.

Empowering Others:

Leadership is not a solo performance. It is an orchestration of many parts, each contributing in its way to the accomplishment of the whole. Think of a symphony orchestra and the ability of each of the members to play their different instruments, sometimes alone, often with like others, and always in harmony with other instruments. The whole is connected through the music, the underlying text that lays out the story and gives each person their part to play. The orchestra conductor doesn't try to play all the instruments – doesn't even play one! She knows the music, knows the capabilities of the instruments, the skill levels of the musicians, and the pace required for the best performance of the piece. She sets the direction and the timing and empowers the musicians to use their talent in concert with each other to perform at their best.

As a musician, under the leadership of the conductor, you feel motivated to do your best, to learn your part and to play it as flawlessly as possible. She isn't simply telling you how each note should be played but rather evoking the notes from you in a way that taps into your soul as well as your skill. She is unleashing your emotions as well as your talent. You feel responsible not only for yourself and your own performance but obligated to the other members of the orchestra as well. You are a team. Only by working together can the music succeed.

This is one example of a leader empowering others. You have undoubtedly been part of a team where you felt empowered to give your best and may have led groups where you empowered others. As the word implies, empowerment is about sharing the traditional leader power with others so that they are as invested in the outcomes as you are. The paradox of power is that by giving some of it away, freely, in the knowledge that power exercised by one person alone cannot accomplish the task, the leader can actually generate more power. This requires an inner strength and maturity in the leader. She must be able to grow beyond her ego, to see the goal not as simply a confirmation of her own power but as the development of shared commitment to a common goal. In contrast to traditional concepts of power, we do not see it as a limited resource; rather it can be magnified by sharing it, by having everyone feel powerful enough to play their part, to make their music in harmony with others. Rather than diminishing the leader's power, empowerment expands it.

This is not to say that the leader gives all power away and becomes passively over-powered by her team. There are some things that are constant -

values are an example – and cannot be delegated away. The score of the music cannot be changed by the musicians just for fun! The leader must be explicit about what is "tight", that is, non negotiable, and what is "loose" and can be implemented in various ways depending on the talent and style of the person responsible. These "loose-tight" couplings allow power to be shared appropriately without turning the music into noise.

Leaders use their vision of the future as an energizer to attract people away from the comfort of their current situation towards an unknown destination. Because they themselves are energized by future possibilities and can paint a clear picture of how tomorrow will be better than today, they "pull" others along with them, like a magnet, toward their vision. Being drawn into a new future, like starting a new mystery book, has an excitement that propels the reader forward even though the details are unknown. Being drawn toward a vision is empowering. This is quite different from being handed a book and told to read it. Being pushed from behind is a disempowering experience.

There are four things people want in their work. They are well known and documented. We all desire:
–   Significance – our work means something in the world.
–   Competence – our work uses our skills and abilities.
–   Community – we work with others in pursuit of a common goal.
–   Satisfaction – we enjoy what we do and are recognized for it.
When we have these four elements we feel empowered to give our best. We feel like leaders in our own right, responsible for producing something of value using our talents in harmony with others and enjoying the process. Empowerment turns followers into leaders. At every level in the organization, leaders are needed to succeed in a turbulent world.

Byrd's fifteen-year-old definition of empowerment still captures its essence:

"Leaders don't invent motivation in others, they unlock it…The skills associated with empowerment entail being willing to share power; taking delight in others' development more than in having control; and realizing that visions are achieved by teams, not by single leaders." [28]

In demonstrating behaviors of mastery in Empowering Others, the leader:

- Uses vision to motivate others to change, to pull them into the desired future.
- Paints a picture of a future that has something for everyone; is honest about the requirements but passionate about the journey.
- Gives people a stake in outcomes.
- Demonstrates the need for and significance of change and invites people to buy in, to catch the wave, to be part of the team.
- Builds effective teams of people who want to work together to achieve a valuable goal.
- Gives direction, shares power and profile, acknowledges and rewards accomplishment, encourages development and coaches high performance.

Learning and Change:

The leader is a master learner, seeing all experiences in all contexts as providing opportunities for continuous, rapid learning. The leader's language is that of one who understands and relishes change...who has mastered the art of reflection, in the moment and in every moment. Reflection cannot be seen as something apart from the daily life of the leader and the organization. Rather it is another 'and' in that there is the need for simultaneous action and reflection. This is because contexts are continually changing and to ignore or respond slowly to these changes might be to miss an important shift in market dynamics.

Learning and change, as a competency cluster, is interconnected with Strategic Anticipation, in terms not only of observing and learning from the change but also of conceiving responses to those changes. At its heart, mastery of this competency means seeing change not merely as a constant and an inevitable reality. It means eagerly seeking out change, resisting the temptation to try to control it but preferring to master being "in the flow".

Leaders must clearly master paradox, be alert to contextual complexity, ambiguity, and constant change and create internal stability in order to encourage the pursuit and embrace of constant change by the employees of the organization. This creative tension creates its own equilibrium, of stability nestled within the state of constant change – stability in motion. Part of this tension is created by the leader's own behaviors...behaviors that include an admission of confusion in the midst of apparently conflicting data, an insistence on the importance of core values, a personal commitment to her own learning and development plan. Not only must the leader challenge assumptions, in setting new directions and creating a sense of urgency for the response required, she must be eager to listen to and to respond respectfully to the challenges of direct reports, peers and customers. This reinforces the linkage to the "Empowering Others" competency.

Such apparently arcane values as modesty and humility are an important part of the personal value set of the leader. Leaders will master the art of creating change without wanton destabilization. Leaders will invoke a clarity of thought and action that includes, at times, the need for creative destruction; the realization that in order to change and begin anew, something must end. As well, the leader is a social architect, a master renovator… continuously improving, reducing, fine-tuning, to ensure that the alignment of the organization is optimally positioned for long-term success. This competency is also connected to Vision and Values, as the values that are core to the individual leader and to the organization, must act as the keel, keeping the ship not only afloat, but moving forward effectively and efficiently.

In demonstrating behaviors of mastery in Learning and Change, the leader:
- Talks the language of change - expresses personal feelings, explores metaphors and change models and makes decisions that reflect an understanding of deep strategic change and how change affects people as employees, leaders and customers. Models this change personally through adopting new patterns, challenging the status quo in meetings, presentations, marketing materials, and strategic plans.
- Demonstrates a personal commitment to lifelong learning, modeling the results of learning, making decisions that reflect the value of learning in action, using all possible opportunities to squeeze out learning, and to encourage others to do the same. Commits personal time to both taking and giving courses, providing and receiving coaching and mentoring.
- Personally models an 'early adopter' and 'frequent adapter' method in the use of technology, in more effective ways of working, and in adoption of methods and models from unusual sources.

The chart below recaps the dimensions of leadership we have been discussing and highlights both the external competency themes and the internal components that have emerged to strengthen and balance them.

Dimensions	External Competency	Internal Component
Focus	Strategic Anticipation	Courage and Conviction
Approach	Vision & Values	Self understanding. Embodying Values
Style	Empowering Others	Passion. Evoking commitment. Servant leadership
Criterion	Learning & Change	Early adopter, frequent adapter. Deep personal exploration

Chart 3: A Framework of External and Internal Leadership Dimensions

To end this chapter, we want to quote from the ex-COO of AT&T, Alex Mandl[29], speaking about his similar view of our concept of *both/and* leadership:

> "…leaders can adapt to a mercurial future and use it to their advantage by cultivating the creative tension that comes from balancing extremes – looking at the world from both sides now. The theory of both combines short term fire fighting with an eye toward long term payoffs and consequences. It fuses traditionally separate strategic and tactical skills, because both will be required of tomorrow's leaders. A domestic and global perspective, already prized, will take on a local component, and the hard side of business will meld with the soft, acknowledging the interdependence not only in the workplace, but of financial, employee, customer and shareowner interests as well. Leadership roles will also straddle extremes, incorporating the skills of the generalist and the specialist, the visionary and the operational whiz."

> "Tomorrow's leader will be both teacher and student, technologist and entrepreneur…there is a singular aspect to the theory of both: a core set of givens that should steer every action and serve as tiebreakers in the leader's ongoing balancing act. The leader of the future will have to be adept at articulating a vision and inspiring others with an imagined future. He or she will find in shared values and beliefs the foundation for commitment, context and creativity. And finally, the leader will delegate real responsibility and accountability – and expect employees to use it."

"These givens speak more to spirit than to skills and, as such, perhaps define the challenges facing tomorrow's leaders."

If you stopped reading here, you would have a good understanding of leadership, past and present, and its requirements. But you would not know how these requirements translate into relationships with others, how the leadership role plays out in everyday settings within the stream of presenting issues and problems. So we need to go further, to look to tomorrow as Mandl says, to see how to extend the *both/and* view.

We will return to these concepts and competencies in Chapter Three after we have had a look at the contributions of the coaching field to our understanding of how leadership is applied in change.

A Personal Reflection:

One of the surprising experiences for those new to the workplace is the apparent prevalence of cognitive dissonance…of the 'say/do disconnect'. For instance, an employee is told in the orientation to the organization that her manager has an open door policy and encourages anyone who wants to, to come and chat whenever….but the rumor mill soon contradicts that. The employee hears that the manager is known for reminding subordinates of the content of apparently private conversations in public meetings….or it's known that the manager has back-to-back meetings from 7 to 7 and is never available for unscheduled conversations. Or, when presented with a situation, she immediately solves the problem and takes the power and credit from the employee asking the question. Another surprising experience is how quickly people inside the organization seem to become numb to the apparent contradiction.

Think about your own workplace and all the ways in which you can accurately characterize it as a turbulent environment. Perhaps reflect on any of these other apparent paradoxes or contradictory polarities and how they have played out in your own career. We've repeated Chart 2 here so you can reflect on it.

Both	And
Self	Other
Inside Out	Outside In
Individual	Community
Change	Continuity
Vision	Implementation
Purpose	Paradox
Leading	Learning
Process	Structure

Now, think of recent examples where the leadership style you observed in yourself or others was one of an autocratic rather than empowering style.
− What do you think prevents you or others from adopting a leadership style that appears to be more effective in leading in turbulent times?
− Who do you think is a true leader, someone who manifests the values needed for turbulent environments?

– Why not write here what makes that true leader your "hero" …and in what ways you might want to experiment with or adopt some of her or his traits?

A Reflection to Share:

For some leaders, building trust starts with trusting their own inner voice…the voice that says, "This isn't right" or "This isn't right for me"….the voice that is at its loudest Sunday evening as you think about the week ahead. Why is it that Monster.com's job board gets the most hits Mondays at noon? After the weekend, people come to work with the conviction, "There's got to be something better than this" And at noon hour, during lunch, they cruise the net to see what else is out there…

Have you an inner voice as a constant companion? An inner voice that is your champion, not your critic? Is it asking you, "Is this what you were put on the planet to do?" "Is this to be your legacy, your 'claim to fame'?" Where do you feel most alive? Is it at work? When are you most aware of your inner voice? Is it a voice that guides you, encourages you, challenges you?

Another part of trust, in addition to being trustworthy yourself, is knowing who you can trust…who has both your own and the company's best interests at heart. Who can you approach, to confess your fears, your insecurities, your anger, your doubts when it would not be appropriate to share them with a larger or perhaps less 'safe' circle?

Trust involves both giving and receiving. Like joy, like love…it can become infectious. It may be that you need to be the one to start taking chances and risks, to trust…where do you hear your inner voice calling you to start, to take a chance? Why not have a conversation about what your inner voice is up to with someone you trust?

A Self-Assessment:

We've talked about the four competency themes for effective leadership in turbulent times. Give yourself a rating on each of these competency areas as you see yourself now, by circling the number that is most appropriate. Consider 1 to be unskilled and 5 to be a master:

Strategic Anticipation				
1	2	3	4	5
Vision and Values				
1	2	3	4	5
Empowering Others				
1	2	3	4	5
Learning and Change				
1	2	3	4	5

Chart 4: An Assessment of Leadership Competencies

Now think about where you aspire to be. Circle the number that represents your leadership goal. Are there gaps in your leadership development? What kinds of experiences or mentoring or training would you need to close the gaps? Think about how you might begin to put some of your ideas into place.

A Team Exercise:

Development can be especially powerful when it is accomplished through teamwork. Have each member of your team do the self-assessment above and bring their ratings to a team meeting.

At the meeting, discuss where each member sees him or herself and what he or she needs to move forward. This is best done in two's or three's so everyone has a chance to talk about their assessments. Allow about 10 minutes per person.

Discuss the themes and common issues in the whole group. Are there areas where the whole team is strong? What about areas where the whole team needs development? Are there areas where one member of the team could use a strength to help another who wants to develop? One way to get the discussion going is to put the assessment scales, as shown in Chart 4, on a flipchart or whiteboard and let everyone put their own ratings onto the common scales. That way, everyone can see where the strengths and weaknesses lie. You can use two different colors for current and desired ratings.

The outcome of the meeting should allow the selection of some action steps for team development. Perhaps one of the competency themes can be chosen for development over the next 6 months, with actions stipulated – what will happen, by when, and by whom. At least one follow-up meeting should also be arranged to track progress toward the goals.

A variation on this exercise is to have members of the team rate each individual so that he or she can compare self-ratings with those of others. Two or three ratings are sufficient to form a 'group' average rating that ensures the confidentiality of each rater. Your HR representative may be able to support this exercise by collecting ratings and preparing a group report for each individual to consider independently prior to a team meeting as described above.

Endnotes:

[1] Given the late twentieth/twenty-first centuries' increasing diversity awareness, we should admit here that we're looking at the classical and western definitions of leadership – that Confucian and African philosophers and First Nations societies everywhere might have very different descriptions of the evolution of this term. And indeed, we use the female pronoun throughout…why? In part, to redress the imbalance, in part to call attention to the rarity of this new kind of leadership with its different kinds of values,…and because we're both women coach/leaders ourselves.

[2] Blake, R.R. and J.S. Mouton. *The Managerial Grid.* 1964.

[3] McGregor, D. *The Human Side of Enterprise.* McGraw-Hill, 1960.

[4] Likert, R. *The Human Organization.* McGraw-Hill, 1961.

[5] Tannenbaum, R. and W.H. Schmidt. "How to Choose a Leadership Pattern", *Harvard Business Review* 36: 95-101, 1958.

[6] Fiedler, F.W. "The Contingency Model: New Directions for Leadership Utilization", *Journal of Contemporary Business* 3(4): 65-79, 1974.

[7] Hersey P. and K.H. Blanchard. "Life Cycle Theory of Leadership", *Training and Development Journal*, May 1969.

[8] The term was coined by Eric Trist and Fred Emery in 1965. It was then a future concept based on insightful consideration of environmental trends. The original reference is "The Causal Texture of Organizational Environments", *Human Relations* 13(1): 21-32, 1965.

[9] Mintzberg, Henry. *The Structuring of Organizations.* Prentice Hall, 1978.

[10] Moss Kanter, Rosabeth. *When Giants Learn to Dance.* Touchstone Books, 1990.

[11] See for instance, The Drucker Foundation. *The Leader of the Future*, Frances Hesselbein, Marshall Goldsmith and Richard Beckhard Eds. Jossey-Bass, 1997.

[12] "Breakthrough Leadership: It's Personal", *Harvard Business Review,* Special Edition, December 2001.

[13] Dror, Yehezdel. "Planning as Fuzzy Gambling: A Radical Perspective on Coping with Uncertainty", in *Planning in Turbulence*, David Morley and Arie Shachar Eds. The Magnes Press, The Hebrew University, Jerusalem, 1986.

[14] Greenleaf, Robert K. *Servant Leadership.* Paulist Press, 1983.

[15] Block, Peter. *Stewardship: Choosing Service over Self-Interest.* Berrett-Koehler, 1996.

[16] Senge, Peter. *The Fifth Discipline: The Art and Practice of the Learning Organization.* Doubleday, 1994.

[17] Whyte, David. *The Heart Aroused: Poetry and the Preservation of the Soul in Corporate America.* Doubleday, 1994.

[18] Quinn, Robert E. *Deep Change: Discovering the Leader Within.* Jossey-Bass, 1996.

[19] Goleman, Daniel. *Emotional Intelligence.* Bantam, 1998.

[20] Goleman, Daniel. *Primal Leadership.* Harvard Business Review Press, 2002.

[21] Cashman, Kevin. *Leadership from the Inside Out: Seven Pathways to Mastery.* Executive Excellence, 1998.

[22] Collins, Jim. *Good to Great Why Some Companies Make the Leap and Others Don't.* Harper Collins, 2001.

[23] Kotter, John. *The Heart of Change*, 2002 and *Leading Change*, 1996, Harvard Business School Press.

[24] Deal, Terrence and Lee Bolman. *Leading with Soul: An Uncommon Journey of the Spirit.* Wiley, 2001.

[25] Jaques. Elliott. *Requisite Organization.* Cason Hall Publishers, 1989.

[26] See for instance, *Competence at Work: Models of Superior Performance.* M. Signe and Lyle M. Spencer. John Wiley and Sons, 1993.

[27] Morgan, Gareth. *Riding the Waves of Change: Developing Managerial Competencies for a Turbulent World.* Jossey Bass, 1989.

[28] Byrd, R.E. "Corporate Leadership Skills: A New Synthesis", *Organizational Dynamics,* 34-43, Summer 1987.

[29] Alex Mandl quoted in "Either/Or Yields to the Theory of Both". Alex Mandl and Deepak Sethi. *The Leader of the Future.* Frances Hesselbein, Marshall Goldsmith and Richard Beckhard Eds., The Drucker Foundation, Jossey-Bass, 1997.

Chapter 2
Coaching as Applied *Both/And* Leadership

We have talked about *both/and* leadership and the competencies required of *both/and* leaders in today's turbulent organizations. And we will propose, in the next chapter, that leadership and coaching blend into an alchemy that is more powerful than either on its own, and that they are in fact, in a chaotic world, essentially and intimately interconnected.

First we need to explore what coaching is all about, in our view. The exponential rise in interest in coaching in the last decade has come about precisely because of the increase in complexity and uncertainty in our lives, both at work and at home. There has been a dramatic escalation in the speed of change and the personal adaptation required to keep up. Futurists suggest that the pace of change will continue not simply to increase, but to compound. And coaching is one response to that ever-increasing pace of change. John Kotter, former Professor of Leadership at Harvard Business School, writes:

> "What's really driving the boom in coaching is this: as we move from 30 miles an hour to 70 to 120 to 180....as we go from driving straight down the road to making right turns and left turns to abandoning cars and getting on motorcycles...the whole game changes, and a lot of people are trying to keep up, learn how not to fall off."[1]

We will suggest in fact that the Leader Coach does not merely "try to keep up and not fall off" but rather thrives in an increasingly changing world. A powerful new image which might reflect how to "play the game" in this new reality is J.K. Rowling's powerful description of Quidditch in the Harry Potter series…a fast-paced, and ever-changing game played in at least three dimensions.[2]

For much of the last century, individual employees were protected within thick corporate walls and the battles were fought outside - against governments, financiers, other corporations, competing interests. The cradle to grave loyalty that used to be the employment contract has disappeared, not in the last hundred years or so, but in the last couple of decades. Organizations can no longer protect their workers as the rounds of restructuring, rightsizing, layoffs, contracting out, mergers and acquisitions, and divestitures, have proved. The walls have tumbled. In addition, the internet and worldwide web have meant that there are few barriers to communication, or at least the constant and frequently overwhelming distribution of information and data. One interesting influence of the internet and the proliferation of websites has been the legitimization of personal opinion – and errors, which can be distributed globally with few checks and balances. Employees can comment on their bosses in public websites, can report abuses in 'whistle blower' websites and chat rooms, can comment anonymously on stock variability, and share their opinions with the world. There is no longer any validity, if there ever was, in the notion that the employer could control or limit what the employee knew. Such radical access to information and the encouragement of expression of opinion adds another element of chaos to the world in which Leader Coaches manage.

Turbulence is no longer a theoretical concept – it is a fact of everyday life. It is no longer noise in the wider world; it is noise all around and within each of us as individuals. It's a whole new world out there virtually every day. Most of us don't spend much time thinking about this – it's hard enough to keep up when we're charging ahead with all our energy. Who has time to look back and reflect? Or sideways…to learn, to anticipate what the impact might be, for instance, of there being more VISA cards in India than in North America. We are unprepared as humans for the level of threat that we are constantly under. Remember our evolutionary choices - fight or flight[3] when we are faced with a threat. But what if the threat is ever-present? What if we are constantly doing battle, running for our lives, just to survive? What then?

Enter the coach…

Coaching as a term applied in management circles first began appearing in the early 1990s…though of course it had appeared in sports and sales training circles for many years. But when we stop to consider, it's not hard to see why a new profession is emerging that is designed to help people cope with change. And in fact, the challenge and the gift of coaching is that at its best, leadership coaching can contribute more to our lives, in all aspects, than simply coping skills…it can help us anticipate, initiate, respond to, embrace and be energized by change.

From the beginning of its appearance in the business press, there has been confusion about what "coaching" means. The coaching we are examining here has several core aspects which are important to assert as we begin.

- In coaching, the agenda of the client is the driving force…the client declares both what the challenge is and what her commitment to change is. The role of the coach is to encourage the client to explore her patterns, imagine a vivid, desired future, understand her resistance, create a plan to overcome the resistance and move towards that desired future. The coach's role or obligation is to have "unconditional positive regard"[4] for the client in all aspects of the coaching relationship. The client "owns" her issues and chooses the future that is compelling and uniquely her own.
- In coaching, the assumption is that the client is a healthy adult who is intentionally making choices to change some aspect of her life. The accountability for change, the responsibility to experiment, is with the client herself.
- In coaching, the focus is on a desired future, and the path to get there is developmental, based on the client's desire to learn. To the degree that understanding the patterns and choices of the past will be instructive, the coach may explore some of these aspects; but coaching is not therapy, it is not meant to heal deep wounds of childhood or earlier adulthood. It **is** about renewal, learning, redirecting energy and self-awareness. The coach's role is to promote or facilitate the change through a learning process, directed ultimately by the client's desire, needs and motivation to change. The coach may help the client see her previously unsuspected "blind spots", to see and test her hidden strengths and to support her in leading an authentic life.
- Coaching is primarily about communication – about sharing feedback and exploring visions of the future to get clear about and to define what might be a compelling future. This future is founded in the client's unique sense of purpose and meaning. The client may already know that she wants to

change and seek help from the coach, or the client may simply have a deep and troubling sense that life is not enough…that there is something missing.

- The coach can act as a guide, challenger, supporter, and a role model, in service to the client's agenda for change. The coaching relationship might be mostly the analysis of the current situation and the generation of options, or it might be more specifically crafting and managing a plan of action to achieve desired results.

- With the kinds of changes in the work world, and indeed the planet itself, it becomes more and more important to see the linkage between lifelong learning and change mastery. We all are leaders in our own lives and need to lead those lives with intention and purpose. Coaching may not be only helpful but indeed indispensable to such a challenge.

- Perhaps most importantly, coaching is not simply about something a coach does to or with a client - it is about the nature of the coach herself. To **do** coaching it is necessary to **be** a coach, and to be a coach it is necessary to start from the inside out…from who we are. Coaching is fundamentally different from consulting, which is basically a model of applying an 'outside in' expertise to problems. Nor is it traditional managing, which is normally viewed as requiring accountability for results involving planning, directing, organizing and control. A coach can only coach authentically when she has been coached and has experienced the relationship from the client's perspective.

The Evolution of Coaching

Given how important coaching is to successful living in the twenty-first century, it is appropriate to examine its evolution. But rather than approaching the evolution with a largely bibliographic report on the hundreds of coaching books and articles that have appeared in the last ten years, we would like to present a personal perspective on a representative sample of offerings we feel have made a major contribution to the extension of understanding of the coaching field. We will use the central ideas in five texts as punctuation points to draw attention to some of the evolutionary themes and issues that have marked the last decade, especially with reference to our interest in Leadership Coaching. We will conclude with a statement of our beliefs, principles and assumptions about coaching and an exploration of the implications of these values for the Leader Coach.

The five books we have chosen represent some of the best thinking done over this time period. We chose them because they propose a theory of coaching rather than dealing only with process and techniques and because they concentrate on changing patterns of individual behavior rather than simply on skill building and performance improvement. In other words, they are as much about how to **be** as they are about how to **do**, for the coach and the client. We start with Frederic Hudson's *The Adult Years,* then look at *Masterful Coaching* by Robert Hargrove, *The Heart of Coaching* by Thomas Crane, *Coaching: Evoking Excellence in Others* by James Flaherty, and finish with *Executive Coaching with Backbone and Heart* by Mary Beth O'Neill.[5]

Coaching Concepts, Models and Principles

The Adult Years, published at the beginning of the 1990s, focuses on mastering the art of adult life through self-renewal in the midst of change. This is one of the first books on coaching, written before the term "coach" gained widespread popularity. Hudson uses the term "adult mentor" in a prescient final section that discusses the need for a profession dedicated to facilitating adult transitions.

Our turbulent world is a jumping off point for *The Adult Years*, contrasting our experience of continuous change with our parents' more stable adulthood. Hudson suggests that repeating past patterns is no longer a viable approach. We must learn and evolve throughout adulthood in order to feel fulfilled as individuals and to build fulfilling societies. He draws on adult development theories, primarily from Jung, Levinson and Erikson, to outline the challenges in the adult life cycle and the patterns of self-renewal.

"The Cycle of Renewal" (Figure 6) is made up of life chapters and life transitions that we circle multiple times through adulthood. Each life chapter is a period of relative stability where we successfully play our roles in alignment with our dreams and plans – we "go for it" - until the inevitable time when these roles wear out, leaving us in the "doldrums", stuck in old patterns and feeling out of synch. We often choose to resist endings and instead make a "mini-transition" to extend our current chapter, a surface restructuring to repair and upgrade our life circumstances. Eventually in order to grow we must leave the "doing" world for the "being" world where we more fundamentally change to create a new life structure. The transition begins with turning inward, a disengagement from our old roles and "cocooning", in order to re-examine our life purpose, values and passions. We then experiment with how to take this new sense of self into the world in the form of new roles and activities, "getting ready" to begin the cycle once again.

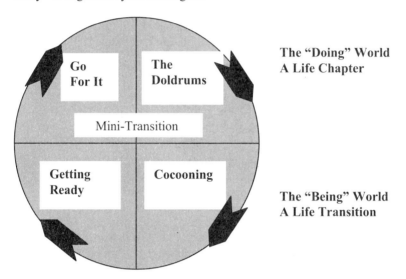

Figure 6: Hudson's Cycle of Renewal

Adult life flows around the circle, each time passing through the same phases in the change cycle but with a different combination of core values that shape our focus, purpose and commitments. With each cycle, we are meant to reassess where our current "juice" for life lies. The six core values of adult life are:

- Sense of self: identity, confidence, autonomy, responsibility.
- Achievement: working, winning, reaching goals, having ambition.
- Intimacy: loving, caring, nurturing, coupling, parenting, being a friend.
- Creativity and play: being imaginative, spontaneous, artistic, funny, joyful.
- Search for meaning: integrity, inner peace, contemplation, ultimate concern.
- Compassion and contribution: giving, helping, mentoring, leading, reforming, legacy.

The strength of *The Adult Years* is that it provides a thorough integration of the theory of adult development and the imperative of change, bringing the underused adult development literature into the current context with a useful diagnostic model for understanding adult lives today. Its weakness is that, because it was written before the coaching field emerged, it lacks some of the attention to applications and techniques present in other later texts. Hudson addressed this by publishing *Life Launch*, a practical companion handbook, with Pamela McLean in 1995.

Masterful Coaching was published in 1995, about four years after *The Adult Years* and reflects the growth of the field. Hargrove opens with the words "Coaching is hot!" While Hudson left the corporate context largely unexplored, Hargrove sees coaching as a new style of management, one designed to teach people to produce breakthrough results in their businesses in response to demands for higher levels of performance and faster, more innovative change. Transformational coaching unleashes the creative energy of people in organizational groups by altering the underlying context of beliefs that block creativity and productive action. He draws on learning theory from authors primarily associated with corporate contexts like Argyris, Senge, and Hamel and Prahalad in discussing how triple loop learning transforms "who people are" by changing their point of view about themselves so they can make different choices and produce truly desirable results.

The coach promotes transformational learning to create a shift in context that is consistent with the client's intentions - changing "rut stories" to "river stories". Hargrove provides four compass points (Figure 7) that are the map of the masterful coaching territory. "Stewardship" is choosing service to others over self-interest so that we open up possibilities for contribution to the future of people, institutions and the world. In so doing, we encourage people to bring to work their whole selves, including all that they care about. "Personal Transformation" involves empowering people to create deeply purposeful lives by challenging their self-limiting beliefs and assumptions. By reframing this underlying context, new avenues for purposeful action are revealed. Communities of "Communication and Commitment" are workplaces made up of teams characterized by shared passion, dedication and pride, where people are encouraged to be authentic individuals but also have a deep appreciation for connection to the whole community. The coach promotes the shift from "following orders to working on causes". Expanding "Capacity for Action" occurs when individuals have a personal calling to the work, when they are challenged by stretch goals, and when breakdowns are acknowledged with the coach intervening to enhance the learning process.

Stewardship

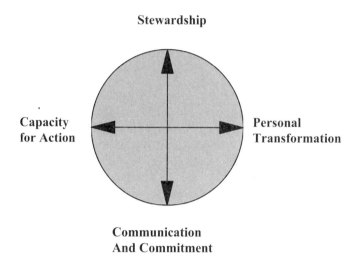

**Capacity
for Action**

**Personal
Transformation**

**Communication
And Commitment**

Figure 7: Hargrove's Four Compass Points

Hargrove also provides some navigation points, some coaching fundamentals to create transformation and learning:
- Stretch, yearning and learning: to motivate breakthroughs requiring deep learning.
- Unwritten rules of the game: to uncover and understand them.
- Theory to action to practice: to identify and question the governing frame of reference.
- Observing and giving feedback: mindful observation, action maps and meaningful feedback.
- New skills and capabilities: to alter practice by transforming mental models.

Masterful Coaching succeeds in bringing together a broad array of guidelines, exercises, cases and techniques for creating learning conversations between individuals and among members of groups. In fact, Hargrove's orientation to "life as narrative" underscores the importance in coaching of telling, listening to, understanding, and learning from the story. Hargrove also includes a complete section on how to be a masterful coach using his transformational learning methodology. The problem is that given this array, the whole can seem unfocused, with no integrating framework to pull it all together.

The Heart of Coaching, published in 1998, develops much the same business case for coaching as Hargrove and even uses the same term, "transformational coaching". However, Crane relates the concept to leadership, describing coaching as the leadership process for the new millennium. He sees coaching as a requisite leadership skill for building adaptive organizational cultures that respond successfully to change and create true high performance. He draws from business writers like Drucker, Kotter and McGregor to outline a new theory of management, Theory "C" for coaching, based on a comprehensive communications process characterized by open feedback, mutual learning, challenge and support between the leader and the employee. Leaders must be open, vulnerable and real, providing *direction*, not *directions.*

There are five roles that are the essence of contemporary business leadership (Figure 8) as it is different from traditional management. Through these roles we bring our leadership to our life's work and relationships. The "visionary" provides people with a sense of direction, lifting expectations to a more desirable common future. Leaders continually connect themselves and others to the business vision. The "servant" sees the organization as upside-down, serving those who serve the customer, and appreciates making a difference in people's lives. Leaders see serving others as a gift. The "coach" connects people to performance through communication. All other leadership roles are enhanced through coaching. The "facilitator" empowers others to act on the organization's behalf by relinquishing control. Leaders facilitate communication, collaboration, decision-making and much more. The "role model" is the heart of leadership, influencing attitudes and behaviors through words and deeds. Leaders cast a long shadow; their influence is what defines the culture.

Transformational coaching as a key element of leadership happens in three phases:
— *The Foundation Phase*: establishes the relationship, sets expectations, allows observation of behavior and preparation of interpretations.
— *The Learning Loop*: is a circular phase reiterated until a common understanding is reached through offering behavioral feedback, sharing perceived impacts, asking learning questions and deeply listening, and using dialogue to gain mutual insight.
— *The Forward the Action Phase*: uses one of three strategies to move forward, depending on the current performance and relationships: a) solicits and suggests options, b) requests specific behavior change, or c) requires

behaviors and states consequences, and ends by clarifying the action plan and offering support.

Crane takes the corporate coaching theme to its logical conclusion – a practical template for the leader/employee relationship at every level in the management hierarchy.

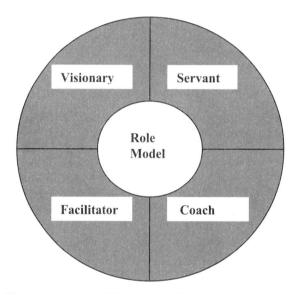

Figure 8: Crane's Five Leadership Roles

The Heart of Coaching does a great job of applying coaching to everyday leadership, taking managers through each of the steps involved in incorporating this essential process into their relations with direct reports. A particular strength is the integration of performance management into the coaching process in a way that managers can accept and adopt. This strength is also a weakness, however, as the text is bounded by the managerial context and the practical considerations being addressed.

Coaching: Evoking Excellence in Others, published in 1999, saves the coaching field from becoming just another management fad by contributing a broad philosophical foundation for coaching. Drawing on phenomenology, a branch of modern philosophy dealing with how we make sense of events in our world, Flaherty cites Flores, Maturana and Heidegger among others in challenging coaches to confront what it means to be human, how human behavior is motivated and how it is changed. He suggests we abandon the manipulative "amoeba theory" of coaching, with rewards and punishments, in favor of understanding the client's "structure of interpretation" - it is not just circumstances but how we interpret them, give them meaning, that leads to action. Coaches help clients change their structure of interpretation by providing new language and practices that create long term excellent performance.

The products of coaching are:
- Long term excellent performance measured by high objective standards.
- Self-correcting by clients independent of the coach, based on observing when they are performing well and when they are not.
- Self-generating continual improvements to performance.

For these outcomes to occur, the coach must account for, or make sense of, the clients' behavior (Figure 9) and help them understand how the meanings they attribute to life circumstances, the "structures of interpretation", lead to particular actions. The way we see the world at a moment in time determines how we react. The coach provides, first, a "language" of new possibilities that allows clients to observe their own behavior and assess it with new information; and second, new "practices" that, through repeated cycles of observation and assessment, embed the new language in the clients' behavior. The altered structure of interpretation with its language and practices allows clients to respond effectively to similar situations in the future without the coach.

Coaching almost always involves an uncoiling and reconstruction of clients' notions of being human. Therefore it is essential to understand the fundamental aspects of what it is to be human in order for coaching to happen. These include:
- Relationship: we enter into relationship with all we encounter, using language to make distinctions.
- Language and time: we exist simultaneously in past, present and future time, so coaching always begins in the middle of something.
- Mood: tells us how open we are to encountering other people and events.
- The body: tells us how open or closed we are and what concerns us.
- Death: our acknowledgement of death allows us to prioritize life.
Coaches, then, use observation and assessment to support clients in crafting their own humanity.

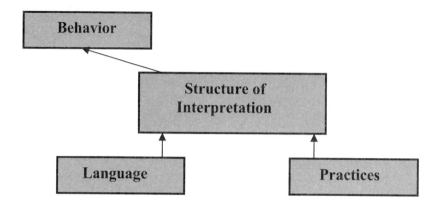

Figure 9: Flaherty's Premise of Coaching

Coaching: Evoking Excellence in Others offers a unique perspective, locating the coaching field within a broad range of literature in the humanities and asking challenging questions about the foundations of the practice. Although the breadth of philosophy makes it less accessible than other texts, it does provide detailed descriptions of coaching conversations with exercises, worksheets and examples. Perhaps the weakness here is that these examples seem somewhat simplistic given the historical sweep and the complexity of most business and personal coaching situations.

And finally, ***Executive Coaching with Backbone and Heart: A Systems Approach to Engaging Leaders with their Challenges***, by Mary Beth O'Neill, focuses specifically on the unique challenges of coaching top executives, from the point of view of external executive coaches. However, her central notion of "signature presence" is an important construct for all coaches to consider. She draws on the consulting field from authors such as Schein and Block as well as previous coaching texts including Hargrove. O'Neill views the executive job as requiring a specific coaching style which blends backbone and heart. To bring backbone is to state your positions clearly, and to coach from heart is to tune into the relationship with understanding and compassion. This style also requires a blend of bringing one's own signature presence (Figure 10), using a systems perspective to uncover the context, and an action research model of the coaching process.

In order to coach executives effectively, O'Neill suggests that there are four essential ingredients:

- A results orientation to the leader's problem.
- Creating a partnership in the executive's journey towards greater competence and effectiveness.
- An ability to engage the executive in his or her specific leadership challenges.
- An ability to link team behaviors to bottom-line goals.

These ingredients underscore how vital it is for the coach to be grounded in a strong sense of self, her "signature presence", to provide an effective sounding board and learning partner for the client.

Signature Presence

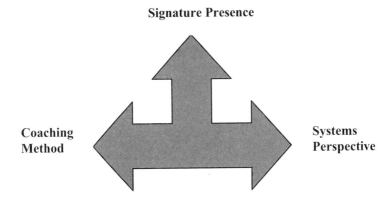

Coaching Method

Systems Perspective

Figure 10: O'Neill's Core Principles

Specifically, O'Neill encourages coaches to be highly tolerant of uncomfortable situations and recover quickly from "reactivity". There will be times of increased anxiety, both personally for the client, and for the organization, that will be important for the coach to acknowledge and work with. It is also vital that the coach not "catch" the anxiety of the client or organization because she will lose access to her own strengths and resources. The coach's challenge, therefore, is to work to keep from taking on the client's burden, or rescuing the client from her situation.

In terms of developing and using a systems perspective, O'Neill guides coaches to explore the specific effects and contexts of the client's stress and reactions. From family systems theory, O'Neill draws on the interactional force field concept in which relationships are explored, including the relationship between the client and the coach, and the many relationships between the client and her system.

O'Neill presents a coaching process model which includes quickly beginning to give the client feedback and testing her ability to own her part of the issue. O'Neill describes *live-action coaching* as blending the roles of coach and consultant, with the coach intervening to offer suggestions, take a facilitator role, or stop the meeting to conduct on-the-spot evaluations and feedback. While there are essential planning and structure considerations to negotiate ahead of time, the coach is "in the picture" in this type of coaching rather than behind the scenes.

O'Neill's call to coaches to develop a strong signature presence, particularly in working hard with resistance and taking risks to help the client learn and grow, may be her central contribution. However, in her responsiveness as an external coach to her executive client, O'Neill may overestimate the need for speed and give short shrift to the learning available through reflection and experimentation.

Themes and Distinctions

Based on this personal assessment of the work of the five authors, then, what similarities and differences are evident across the texts? Are there themes and distinctions that can inform our understanding of the central tenets of leadership coaching? And what ideas are new and emerging?

Leadership Competencies	Coaching Themes and Distinctions
Strategic Anticipation	Deepening Context Working through Stuckness
Vision and Values	Living on Purpose Being in Service
Empowering Others	Using Conversations Sustaining Diversity
Learning and Change	Modeling Change Continuous Learning Reframing Paradox

Chart 5: A Framework of Leadership and Coaching Competencies

We imagine you will be struck, as we are, with the similarity of philosophy and practice between recent leadership and coaching writing. So rather than repeat the major competencies, in this section we have outlined some issues and themes that have emerged for us. In Chart 5, we headline these themes as they relate to the Leadership Competencies from Chapter 1.

Deepening Context:

The authors all speak of the importance of understanding the underlying context within which behavior occurs in order to bring about change. For Hudson, the context is the cycle of life chapters and transitions that must be navigated to grow and develop as an adult. For Hargrove, the context is the individual's current mental models and governing frames of reference that need to be in alignment with intentions. For Crane, it is the unintended consequences of the command and control organizational culture and the adaptability required to sustain high performance. For Flaherty, our use of language and our daily habits and practice are the context that shape our interpretations of events and lead us to the behaviors that may or may not achieve long-term excellent performance. O'Neill requires a systems perspective and awareness of the interactional force field - seeing the system the leader is in.

Although the context in each author's work is critical, there are distinctions between corporate and life settings. Hargrove, O'Neill and Crane concentrate on corporate contexts – the leader/manager, employee, team and organization. Hudson and Flaherty look more generally at life contexts – individual behavior and adult development phases. This distinction is true of the coaching field as well. Corporate coaching and life coaching are two separate, somewhat overlapping streams or specializations that have emerged over the past decade with their associated authors, education, skill requirements and practices.

As corporations have come to see coaching as a fundamental aspect of leadership development, there has been an evolution from remedial coaching of single executives to developmental coaching of larger pools of managers and executives and an emerging desire to create corporate coaching cultures embedding the principles throughout the organization. Coaching is becoming the leadership style for managing in turbulent times. Group and team coaching have grown in tandem as a powerful reinforcement of individual learning as well as a practice in its own right. Among the authors represented here, only Hargrove deals with group coaching to any extent. This aspect of coaching as a distinct process, apart from existing group and organization development methods, is still in the formative stages. Indeed, O'Neill blends the notion of group coaching and Organization Development consulting.

In life coaching, there has been a similar explosion of specializations. Some, like career coaching and couples coaching, build from current professions, while others, like transition coaching and longevity coaching, have evolved from social and demographic realities. While it is appropriate that there is some separation between the two streams, the blending of human development and leadership development is long overdue and adds value to both. As a Leader Coach, this *both/and* blending of life and work, learning and leading, individual and group, is a central tenet.

Working through Stuckness:

One of the most common presenting issues in coaching is when someone is feeling stuck, sensing that things are not what they could be but unable to move forward on their own. Hudson calls this state the "doldrums", the wearing out of previously purposeful roles over time. Hargrove refers to clients telling "rut stories". Crane sees organizational leaders as responsible for changing a culture stuck in a command and control paradigm to one of high performance. In these coaching relationships, the coach's role is to uncover what the stuck point is, what Flaherty calls the "structure of interpretation", that is limiting the ability to take effective action. O'Neill refers to the need for "backbone" to confront the resistance. Being stuck is a natural occurrence in a changing world and can be a catalyst that creates momentum for taking new action.

The distinction here comes from the varied sources the authors draw on to center the coaching need, the stuckness. All agree that some form of barrier, beyond our awareness, is where coaching starts, but they differ with respect to the source of the malaise. Flaherty sees it embedded in our everyday language and practice; Hudson sees it as the inevitable erosion of energy in life roles; Hargrove sees it as our inability to confront our defensive routines; Crane sees it as endemic in our assumptions about what makes good leaders. O'Neill introduces the helpful notion of "loyal resistance" to describe a form of advocacy, clearly standing in a different, sometimes opposing, place from the client.

From a Leader Coach point of view, understanding and managing 'stuckness' or resistance, is a central part of the role. One of the most common outcomes of chaotic change for us as individuals is that we tend to become paralyzed, we don't know which way to turn so we don't do anything at all. The Leader Coach must understand, as Hudson does, the cycle of change that individuals go through to learn and grow; must be able to surface structures of interpretation that inhibit forward movement, as Flaherty does; and be able to reframe them, as Hargrove does, so that action is possible. Resistance doesn't happen only within the person being coached. It happens with the coach as well, and can tell her much about how to be effective in the moment. The Leader Coach moves *into* the friction knowing it has also to do with her. When the performance or results aren't there, for instance, she doesn't retreat to an autocratic model, but rather, staying in a coaching role, works it out by raising awareness and staying connected.

Living on Purpose:

So what drives this transformation? What motivates change? These authors believe it is a continuing reference to a central life purpose, a passionate intent, an inner compass, that helps us to make difficult choices and tradeoffs. It is this awareness of purpose that allows us to align our behavior with our desired outcome, to be intentional in a complex and uncertain world.

For the client, purpose underpins the change plan - what Hargrove calls "the passionate goals" and Hudson calls "the core values" - and supports its implementation. Flaherty believes language and practice provide a mirror of our purpose and values; it is our examination and reassessment of them that allow us to shape new behaviors.

For the coach, purpose fuels the process and connection between the coach and client. Hargrove refers to "calling forth" those inner values, an almost involuntary seeking, expressed through the coaching role. In other words, a coach is something that you **be**! Crane suggests that the "heart of coaching" is bringing our whole humanity to our work and relationships. We believe that coaching includes body, mind, heart and spirit – the whole person. Leader Coaches live "on purpose" and model this way of being for their clients. The transformative power of coaching lies in this drawing or calling forth of our inner purpose to align with our outer vision, a process that is often ignored in our culture where speed and outward focus are seen as paramount. Coaching happens from the inside out and in all facets of our being.

Being In Service:

There is an underlying philosophy of service to the needs of the client. Crane sees service as one of the key roles that the "new leader" models for others. Those in leadership roles must see the organization upside down, empowering those on the front lines. Similarly, Hargrove sees stewardship as one of four "compass points" for transformational coaching. The corollary of the coach in service to the client is that the client is then in control of the outcomes of the coaching relationship. Leader Coaches use a variety of methods to evoke new awareness but it is up to the client, with the coach's support, to commit to change. As Hudson says, coaches "lead from behind".

This leading from behind is one of the many paradoxes of leadership coaching. It requires letting go of ego and control, trust in the process, and true desire to listen to understand. If the people we lead are willing participants in the journey and see a positive outcome from making it, then as leaders we only need to gently guide the process, to give a hand over the hurdles and a pat on the back for the achievements.

Our innovation can then center on the larger human systems that can benefit from our service leadership. Coaching can have an impact on organizational cultures, including the way power is shared. It has been suggested[6] that coaching as a broad leadership change movement plays a strategic role in helping leaders develop synergistic, or shared power, leading for example to more democratic organizations.

Using Conversations:

The central tool in the process of coaching is conversation - the dialogue between coach and client that reveals the client's current story and then composes a new and more fitting one. Hargrove, for example, sees life as narrative. By reciting our stories and becoming aware of the breakdowns, we can transform them into breakthroughs. Crane frames conversation as the dialogue between the manager and employee, peer or boss that builds not only better performance but better relationships as well.

Language is a key to these conversations. For Flaherty, language is central to understanding why we act the way we do. It is through language that we express our deepest selves. For both client and coach, it is critical that our language reflects the behavior we want. Crane contributes a practical framework of appropriate coaching language, including body language, that leaders model for others. For Hargrove, it is often the unspoken, the "undiscussables", that must surface to promote true learning conversations. For Hudson, the language of adult development in change allows us to diagnose our current phase in the cycle and plan strategies for self renewal. O'Neill stresses that the key to successful coaching lies in getting into the *right* conversation with the client.

Leader Coaches, then, use the art of conversation to express themselves and understand others so that problems can be solved and relationships developed. They are students of language and feelings, as they reflect the underlying assumptions that lead to certain behavior, and strive to bring to the surface and realign mismatches in word and deed, in thinking and feeling.

Sustaining Diversity:

Four of the authors' views presented are from a male perspective. This is not intentional; it is just a reflection of much of the coaching literature over the decade. There have been, of course, female authors but they are fewer and usually less well-known, particularly in the corporate coaching frame. And despite being a female author and making an important contribution to the notions of coaching executives, O'Neill does not address gender or diversity issues.

In contrast, practicing coaches in the field are predominantly female, including those in corporate coaching settings. The imbalance is beginning to be rectified with the growing number of female authors contributing their unique views. In fact the role of coach may be more about 'the feminine' than strictly female-ness. It is the invitation, the opportunity for a different, deeper kind of conversation that is at the heart of coaching and that is its true magic.

If this imbalance between perspectives is true of gender, it is all the more true of diversity in general. We are threatened in the emerging coaching profession with an extremely limited field of view. We need to learn about other cultures, other perspectives, experiences other than our own and to incorporate them into our deepening understanding of coaching and its potential role in social and organizational change. This is beginning to happen as some multinationals extend coaching to their operations in other countries. Much more is needed. Our challenge is to move into the relationship, move into diversity, and work to understand, knowing it has everything to do with us. The final potential is far beyond organization and community – it is socio-ecological and leads to global sustainability[7].

Leader Coaches need the broadest possible perspectives on issues in order to match the variety and complexity we find in everyday problems. A narrow view is simply not going to afford the range of alternatives necessary, and may in fact be a very dangerous standpoint. When creativity and innovation are the order of the day, diversity of every kind is the best strategy.

Modeling Change:

For all of the authors, the reason for coaching is that change has added such complexity and uncertainty to our work and personal lives that we have trouble coping with being adults. Hudson focuses on the challenges of adulthood in general; Hargrove and Crane look at the requirement for performance in the corporate world; Flaherty concentrates on individual self-monitoring to adapt behavior. O'Neill sees the coach in the role of change agent. All take as their starting premise that we need to grow and improve to keep pace with our changing times. It is interesting to note, though, the decreasing need to explain, describe and justify change over the decade. Change itself changes, from needing to be carefully considered (a couple of chapters in Hudson) to being simply a given (a couple of paragraphs in Flaherty).

Also noteworthy from a change point of view is that coaching as a distinct field of inquiry and practice is the first would-be profession to be born out of change and specifically focused on supporting people in responding to it. So, too, leadership coaching is about change, its endemic and pervasive nature in our society, and the way leadership is expressed in order to survive and thrive in it. Leader Coaches evoke better, faster, deeper change. They recognize change as a way of being and as a process that is as natural as our progression from birth to death, as the changes we make as we live through every day.

Reframing Paradox:

New understandings lead, with the coach's help, to a reframing of perspectives and the vision of new possibilities for moving forward. Crane speaks of the learning loop that generates mutual insights about next steps; Flaherty recommends altering the structure of interpretation; Hargrove changes 'rut' stories to 'river' stories; Hudson legitimizes people's experience and provides strategies for moving on. O'Neill sees ambiguity as something to "get through". Whatever the metaphor, the coach helps the client gain greater self awareness about the "stuck" points and provides tools and support for looking at current circumstances in a new, more positive way.

However, sometimes the reframing is just about acknowledging the reality of paradox. Paradox is real. Sometimes, the only help you can provide is to help the person hold the paradox, not solve the problem. Having the Leader Coach model the ability to stand **in** the paradox and hold the ambiguity in mind, resisting the temptation to sink into an easy right or wrong, good or bad dichotomy will aid the client to do the same.

Continuous Learning:

Learning is central to coaching, both for the client and the coach. Crane and Hargrove both use transformational terminology to stress, as Hargrove says, "The person who was there before is not there now." It is fundamental change, triple loop learning, transforming who we are and how we see ourselves in the world. Flaherty sees coaching as changing our very notions of what it is to be human. Hudson compares our life transitions to undergoing major surgery. All stress the importance of the coach being a learning partner with the client. As the client is changed through new learning and insight, so too, through the process, is the coach.

This continuous learning is a hallmark of the Leader Coach. It is the antidote to change and the route to self-understanding. In a world of rapid change, we must be constantly learning new things just to keep pace with what's happening around us. And we also need to keep pace with what's happening within us, our emotional responses, our needs, desires, and fears. Learning both from the inside out and the outside in provides the basis for effective leadership coaching.

So, we've explored with you a lengthy list of themes that we believe highlight why the interest in coaching has developed. We have extended these themes to include some of our own thinking. We'd like to conclude the chapter with Chart 6 which summarizes how we have been describing Leadership Coaching stretching beyond its already impressive history to move into its potential future.

Coaching Competencies	Common View	Emerging View
Deepening Context	Separation of life coaching and corporate coaching	Blend of both leadership development and personal development
Working through Stuckness	Coaching starts at the stuck point	Resistance is natural in both the coach and the client
Living on Purpose	The primary driver of transformation and motivator of change	Coach the whole person - alignment of body, mind, spirit and heart
Being in Service	Stewardship, client owns agenda and outcomes	Service leadership toward more democratic organizations
Using Conversations	Central tool of coaching Stories and language	Alignment of language and feelings – intellect and emotion
Sustaining Diversity	Imbalance of perspectives between genders	Variety and complexity of diversity prompts socio-ecological sustainability
Modeling Change	Creates difficulty coping	Way of being, in the world and in us
Continuous Learning	Transforms coach and client through learning partnership	Continuous learning about self, as coach, and client, in deep partnership
Reframing Paradox	New perspectives to lead to new choices	Paradox is real - standing in the paradox may be all one can do.

Chart 6: A Framework of Emerging Leadership Coaching Competencies

As we move to the heart of our book, to the alchemy we propose is more than the sum of these two parts, we want to draw some distinctions between our concept of leadership coaching and just leading or just coaching. We've explored leadership and its evolution; we've looked at how coaching has emerged over the past decade. How do they blend together and what are the implications of this *both/and* view?

Leader Coaches encompass:

BOTH	AND
Leading	Coaching
Results	Process
Challenge	Support
Reflecting on experience	Planning the future
Assessment	Development
Stories	Dreams
Coach as "Showing Up"	Client as central
Accountability	Trust

Chart 7: A Framework of Both/And Leadership Coaching

What makes leadership coaching different from just leading or just coaching? Most books on *leadership* talk about what it is, what it takes, who does it well, and so on but they don't often tell you exactly, practically, how you can become one, how to apply what you now understand to your day-to-day work life. What does it mean to get out there and **do** it. Most books on *coaching* are positioned for a general audience of people who may or may not be leaders in organizations so while they, again, give you a sense of what coaching is, what it takes, who does it well, and so on, they don't specify how to coach as a leader or lead as a coach. What does the leader **do** as a coach? How does a coach demonstrate leadership through playing the role?

Carol has been a manager of people and processes for most of her career, in one way or another, and has this reflection on her own evolution from traditional supervisor and manager to coach manager.

> When I was first made a manager, the situation was typical of the early 80's: I was called into my boss's office and told I had a promotion. While I wasn't unhappy about this recognition, I had not directly asked for it. I wasn't sure it was in my career plan. And I certainly had no training for it, though perhaps I had an intuitive sense of it that my 'boss' saw. Virtually immediately, I was instructed that, as the manager, I was required to terminate an employee who had been an underperformer. It may have been my compassion or sense of justice, rather than anything more managerial, which prompted me to protest that he and I hadn't had a chance to establish a working relationship

and that I hadn't had a chance to turn the situation around. I certainly saw this as my challenge and responsibility. I met frequently with the employee and discovered that there were structural impediments to his performance, both in terms of job design and his own life constraints that we could actually do something about. I also learned that he absolutely did want to continue to do this work in this company if he could. He told me he realized he had a chance to start over and prove himself with me, and that prior to my appointment he had thought he was already fired.

Once we'd had the conversations where he realized I would support his attempts to start over, his performance improved dramatically and quickly. I was not really a Leader Coach here, as we've defined it, but I was a manager who was intent on discovering what the central goals were of this employee's life and how much responsibility he was willing to take for turning the situation around. He taught me that while it was my responsibility as the manager to deliver results from the team, it was in fact his responsibility to manage his own contribution in ways that honored his goals and values. This learning helped to define my leadership style for the next twenty years, and has been validated repeatedly.

We believe the leader in an organizational setting who is accountable for a group of direct reports and the products or services they produce must be a coach, a Leader Coach, to evoke high performance in her team. This *both/and* blend of competencies is the prerequisite for organizational success. There are several reasons we believe that this is so.

– Employees look to their bosses for information, direction, support and learning. In survey after survey, the leader is the person the employee chooses as her coach.
– Leaders have a broader view of the organization with its challenges and possibilities, as well as a detailed picture of the day-to-day operation. From this viewpoint, they can advise, mentor, guide and develop members of their team.
– Coaching, as does leading, requires a level of mental complexity sufficient to not only understand but to extend the client's perspective. Jaques[8] has shown in his research that appropriate levels of mental complexity are associated with successful leadership and coaching relationships. Where these are out of balance, there is either a communications gap between

leader and direct report or there is frustration on the part of the direct report that the leader can't really stretch her thinking.

– Leaders have a stake in the outcomes of coaching. They are not just interested third parties but directly accountable for the results produced by the team. Coaching is about change – better, faster, deeper change. Leaders are in a position to measure their success with coaching over longer periods of time and see the results in tangible terms.

– Leaders have the means to reward high performance, the outcome of coaching. They can ensure that members of their team who excel are rewarded not just with acknowledgements from an outsider but with increased compensation, opportunity and profile.

Exploring these distinctions and addressing the questions raised in them is the work of the remainder of the book. We have now set the stage – on with the play!

Personal Reflection:

One of the greatest gifts a coach can bring to her client is a great question. So we've collected a few questions, both to get you dreaming about what your life might be and to model for you through your interaction with these questions how you can experience "the coaching voice within" during stuckness and change, learning, reframing and perhaps even conversation.

So you might choose two or three questions to have an internal conversation about, perhaps writing down your thoughts in your journal. When you do, you might try this: draw a line vertically down your page and write only on the left hand side of your line. Answer the three questions as fully and deeply as you can, practicing the reflection gift as well. Now, go back and start reading...whenever it seems to make sense, ask yourself, "Why is that important?", and write your thoughts about **that** question on the right hand side.

- Many people believe that we come into the world with a purpose, a raison d'etre. What is the number one problem you believe you were born to solve or the number one question you were born to answer?
- In many myths, the hero is granted three wishes. If you were the hero of the story, what three things would you ask for? What is one action you could take right now to begin to make your wishes come true?
- What is the most consistent message you have heard in the last year? This message is a persistent prompting to make a course correction or take a next step. It is a calling to make an affirmative departure from the status quo. What are your messages in a) your work, b) your relationships and c) your lifestyle?
- What is the most important thing missing from your life right now?

Perhaps jot down some of your own questions and journal to explore your answers to them.

A Reflection to Share:

Speaking your dreams out loud can be a powerful experience. It can also be risky, so for this exercise we encourage you to find a partner with whom you can experience and receive "unconditional positive regard".

From the questions that you've explored in the "Personal Reflection", try selecting one to talk about. Ask your partner simply to listen as you describe the question and your answers to it…and have your partner ask the question when you've finished, "Why is that important?". See if hearing that question from someone else's voice prompts you to new levels of self-discovery. It might be helpful to have your journal nearby to jot down some of your learnings.

When you've finished or think you're done, you might also ask your partner to ask you, "What do you want?" …you may now find yourself able to articulate that more clearly.

A Team Exercise:

One of the surest ways to embed the coaching principles we've discussed in this chapter is to begin…here and now. You might want to share some of what you've read here, and already know about coaching principles.

Why not convene a team meeting to explore what the coaching principles are and where they could be applied to improve effectiveness. You might have a recent experience with some kind of change that the team could use to explore the topics of stuckness, context, learning, reframing and so on.

A Self-Assessment:

To get a sense of how you are now with your coaching competencies, we've adapted the chart presented earlier in this chapter. We invite you now to assess yourself as a coach, both currently and as you see yourself in the future.

– How strong are you currently at displaying these competencies?
– Where do you consistently display these attributes?
– Where, in times of stress, high anxiety or other provocations, do you not model these behaviors as much as you might wish?
– How do you want to be as a coach?
– What particular competencies do see as your future strengths?
– What are the areas where you may want to improve or develop?
– What might you do to move in this direction?
– Who can you call upon to help you with continuing feedback, challenge and support?

Coaching Competency	Emerging View	How am I? How do I want to be?
Deepening Context	Blend of both leadership development and personal development	
Working through Stuckness	Resistance is natural in both the coach and the client	
Living on Purpose	Coach the whole person - alignment of body, mind, spirit and heart	
Being in Service	Service leadership toward more democratic organizations	
Using Conversations	Alignment of language and feelings – intellect and emotion	
Sustaining Diversity	Variety and complexity of diversity prompts socio-ecological sustainability	
Modeling Change	Way of being, in the world and in us	
Continuous Learning	Continuous learning about self, as coach, and client, in deep partnership	
Reframing Paradox	Paradox is real - standing in the paradox may be all one can do.	

Chart 8: An Assessment of Coaching Themes

Endnotes:

[1] Quoted in Silzer, R., Ed. "Coaching Executives: Individual Leader Development", in *The 21st Century Executive: Innovative Practices for Building Leadership at the Top.* Jossey-Bass, 2000.

[2] See for instance, J.K.Rowling. *Harry Potter and the Sorcerer's Stone.* Chapter 11, p. 180. Scholastic Press, 1997.

[3] Recent research shows that women may respond to stress entirely differently than men, "tend and befriend" rather than fight or flight, and that a coaching relationship in fact might be essentially a 'tend and befriend' relationship, regardless of the gender of the coach and client. "Study after study has found that social ties reduce our risk of disease by lowering blood pressure, heart rate, and cholesterol. There's no doubt, says Dr. Klein, that friends are helping us live longer. In one study, for example, researchers found that people who had no friends increased their risk of death over a 6-month period. In another study, those who had the most friends over a 9-year period cut their risk of death by more than 60%." S.E.Taylor, L.C. Klein, B.P. Lewis, T.L Gruenewald, R.A.Gurung, J.A. Updegraff. "Female Responses to Stress: Tend and Befriend, not Fight or Flight", *Psychological Review* 107 (3) 41-49, 2000.

[4] Rogers, Carl. *On Becoming a Person.* Haughton Mifflin, 1961.

[5] Crane, Thomas G. *The Heart of Coaching.* FTA Press, 1998; Flaherty, James. *Coaching – Evoking Excellence in Others.* Butterworth Heinemann, 1999; Hargrove, Robert. *Masterful Coaching.* Pfeiffer, 1995; Hudson, F.H. *The Adult Years.* Jossey-Bass, 1991; O'Neill, M.B. *Executive Coaching with Backbone and Heart, Jossey-Bass, 2000.*

[6] Warah, A.A. "Governance, Synergistic Power and Coaching: Towards the Democratic Organization". University of Ottawa, awarah@uottawa.ca, 2001.

[7] Another aspect to this reflection on diversity and sustainability is in relation to the natural environment. We need to be 're-minded' that the world is finite, we're all on the planet together and therefore interdependent with each other. As long as we feel 'dominion' over some aspect of nature, or each other, we won't be free. To be self-responsible, to be a whole person includes being aware of, celebrating and in-corporating the natural environment - learning from it, contributing to its health and healing. As an example, leadership development is moving out of corporate training centers and into the deserts of Africa… to explore different cultures, different physical environments, different relationships with nature, different learning processes, different experiences of time, and so on, enabling leaders to return with a greater understanding of global diversity.

[8] Jaques, Elliott. *Requisite Organization.* Cason Hall Publishers, 1989.

Chapter 3
Leadership Alchemy as a Metaphor for *Both/And* Leadership

We have discussed the evolution of leadership themes and approaches, and looked at the recent explosion of coaching as a leadership tool. This background gives you a sense of our point of view on these topics and a common frame of reference, so that we can go forward from here together. Our hope is that what we have provided so far gives you a map of the territory of both leadership and coaching and the extent to which they are merging in terms of their underlying philosophies and competencies .

So, here is the heart of the matter. We believe that leadership and coaching are coming to be inextricably intertwined and interdependent. Although each can stand alone, together they become more powerful and in the end a different, more complete and more valuable entity. We propose that the concept we define as Leadership Alchemy is essential for any Leader Coach working with and through others to achieve high performance results in dynamic, constantly changing organizations.

Let us explain. When we think about combining known things to make something different we think of the ancient art of alchemy. Beginning with base metals and some natural ingredients, the fabled chemists turned ordinary items into gold. Each of the ingredients stood on its own and had other uses, like the brass used at that time for most utensils. Put together with some skill, however, they transformed into a completely different and more precious metal – gold, one of the strongest and rarest metals, cherished both for its intrinsic value as beautiful to behold and its symbolic value as currency.

So it is with leadership and coaching. The alchemy is in the blend of *both/and* to produce powerful results through others. Leadership without coaching is autocratic control or blue-sky visioning - it is not valueless in itself, it is just incomplete. Together, leadership and coaching produce an alchemic reaction, transforming the essential ingredients into something quite different and highly valuable.

The transformative element that has been lacking, as organizational change has dramatically increased, is the "inside out" aspect, the focus on self leadership. Our most common experience with leadership is that it is practiced almost flawlessly in technical terms but is badly, sometimes fatally, flawed in personal and interpersonal terms. In competency studies of managers and executives, their greatest strengths tend to be intellectual capacity, functional skills, action orientation and the like, while their greatest weaknesses tend to be developing and confronting direct reports, patience, personal learning and understanding others.[1] So it is no surprise that coaching has emerged as a way to try to close this growing gap.

The problem is that coaches outside the direct line of accountability can only go so far… they can guide, support, model and assist but they are not part of the daily leadership context and therefore, while they can make a substantial contribution to specific development challenges, they are limited in their ability to embed the principles and approaches into the leadership culture and systems of the organization to promote their broader diffusion. And leaders themselves can only take on this role if they have developed a strong sense of self that allows them to lead through engaging with others in coaching relationships.

So our proposal is that leaders must become Leader Coaches to be effective in turbulent times. Coaching adds the transformative potential. Coaching is applied leadership. Leadership is manifest through coaching. It is how the best leaders lead - all of the time, in all aspects of their work and life. And, in fact, the competencies of the transformative leader and the transformative coach have extensive overlap, a "likeness" to each other. They are internally fundamentally the same, at their foundations, as shown below the line in Figure 11. Above the line, the roles may be distinct – they have not yet merged in most cases. The current leadership role looks quite different from the role of the coach but this is rapidly changing as leaders and their organizations see the value in this new style of leadership. So our belief is that expressions of leadership and coaching may continue to differ at their edges and farther extensions but as we see them, they share a common destiny, a common foundation of shared values and shared competencies.

We therefore invite you to imagine, for the purposes of this exploration, that leadership **is** coaching, that the two are for most purposes the same. We invite you to seek the common ground, the similarities, the gold in the alchemic blend rather than the distinctions we know are also there – to take the *both/and* view. Let us begin with Leadership Coaching as a state of mind, a state of being in the world, where we add value through our stand, the expression of our point of view. After all, we lead and coach from who we are.

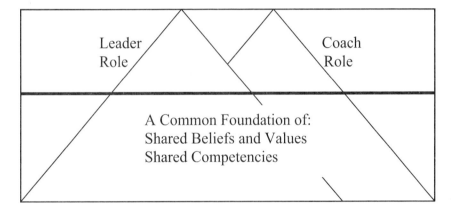

Figure 11: A Model of A Common Foundation

That is the concept. But that is just talk. We propose that there are some invaluable benefits from looking at leadership and coaching as an interdependent set. In the next section, we will outline these benefits in relation to our leadership competency clusters from the first chapter. Our purpose is to extend our thinking into the alchemic realm to see what transformative results we can achieve by blending leadership and coaching together.

Let's start by reminding ourselves about the context in which we are placing our "story" of leadership and coaching. It may have always been true to some extent that leadership is manifest through coaching and coaching is applied leadership. However, the pace, the scale and the complexity of change makes it more imperative now that we integrate our thinking about these two concepts. There are many reasons why this is so.

– We live in a world of crisis – not out there somewhere but right up against us, in our faces. There are no longer any institutional protections from our turbulent environments. We live with the crisis at our very skin. In the past, our organizations, our churches, our families provided buffer zones. They shielded us from being at the front lines of change by providing us, at least, with an interpretation that made sense of the chaos and our place in it. Information was not as widely or quickly available. Now there are no buffer zones. We don't trust our organizational leaders to protect us; in fact some have shown they will push us off the edge so they don't have to jump. Some of our religious institutions lack integrity and others perpetuate violence against each other. Our families are scattered, broken and patched. Technology allows us to see shocking events around the world within minutes, and to give and get mostly uncensored opinions on virtually any topic. This means we have to draw strength from within rather than without. Leadership becomes modeling that inner strength, to inspire others to do the same. The leader creates coaching communities that support and buffer each other.

– Individuals can no longer assume they can lead single-handedly; it takes communities to lead. There is too much information and change for power and control to rest with one person. Power is no longer held by a few at the top; it is, by default, shared. The sheer immensity of the actions and decisions that must be made, the incredible complexity of systems and processes that must be followed, dictate that control is shared by many. If you ask ten CEOs, you will find they claim to have very little power. It is widely dispersed throughout the culture. Positional authority, the traditional basis for power and control, has broken down. Authority now comes from stance, from presence, from inner strength, from adding value. It is earned as much as bestowed.

– The pace of change means no one can legitimately claim to understand most of what is going on at any level of detail. The Leader Coach models learning, asking questions, admitting confusion, making mistakes, responding to changes in the environment, applying new technologies. She does this both for her own development and performance, and to demonstrate to others. Today, if you are standing still in terms of your own learning, you are on a fast track to extinction. The pace of change demands that we pull ourselves constantly into the future not hold timidly on to what worked in the past. We must be adaptive and responsive to change rather than hesitant or resistant.

Within this context, then, let's take an alchemic view of our four competency clusters and see how the addition of coaching to the mix transforms them. Remember, they are:

– Strategic Anticipation

– Vision and Values

– Empowering Others

– Learning and Change

We'll explore each of the four in turn.

Strategic Anticipation - The Co-creation of Futures

It's true, despite all we've said about the unpredictability of turbulent times, that ideas still need to be generated about the future, events anticipated, strategies created and implemented, and decisions made. And there needs to be some stability in this – strategies can't change moment by moment, although the tactics required to accomplish them may. The distinction we want to make, with regard to Strategic Anticipation, is not so much about what happens as how it happens – it is about the creative process and its application. It's about the leader acting as the coach of others when seeking and choosing a common strategy and action plan. We see it as a co-creation of futures. It's the process of getting there that is different, not the fact that you eventually have to decide. What you must decide is to move among a range of scenarios, rather than a tightly defined and highly predictable path.

Here's a story from Susan.

When I was a graduate student, learning about organizations during turbulent times, one of my most profound moments was when Eric Trist said, "Future is not a single word, it is a plural word…it is not future, but futures." It was such a small distinction, a single letter, but such a huge moment for me. I realized the future doesn't have to be either/or; there will be many futures, none of which will specifically come to be but all of which will have some grains of the future in them. There is not one future but many futures. We all have our own sense of futures and if we share them, we will have a rich set of futures to guide our planning and decision making. There is no right answer. The future cannot be known. But futures can. They can be created, debated, analyzed, compared, assessed, changed. No one opinion is correct; it is the sum of them all that encompass the future. "Futures We Are In" was the title of a book that Eric's friend Fred Emery wrote. It has stayed with me and I often think about what a wonderful concept it is.

Exponential change means that we are "in" our futures, not waiting for them to happen. We must be creating them, and co-creating them, all the time. How do we do that? Fortunately, there are many processes and techniques for co-creating futures. Many have been used for decades with a wide variety of groups. One example is what is now called the "Future Search", a term coined by Marv Weisbord and the title of his 1995 book[2]. It looks at how futures can be co-created by people in organizations and communities, by taking advantage of the many perspectives and insights of workers at every level and often including customers and suppliers as well. The outcome is a more complete picture of the issues, leading to a more effective set of directions for future actions. The sense of common vision and community created in a process of "searching" for futures we prefer builds energy and commitment that is much different than having the decision handed down from on high without context or input. As the Leader Coach co-creates the future with the employee, it is perhaps more about the process of discovering the common ground and the possible future scenarios than the particular results, that is so powerful an outcome of a "Future Search".

In fact, the "Future Search" has a long history of finding common ground between diverse groups around the world. It began as the "Search Conference" process[3], invented by Fred Emery and Eric Trist in the post war period as a means of involving ordinary people in choosing futures they preferred rather than being passive recipients of someone else's ideas. "Searches" were held with the Aborigines and the federal government in Australia, with the coal miners and their bosses in northern England, and in places like Ahmedabad, India with textile workers and their overseers. The conflicts were fundamental and the viewpoints entrenched. Many of the participants could not read or write, they were not educated or steeped in process. But they were able to come together in community to deal with issues that were important to all of them and to envision better choices for their lives. They found a common voice and used it to precipitate change.

Similar processes are gaining recognition and being used with groups inside, outside and across organizations all over North America and the world. "Open Space" is a related process begun by Harrison Owen and detailed in his 1992 book on the subject[4]. An open space is a forum in which the participants select issues critical to the community and then gather in groups to address them. When people are involved in Open Space, they express themselves in the context of "passion bounded by responsibility". They do not need to claim expertise about a topic or issue; instead, they declare their passionate intent, that they care enough about it to act with commitment. Again, it is a co-creation of futures that are meaningful and empowering those affected to do something to bring them to life.

Another example within the same family is "Appreciative Inquiry" where groups discover their strengths that can pave the way to better futures. Sue Hammond wrote a primer on this topic in 1996.[5]   The concept of "appreciation" is important. An appreciation is not simply an understanding, an analysis, a judgment. It is a study of an issue or set of issues from all sides, from all points of view, not to reach a definitive conclusion as much as to sit in the questions, the contradictions, the paradoxes and to appreciate them all as futures we are in, knowing that any one path will require trade- offs and difficult choices.

Finally, there are many processes that have come as a group to be known as "whole scale change" where organizational change and design can be rapidly accomplished with the participation of hundreds, even thousands of people who will be affected by it and choose to have a voice in the outcome. Kathleen Dannemiller is widely recognized for this approach[6], as are Barbara Benedict Bunker and Billie Alban.[7]

There are a set of principles common to all of these methods:
- An issue of critical importance to the community with regard to their futures – passion bounded by responsibility.
- A ground rule that all voices are heard and are equal regardless of position or power.
- A value in creating multiple ideas, wide ranging alternatives, thinking outside the box, where every idea is valuable.

– An intent to find common ground among apparent contradictions, to move beyond the differences to the shared beliefs uniting us at a deeper level than our differences divide us.
– An assembly of interested persons from as diverse a social field as is required to present the issue in its full complexity.
– A planning process that reveals the gap between preferred and probable futures and leads to actions to close that gap.
– A reliance on the knowledge and experience of the group rather than on expert opinions or answers to guide choices.

These are some examples of the processes that can transform the concept of Strategic Anticipation into the Co-creation of Futures.   Anticipating possible futures becomes everyone's responsibility. Thinking strategically becomes critical for all of us in choosing the futures we prefer. We each need a personal strategic plan that fits, like a series of "babushka" dolls, into the larger systems of which we are part. From our personal goals to our family, work, community, and larger global views, we strive to align ourselves so that although each system level is different, there is a 'likeness', an expression of our own purpose and its manifestation in the world around us.

By extension, the alchemic leader coaches the members of the team and the organization through participative processes that anticipate the widest possible range of future alternatives and generate the best choices among them, the best 'likenesses' for taking dispersed action on multiple fronts. Strategic Anticipation becomes co-creative community building for choosing the futures we are in. The magic is in the unleashing of the talent, energy, commitment and enthusiasm necessary to make the dream come alive.

Vision and Values - The Holographic Metaphor

We know that in turbulent times the only anchors we can count on are our values. They are the constant in change, the guide to choices in uncertainty. And a common vision of where we are headed, based on these values, is the magnet that pulls us into the future. It is this magnetic force that allows us to persist through the chaos and complexity and to keep our eyes on the goal. The leader's role is to articulate and model the values and to shape and communicate the vision. Which is fine as far as it goes but as we have said, leaders can't do this alone.

The emphasis we want to make draws on the metaphor of the hologram…the notion of the whole in all the parts, however small. The hologram is constructed in such a way that when it is broken apart, rather than having a fraction of the whole in each part, the fundamental elements of the whole are replicated in each of the parts. The "code" – the DNA - is never lost, no matter how many times the pieces are separated. This concept is very different from the one most of our organizations have been designed around. Since the early part of the last century when Frederick Taylor revolutionized industrial production through the assembly line, the underlying basis of organization has been breaking the work down into separate tasks under direct supervision. Each person can do their specialized piece either alone or in teams, in contribution to the whole but without necessary reference to it. The leader's role in this task specialization model is to orchestrate forward motion through a common vision that is consistent with the workers' values. In Taylor's case, this vision was that every family in America would own a Ford and every worker would be treated and paid fairly. It worked well in its time…

Our purpose in introducing the hologram is to suggest an alternative model that is more appropriate to the needs of organizations and their members today. So how are leadership and coaching reflected through this holographic lens? At the team and organization levels, the cultural code is carried throughout the organization, into all roles and relationships. Because the vision of our futures and the values on which our choices rest have been co-created, the whole vision and the common values are carried *in* each member of the team and of the organization…"at the cell level". Because our choices are based on passionate intent, on eager commitment to a common direction, the whole is reflected in each of the parts. It is up to the community to create shared futures based on common values, and to have each member carry the whole within her while doing her part. So that together, the organization flows in the desired direction without the need for constant supervision and control. People are willing to stand for, in the face of conflict and all the inevitable hurdles, not only their own values but also that sense of the whole that they are a part of co-creating. They own the vision.

Here is an example of what we mean. It's a vignette about the "moment of truth" when a customer-facing employee who has "got it " at the cell level exercises authority, makes decisions, spends company resources to please the customer, taking what would have appeared in the old paradigm to be a risk but in the new order, is doing exactly what is expected.

Jane had been part of the "customer intimacy" strategic planning initiative where all the call center employees participated in the "challenge" session to improve the work of the management team. So when she got a call from an angry customer claiming that his last statement charged his annual fee twice, Jane knew she had to do something. Policy said that she should speak to her supervisor before changing a customer account but Jane could see on the screen in front of her the two charges. She didn't know what they were for but the amounts were consistent. Jane decided to tell the customer right there and then that the second charge would be immediately reversed and further, that she would call the customer in a month to be sure the statement had been corrected. The customer was more than satisfied with the quick action and Jane's supervisor was pleased that she had taken the initiative to solve the problem.

At the individual level, we believe the hologram concept is about showing consistency in all roles, at all times, no matter how diverse or multiple or challenging. It is being present consistently in all aspects of your work and life. It is congruence, authenticity, and transparency. You are a Leader Coach. It's not something you do sometimes. It's not something you move in and out of. It's not an event. It's a way of being, in the whole and all the "parts". It is indivisible. The coaching application of leadership implies that we are, we wear, we show up as, our values and our vision.

It is almost redundant to mention "walking the talk", it has been said so many times. It bears repetition only to reinforce how important it is to **being** our values and vision, as opposed to merely **doing** values articulation and vision communication. Richard Leider[8] describes this beautifully as "pulling who you are through what you do"…your work, your purpose in the world is the arena in which you can express, work out and refine your values. They are not separate from but integral to your everyday life and every encounter in it. It is in the constant learning and changing that the Leader Coach models what is needed and valued by all members of the organization. It's not all figured out but the learning journey continues.

It is absolutely right that employees challenge us when we are inconsistent - when in the midst of the merger, for example, we suddenly stop communicating as much as we had promised. It is in the moment, in the heat of the "battle" that our values are tested…as much as it is in the everyday, mundane encounters - the budget review meetings, the performance review conversations, the chance encounters in hallways, at staff parties, at community events.

One of the realities of leadership in the twenty-first century is that there is no distinction between work and life – it's about a blended life, not a balance of separate entities. It is from this blend of roles that the Leader Coach emerges…applying the learnings from an organizational context to those of a community volunteer, applying the learnings from parenting to the role of colleague, using the same admission of need to learn and improve from taking up a new sport or hobby to the constant revision of business processes.

It is easy to see the benefit to organization effectiveness of this dispersed commitment to living the vision and values. But there is a corollary that benefits the individual members. Just as they carry the organization's "genetic code" in the performance of their roles, so too the leaders carry the needs and desires of the members into their decision-making as a profound commitment to the wellbeing of both the whole and the parts, both the results to be achieved and the member satisfaction to be ensured. It is not the "job for life" dogma of the previous generation; being a part of the organizational community must be earned. It is more that the "I" - the ego of the power-based leader, transforms to become the "We" - the self expands to include others, which again transforms to become the "It" - the unity of hearts and minds directed toward a common goal.

Vision and Values extended to a Holographic Metaphor transforms a future direction created by mostly by leaders themselves into a genetic imprint that guides decisions and actions at every level in every role in the organization. What is co-created is also co-acted. The magic is that as people begin to trust the authenticity they see, a new organizational culture is born. It's just the way things are around here. It's not perfect, but it feels real, compelling, attractive, and it fits the nature of the world in which we all live and work together.

Empowering Others - From Hierarchy to Heterarchy[9]

In empowering others, leaders share their power with their team and wider constituents in order to motivate them to take action. It is a giving away of power to get results back. Empowerment recognizes that a passive following of orders and instructions is insufficient for today's jobs where judgments and trade-offs must constantly be made. In fact, it recognizes that power **is** shared, by virtue of the kind of environment in which organizations do business. The service representative who answers calls won't delight the customer by referring to the manual and apologizing if the answer isn't there. She needs the knowledge, the experience, and the interpersonal savvy to solve the problem and keep the customer relationship intact.

This empowerment assumes, though, that there is a hierarchy in which someone has more power and someone less, that power is a scarce resource doled out in measured quantities by virtue of level and position, and is at the discretion of the more senior to grant. The notion that power is held to be given away is itself anachronistic – employees choose constantly to give their energy, their creativity, their maximum effort, to the organization, and likely to the Leader Coach, or not to. So what if power was not a scarce resource? What if power was attached to the person and not the role, by virtue of their presence, their authenticity, and their contribution? What if power was an abundant resource, limited only by the ability to know our selves and express our gifts appropriately in the world? In that case, using power authentically would never reduce it. In truth, it is through this knowing of our self, this self-awareness, that we realize we have the power to choose…and that by choosing, we are in fact powerful.

We believe that this is where leadership and coaching can take Empowerment – into Heterarchy, the sharing of leadership and power according to the needs of the moment, of the individuals and the business. Heterarchy is shared leadership in the sense that each person's individual strength and talent is exhibited in response to a need in the community as a whole. Rather than authority bestowed, it is an earned expression or demonstration in response to a particular situation. So someone is always leading, according to circumstance and ability to contribute, and everyone leads in their time. One can be both a leader and a follower - a leader perhaps in an area of content expertise and a follower in the process of getting that expertise marketed within the organization. And this can be repeated in all facets of the leader/follower role.

There are many familiar examples of heterarchy in our organizations today. A simple example is that the CEO role has become so impossible for a single individual to take on that several companies have tried putting two individuals in the role, sharing leadership according to capability and need, often supported by a team of advisors who take the lead on issues in which they are experienced. GE and Citicorp are examples of the co-leadership idea. In GE's case, Jack Welch needed to ensure that his successor was ready for the role before he stepped down and he wanted to see Jeffrey Imelt in action. In the Citicorp case, although the merger-based pairing didn't work out, ending in a power struggle between Sanford Weill and John Reed, its failure was arguably more about the personalities and expectations of the two players than the efficacy of the idea itself. Weill, who has been battling unethical practices on his watch, has recently been quoted by Fortune as saying that the job is too big for one person to manage, although he should have known what was going on.[10] As more and more ethical malpractices are unearthed, the case for shared leadership and less autonomy, secrecy and insider dealing by single power holders, grows. This is especially true for boards but also advantageous to top management as well.

Lead roles in government are similar, right up to heads of state who can't possibly be experts in the deluge of issues and problems that challenge them every day. Think of the team of key people around President Bush following the 9/11 attacks – Cheney, Powell and others. It was difficult to tell who was making which decisions – they acted from their unique capabilities to cover the issues needing to be addressed. Many self-directed teams are heterarchies where leadership is shared - people automatically refer to the conceptual thinker when a new problem needs to be framed, and move to the relationship builder when conflicts arise, or to the most experienced member of the team when prior solutions will add to the alternatives.

Heterarchy recognizes the need for diversity in turbulent times, the strength in diverse views, and the need for multiple perspectives in leadership systems. We should be clear – we are not suggesting that heterarchy replace hierarchy but that both hierarchy and heterarchy are required. Hierarchy is necessary in complex systems and contributes to role clarity and accountability. The team leader is accountable for the results of the team and those results are achieved through the team members. The way that leadership is **applied** should be heterarchical, that is, in community and not in a chain of command. It is this exclusivity of hierarchy and the 'class system' that hierarchy creates - you obey the chain of command, you turn to a superior for the information you need and are allowed to have, you are a passive follower, you accept the word of the 'boss' – that is outmoded and dangerous. We need as much diversity in our organizations as we can get. We need as much leadership as we can get.

Let's step back a minute to hear from Susan on the reason for valuing diversity.

I really like Ashby's Law. I learned it when I was studying systems theory, much of which was conceptually appealing but mathematically challenging for me. Ashby's concept is a good example. His systems concept is called "Ashby's Law of Requisite Variety"[11]. He proposed that any system, in order to sustain itself over time had to contain enough variety to match the variety in its surrounding environment. If it did not have sufficient - or requisite - variety, it would simple dissolve, unable to hold its boundaries. Now, this was way back in the 50s, long before the waves of mergers, acquisitions, dissolutions and bankruptcies we have come to experience. Or the global terror. It was just a systems concept. But when we say that turbulent times have eroded the buffer zones between us as individuals and our environment, it is all about requisite variety. Our historical institutions have lacked the requisite variety to hold their boundaries against the complexity in the environment and the result is breakdown. We have had insufficient variety to match what is happening in our wider world. This is as true of us as individuals as it is of our organizations, our nations, our religions. We must embrace diversity if we are to survive.

One of the ways to embrace diversity is heterarchy. It is no longer true, if it ever was, that a single person can perfectly model and embody organizational leadership. In our holographic model, all of the required leadership, as well as all of the required variety, is embedded in the parts, the members of the team and the organizational community. This is not simply replication. The parts, the team members, are not all the same but they have the DNA, the vision and values, within them and are able to express their differences through their leadership in contribution to the needs of the whole, not the role. They lead from who they are. And in a heterarchy, they lead from their diversity. It is precisely the difference and not the sameness, which is valuable. We are not all trying to be replicas of the one leader at the top of our heap. We are striving to express our unique gifts in order to generate variety of perspective, to add value through our own self expression. We lead from the *inside out*, from our values and shared visions, where needed from the *outside in*, to respond to continuous change.

Heterarchy also implies community. Variety is created by banding together and supporting each other, not counting on ourselves for all our needs but sharing the load, building relationships that expand and fortify us. It is not surprising that the need for community has never been greater, at work and at play. Community creates a buffer zone to provide respite from the bombardment of environmental variety. Many of us turn away despite our need, becoming isolated and rigid, paralyzed by complexity. Although this is a natural response, it is the wrong one. It robs others of our uniqueness, the diversity we bring, and it robs us of the opportunity to draw strength from those around us. Leader Coaches encourage community and interdependence in relationships because they know this is the source of power and its means of expression. Leader Coaches model embracing diversity in every aspect of their lives - she who is an employee is also parent, partner, consumer, activist. It is not too much to claim that developing and encouraging an organization of Leader Coaches at all levels can have a transformative, magical effect on a community.

We know of a senior person in charge of organization effectiveness for a global financial services firm. Whenever he brings a team together, he introduces something unexpected, out of the ordinary. He has used drumming, mime, clowning, art, cooking, and so on and he has become widely known for these celebrations. The people who experience them come away with a different point of view, a different understanding of others, and a deeper insight into their own strengths and challenges. Variety adds interest and perspective.

One last point before we leave this discussion. There is a process for dealing with environmental variety: we become aware of it, we acknowledge it, and then we incorporate it. The awareness may be nothing more than a sense of the "noise" in our surroundings, that things are hyped up, moving fast - the way you feel in downtown Manhattan. Acknowledgement brings things into focus and attention, gives them an identifiable source and impact, like there's an airplane overhead and I'm unable to hear you. Then incorporation means that the body literally takes it on, responds and adapts to it, making necessary adjustments not only to the body itself but to the interconnections of the heart, the spirit and the mind. When someone I trust has sabotaged my project proposal, my body tightens, my heart beats faster, my spirit deflates and my mind goes into overdrive about the causes and consequences.

This is an important process because the more we have to cope with, the harder all of these body/heart/spirit/mind interconnections have to work. In fact, there is so much environmental noise in our lives that we are taxing our systems far more than we acknowledge. Have you felt at the end of the day that your shoulders are way up, stiff and tensed from stress? Or that your temper is short with your kids because you have used all your tolerance just getting through the frustrations at work? And the drive home? Are there Monday mornings when you don't feel you have the spirit to face another week? It is perhaps not an accident that we are all seeking life balance, fitness is a constant goal and health is a huge issue. Stress-related illness, including depression, is at the top of the list of most prevalent diseases in America. The Canadian Health Network estimates that one woman in four and one man in eight will face depression in their working life.[12] The International Labor Organization calls workplace stress a "global epidemic". Incorporating variety demands that we adapt. When we have a sense of power, of control, of community and support, we increase our adaptability immensely.

So through our alchemic chamber, we transform Empowerment in a traditional hierarchical sense into shared power in community through Heterarchy. The magic is that when we co-create our futures and carry the holographic code of our vision and values in each of us, we can step up and lead when the situation calls us forward. In so doing, we increase the adaptability and contribute to the goals of the community as a whole. Heterarchy makes leadership everyone's right and everyone's responsibility.

Learning and Change – Interdependence and Meaning

Learning and change, the final competency cluster, underpins the other three. We have talked a lot about change as a constant and the need for continuous learning in order to adapt, to reduce the variety to a sustainable level. Learning is the antidote to change. The key competency for today's leaders is their learning agility. We want to extend that notion to include the interdependent relationship we have with change and how that gives meaning to us as humans, as leaders and as coaches.

When we speak of change, we tend to think of it as an external force weighing in on us, forcing us to adapt. We want to beat back the variety that constantly attacks our stability, our homeostasis. While this is true, it is only half of the picture. The other half is that as humans we are naturally in constant flux. From the moment of our birth to our last breath, we are evolving: learning, moving, thinking, feeling, doing, interacting. We are not passive recipients of change. Far from it! Every time we express ourselves in the world, we change it. When we co-create futures, when we articulate our values through our visions, when we lead in our turn with others, we change our world. And if we are open and connected, we also learn and grow from the experience. There is an expansion in both directions.

Being aware of this interdependence with the world around us is uniquely human. Other species interact with the environment but they are not aware of change, of growth, or of death. We understand as adults that our time here is temporary, that we have a limited span in which to contribute, and this makes us uniquely human. It provokes in us a search for meaning in our lives. What are we here to do? How do we make our mark? What is the purpose of our life? Our work? What legacy will we leave? How will the world be a better place than we found it?

This leads to the second distinction we want to make - that the search for meaning is a striving to contribute beyond our own wants, to transcend ourselves by offering something of our own unique humanity to others. In this uniqueness is our authenticity, seeing the truth of things and choosing to respond to what really needs to be started or stopped. Meaning is beyond power and pleasure. It is self-less, beyond ego. It is a sense of aliveness, fulfillment, vitality. Meaning adds purpose to all that we do.

So the alchemic transformation of Learning and Change is moving from our sense of merely adapting to, coping with, the environment to a proactive relationship with change and learning, in ourselves and in our world, to better reflect our vision and values. And that means learning everywhere – from our children, from our clients, from our colleagues at all levels, from our daily activities and from surprises. Everyone is our teacher, every situation presented is one to learn from. It is interesting that learning occurs more in the heart, spirit and body than in the mind...we need to acknowledge and integrate learning from all sources, both within and without. The magic in the extension of our interdependence with those around us is that it is in these relationships that we find the meaning we so desperately seek in life. Learning becomes deeply purposeful. Change becomes deeply meaningful. In fact, it is a visceral sense that change **is** energy, that it is the transformative fuel that powers us to contribution, to opportunity, to growth.

To balance this abstract thinking, let us give an example of a place of learning and change.

Richard Strozzi Heckler[13], an expert in the martial arts, has spent years learning from masters in a variety of dojos, and facilitated exercises at a recent conference to allow participants an experience of what it feels like to be part of a dojo. One exercise contrasted our usual limited field of view with an expanded awareness of things around us when we are deeply centered in ourselves. Another demonstrated the incredible strength we can muster when we concentrate our total energy. A dojo is a learning lab, a place for practice and refinement of the physical, mental and spiritual components of one's art. It is also a place of awakening – through mental and physical discipline over time, awareness of the whole self and our place in the world is raised.

The "Karate Kid" movies, if you remember them, are wonderful examples of the concept of the dojo. We believe the dojo is an apt metaphor for the kind of place we are imagining here. A dojo has four aspects according to Heckler. We have extended them here to relate them to our four competency clusters:

– A place of teaching, coaching through demonstration and support, a place of **co-creating** the path forward, the vision of self mastery with those who are more experienced.
– A place to practice the applied arts, where discipline and commitment to a vision lead to deepening awareness and refinement of choices, of how the **holographic** principle, the values code, is applied to all life's situations.
– It is a place of practice in the art of community with people playing a lead role at some times and a follower role at others, an expression of **heterarchy** where everyone is both a teacher and a learner.
– It is a way of being, an intentional path, a Tao, where our own **interdependence** with others in the world leads us to clearer understanding of our place, our **meaning**, our goals in life.

Through practice, this place of learning becomes reality in all aspects of life, in a lifetime of dedication to continuous improvement.

Developing leaders and teams is a continuous process. Perhaps it starts as an explicit strategy, a dojo, but over time as leaders change, as members change, as the external environment changes, the dojo becomes the way of the team, an ongoing attention to the direction and growth of community through the practice of living the values. What kind of dojos can you create in your life to practice the discipline of alchemic leadership with others?

One of the central roles of leaders is to invite others to explore meaning with them. They do this by offering their own meaningful visions of futures for others to contribute to. They do it by embodying those visions in all they do and all they are. They *become* the visions, speaking and acting from futures they are already in, finding meaning for themselves and pulling others forward with them. In a recent survey of CEOs, the Center for Creative Leadership and *Chief Executive* magazine asked about the personal characteristics of leaders. "People-management skill was cited as the number one success factor for CEOs, executive teams and mid-level managers alike…The higher the level of management, the more important personal characteristics become…The personal characteristics of top leaders set the example for others to follow and create norms of acceptable behavior."[14]

You will know the Gandhi quote, "Be the change you want to see in the world." Don't only talk about it, don't only do it, but BE it. Take it on, stand for it, mean it. Be brave, even in the face of challenge, censure, constraint from others. When we step forward to play a leadership role in our own life and work, when we stand for something despite all odds, then we find meaning and happiness. The irony is that when we seek happiness as an end in itself, what we find is emptiness. When we seek to serve a cause greater than our own, happiness ensues.

It is one of the sad realities of our time that many of us have a great deal of material success but very little fulfillment in our lives. Viktor Frankl in his classic text entitled "Man's Search for Meaning"[15] called this an existential vacuum, the malaise of our generation. His belief was that meaning was not attached to material success – in fact meaning was associated more with giving than receiving. Here is a way of portraying this experience.

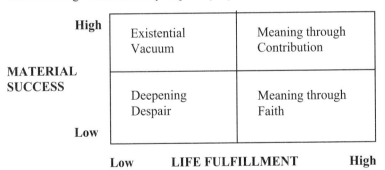

Figure 12: A Model Relating Fulfillment and Success

Frankl himself suffered the horrors of a concentration camp, finding meaning through his own suffering and that of others around him. He wrote about it and it changed our understanding of mankind. Terry Fox, a Canadian athlete, had his leg amputated due to cancer and still ran most of the way across the continent to raise money for others. He stretched himself and it changed our view of cancer.

There are many examples of people finding meaning in the direst of circumstances. But where do we find it in our ordinary lives? We believe it is through the transformations we have suggested: stretching beyond our own interests, seeing the globe as our neighborhood, leading with our unique gifts in contribution to others, and finding meaning in doing so. This is how we transform the world. This is where the magic of alchemy is found.

Here is a summary of what we have been discussing.

Leadership Competency	Coaching Theme	Leadership Alchemy	Description
Strategic Anticipation	Deepening context Working through stuckness	**Co-creation of Futures**	Co-creative community building for choosing futures we are in
Vision and Values	Living on purpose Being in Service	**Holographic Metaphor**	Holographic imprinting guides all decisions and actions
Empowering Others	Using conversations Sustaining diversity	**From Hierarchy to Heterarchy**	Heterarchical leadership according to capability and the needs of the situation
Learning and Change	Modeling Change Continuous learning Reframing paradox	**Interdependence and Meaning**	Interdependence with the world around us and within us, providing meaning to life

Chart 9: A Framework of Leadership Coaching Alchemy

Alfred Lord Tennyson wrote these inspiring lines which we feel express the challenge.

> "The long day wanes,
> The slow moon climbs,
> The deep moans round
> With many voices.
> Come, my friends,
> Tis not too late to seek
> A newer world."

We know this may be a lot to absorb and the challenges of applying the ideas in traditional work settings may seem daunting. But this is our task as leaders today – a transformation that only we can accomplish. We must begin.

A Personal Reflection:

Transformation is a word that is used frequently and rather loosely to imply a major change. It really means that you become someone you were not before...that the change you experience is so fundamental that you, as a person, are different. You can't go back, you can't unlearn what you have learned. You are in a new place of awareness.

Think about a time when you experienced a transformation in your beliefs, assumptions, knowledge and attitude – something that changed you fundamentally. It might be a simple insight – like Susan's story of Eric putting an 's' on the end of future – that changes perspective in an instant. Or it might be a longer-term process of education, realization or experience from which you emerged with a different sense of yourself and your place in the world.

What were the circumstances surrounding this transformation? Can you identify the significant factors involved? What led up to it? How did it happen? Who was part of it? What elements of the 'story' are key? If you have had more than one transformational experience, do the factors vary or is there a common theme? Is there an environment, a setting, a chrysalis, in which you can cocoon and emerge a butterfly? Often, the transformational settings of our lives are where we intuitively go to regroup and, once aware of them, we can seek them out as supportive environments for our transformative needs.

If you are not able to identify a transformational experience in your life, think about that... Does it mean you have not yet had the opportunity? If so, how can you explore the possibilities? What in your circumstances presents itself as an opportunity for new learning, new meaning? If you have had the opportunity but not taken it, how does that feel to you? Are you living life to the fullest? Are you engaging in whatever you are doing in such a way that you draw meaning from it?

Write in your journal about transformation. Be a storyteller, relate your personal stories and their life lessons, or tell the story of someone you know and the circumstances of their transformation.

An Exercise to Share:

Share your stories with someone you trust. Tell them as stories, in the first person, expressing all the feeling you experienced as you went through your transformation. Then listen carefully as your partner tells her stories. Watch her emotion while listening to her words. Discuss the themes that run through both your stories.

- What are the common elements?
- How do they relate to the alchemic leadership competencies we have discussed in this chapter?
- Are there similarities? Differences?
- What can you learn from this discussion that will help you in future transformations?

A Self-Assessment:

We have now talked about the four alchemic leadership competency themes – the competencies of effective leadership coaches. Give yourself a rating on each of these competency areas as you see yourself now, by circling the number that is most appropriate. Consider 1 to be unskilled and 5 to be a master:

Co-creation of Futures				
1	2	3	4	5
Holographic Perspective				
1	2	3	4	5
Heterarchical Leadership				
1	2	3	4	5
Meaning from Interdependent Relationships				
1	2	3	4	5

Chart 10: An Assessment of Alchemic Leadership Competencies

Now think about where you would like to be. Circle the number that represents your alchemic leadership goal. Perhaps use a different color, a color that represents growth and hope to you.

Consider what you see on the rating chart:
- Are there gaps in your leadership coaching development?
- Are they things you would be interested in pursuing?

- What kinds of experiences or mentoring or training would you need to close the gaps?
- What can you do to put some of your ideas into place?

A Team Exercise:

Have each member of your team do the self assessment above and bring their ratings to a team meeting. You may want to open the discussion by reviewing the concepts in the chapter to be sure everyone is familiar with them and with how they have, or have not, played out in your team setting.

Discuss where each member sees him or herself and what he or she needs to move forward. This is best done in two's or three's so everyone has a chance to talk about their assessments. Allow about 10 minutes per person.

You may then want to have each person transfer their ratings to a common whiteboard or flipchart where the rating scales above have been outlined. You need not put names on the ratings, just circles in one color for current skills and another color for desired skills, so that you can then see how the team as a whole maps out.

- What are the themes and common issues in the whole group?
- Are there areas where the whole team is strong?
- What about areas where the whole team needs development?
- Are there areas where one member of the team could use a strength to help another who wants to develop?
- Where are the largest gaps between current and desired skill levels?
- What could the team do to close these gaps?

The outcome of the meeting should be selecting some action steps for team development. Perhaps one of the competency themes can be chosen for development over the next 6 months, with actions stipulated – what will happen, by when, and by whom. At least one follow-up meeting should also be arranged to track progress toward the goals.

A variation on this exercise is to have members of the team rate each individual so that he or she can compare self ratings with those of others. Two or three ratings are sufficient to form a 'group' average rating that ensures the confidentiality of each rater. Your HR representative may be able to support this exercise by collecting ratings and preparing a group report for each individual to consider prior to a team meeting.

EndNotes:

[1] Lombardo, Mike and Bob Eichinger. *The Leadership Machine.* Lominger Ltd., 2001.

[2] Weisbord, Marv and Sandra Janoff. *Future Search: An Action Guide to Finding Common Ground in Organizations and Communities.* Berrett-Koehler, 1995.

[3] Emery, Merrelyn and Ronald Purser. *The Search Conference: A Powerful Method for Planning Organizational Change and Community Action.* Jossey Bass, 1996.

[4] Owen, Harrison. *Open Space Technology: A User's Guide.* Abbott Publishing , 1992. Also Michael Herman's website www.invitingorganization.com for current information on open space.

[5] Hammond, Sue. *The Thin Book of Appreciative Inquiry.* Thin Book Publishing, 1996.

[6] Dannemiller, Kathleen. *The Thin Book of Appreciative Inquiry.* Thin Book Publishing, 1996.

[7] Benedict Bunker, Barbara and Billie Alban. *Large Group Interventions: Engaging the Whole System for Rapid Change.* Jossey Bass, 1997.

[8] Leider, Richard. *Whistle While you Work.* Berrett-Koehler, 2001.

[9] You might not have encountered the term 'heterarchy' before – we define it for these purposes as the organization design principle of power distributed to and enacted by the many, rather than the few or the one, based on capability and the needs of the community.

[10] *Fortune,* November 24, 2002.

[11] Ashby, W.R. "Self-Regulation and Requisite Variety", in *"Systems Thinking".* Fred Emery, Ed. Penguin Books, 1978.

[12] The Canadian Centre for Occupational Health and Safety web site, www.ccohs.ca, contains information on occupational stress. See "OSH Answers" and "Workplace Stress" for specifics including a diagnostic tool and resources for addressing the issue.

[13] Richard Strozzi Heckler presenting to the "Edges" Conference, Sante Fe, NM, October, 2002.

[14] "What CEO's Think: A Leadership Survey from CCL and Chief Executive Magazine". Center for Creative Leadership e-Newsletter, www.ccl.org, October 2002.

[15] Viktor Frankl. *Man's Search for Meaning.* Beacon, 2000.

Part Two – Contexts

The Invitation

We now invite you to move from concepts, the principles and ideas that underpin the *both/and* Leadership Coach, to contexts, the domains in which the concepts are applied. Here again, we present a duality, a seeming paradox, and invite you to see both dimensions at the same time and to accord them equal value. The dimensions are the inner and outer contexts in which we function.

We are all familiar with our outer world contexts, the roles and relationships we establish and maintain, the issues we address and the problems we solve. These are the stuff of education and experience. Although we don't often focus on them consciously as contexts – they are the air we breathe, the river to the salmon - we are usually aware that they are there and that we must attend to changes in them.

Less familiar are the inner world contexts, our values and passions, our desires and dreams, our hopes and fears. These are the uncharted territories and we are often unfamiliar with their expression as a part of our whole selves. While we may struggle with these inner domains at a personal level, we seem to have denied their very existence in organizational life   And yet, they are the critical "base metals" that form our character and presence, our alchemy, as Leader Coaches. Our culture has dictated that we ignore these emotions and, as a result, we are less able to access them and to incorporate them into our whole being. Indeed, the dissociation from values, ethics and integrity, has allowed great harm to be done to others by leaders in the name of 'business." For in fact, within the exploration of the inner life is also the acknowledgement of the shadow side, where lie both the opportunity for great learning and, if unrestrained, the shackles that can limit us, the blind spots that can endanger us, the world views that can distort and turn us from our magnificent potential.

It is the combination of these two worlds that fuels greatness. Neither on its own is complete but the interplay of both inner and outer is powerful enough to transform individuals, teams and organizations. Imagine again the chalice, the alchemic container within which these disparate ingredients are united, to produce not merely a combination of two, but an entirely new entity, more than the sum of the parts. Leader Coaches strive to contain both contexts in their 'being' and 'doing' in all aspects of their lives.

Figure 13 looks at these inner and outer contexts in relation to the competencies we discussed in the previous chapters. We have chosen the competencies that reflect most clearly the distinctions in each of the domains of the model.

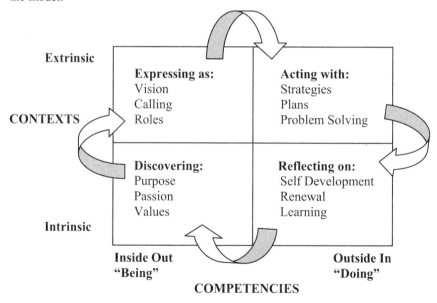

Figure 13: A Model Relating Competencies and Contexts

If we start in the bottom left box of the model, the intrinsic context of the self, we find that the competencies associated with this world involve discovering our values, purpose and passions. These are the inside out dimensions of the self that structure and guide our lives. When these inner competencies are pulled into the extrinsic context of our organizations, the values are expressed as visions and callings. We are en-roled to play our part in accordance with who we are.

In order to make our visions a reality, we need competencies for getting things done: strategic ability, planning, problem solving - the subjects of our business school training. Here we are fully out in the world, confident, competent, achieving our goals. And experience with making reality of our dreams then leads us back into ourselves, to learning from reflecting on our actions. Perhaps all didn't go as planned, unexpected surprises arose, our values were tested. Here we take steps to understand how our outside in experiences align with our inner purpose, maybe taking on some further development or choosing a path of renewal and rebuilding for the future. And we start around the circle again. It may be a minor course correction, or striking out in a totally new direction...only now carrying with us, embodying all that we've learned, to live at a deeper level of awareness and understanding.

If we apply the model at the team and organizational levels, we can imagine why it is so important to co-create the future vision by starting with the expression of common values and purpose. Each of us is enrolled to play our part in making the vision a reality, carrying with us the essential elements and principles, leading in our turn with our particular skills for making it happen. And it is through this experience that we are able to recognize our interdependence with those around us and find meaning in our contributions and achievements.

These cycles happen throughout our adult lives as we move from chapter to chapter of our careers and our other relationships, communities, and roles. We exist in the tension of being in the inner world and doing in the outer world. Being seeks doing; doing seeks being. And so it goes...the alchemic experiments, the breakthroughs, the failures, the learning...as we discover more and more about who we truly are and what we are called to be and do.

In the next three chapters, we will examine these contexts separately but it is important to hold the tension, the paradox of both at the same time.

Chapter 4
Inside Out – Development of the Leadership Coach

In this chapter, we want to look at how the concepts presented in Part One can be applied to the self. In other words, what does it take to be a Leader Coach in the way we have described? What are the competencies required to be successful? We start with the self because, as we have said, the learning journey of the Leadership Coach begins here, on the inside, with an examination of our talents and potentials as well as our frailties and failures. We start with who we are.

This inner context, the self, is a vast territory for exploration and understanding that has been mostly ignored in recent times as we have focused on the outer world of competition, power and, most recently, change. These have been the contexts that have received the attention. But in order to survive and thrive in these outer domains, we must grow strong, resilient inner domains of the self. This terrain is now beginning to claim its rightful place in leadership as we begin to understand the great impact that this 'inside out' perspective has on leadership success.

Seeing Self as System

We begin by broadening our definition of the self to include body, spirit, heart and mind – a full systems view of the interdependence of what have often been seen as separate parts, or denied altogether. We will explore the self as an interconnected and mutually supportive holistic system – the combination of body, mind, heart and spirit - and how this system, when in alignment, can *be* the Leader Coach. Each aspect of the self plays a different role in our lives; each contributes to our whole being. And as we've said, part of the challenge of this notion is that it is not something you sometimes do…rather it is who you are and aspire to be. So, we'll include here some descriptions of what it is like to be the Leader Coach, from each of these four dimensions. Our purpose is not so much to give you traditional competency statements as to invite you to discover their gestalt by taking them on, folding them in, becoming them… We start by looking at the four dimensions of the self. How do we view them as aspects of who we are? What lessons can we learn from what they have to tell us?

Body:

Much of what we've presented so far – words, concepts, charts, four-box models - has been written from *our* heads, and directed to *yours*. We've appealed to the rational thought processor part of you. However, you might have found in some of the assessments that your emotions were involved – perhaps some resistance to or denial of the sensations you were experiencing. Or perhaps some of our stories touched your spirit. And perhaps you've already been moved to act, to behave differently. For our belief is that the Leader Coach *embodies* the values and competencies of *being* a Leader Coach, in everything she does, everything she says, everything she is. So our bodies become who we are – they are an expression of the lives we lead. And yet so often, as leaders, we find ourselves virtually denying we live in bodies…the long hours at a desk, the overnight flights on a Sunday night to be at an important meeting early the next morning thousands of miles from home, the meeting that feels like a school class detention with no windows and uncomfortable chairs, the schedules that allow no time for a workout, or for dancing or for daydreaming…there seem to be many examples of how a leader's life can encourage the separation from, and even the denial of the body.

Here's a story from Carol about this denial of the body.

I had moved across the country to head up a powerhouse consulting team, in a large multinational consulting firm. The previous team leader had collapsed from the demands of the job, and it seemed unlikely that he'd ever (at 48) be able to return to the workplace. I was keen to prove myself in a new market, a new city, and a new firm….one that, of course, I'd competed against in my previous two jobs in rival consulting firms. So I would work the long hours, keeping track of those hours on timesheets requiring every fifteen minutes be accounted for, as billable or non-billable, and I'd ensure that the team members had lots of billable time but that I had lots of billable time as well! I would be making the transcontinental flights, including 'red-eyes', to represent our team at the national level, and our national team in the global context. I was working 15 hours virtually every day, and often had 60 or 70 hour weeks….you know the type!

And then the morning came, when I simply couldn't stand the pain of the shower on my skin….I curled up in a ball on the shower floor, not able even to reach up to turn the shower off. I realized that I too was succumbing to the pressures that had incapacitated my predecessor. I was fortunate to work for a firm that had an "Employee Assistance Program". I phoned my assistant, who snuck into the coffee room, to find me the number to phone. Her empathy was so palpable, I thought I'd cry. I suppose my workaholism and the toll it was taking were apparent to her, and probably my other colleagues, and indeed my clients.

I remember reflecting, as I went to the EAP counselor, (this was before I'd ever heard of coaching) that "if you ignore your body's whispers, it shouts". Thankfully, I'd only had this mini-crisis in the shower, not a heart attack, not a stroke, not a car accident…and of course, because it was a mild warning, I didn't get it, that time. It took several more years of similar incidents – and finally working with a coach - to realize the patterns and themes that were playing out in my life. My body was telling me an important truth about the need for healing from what was toxic in the way I'd been working. For some of my colleagues, like my predecessor, this realization was too late to prevent permanent health consequences and as a result a shortened career.

What seems so obvious to me now as I try to remember what that crisis, and that old life, was like, is that I was 'out of my body'…and that my lifelong struggle to be fit and healthy reflect the gap in my understanding of what it means to live a whole life, to approach living from a whole systems viewpoint. That it should be my skin, the apparent armor between me and the world, that hurt is no accident. And it also seems clear to me now that being comfortable in my own skin is an indication of a life in balance, a life integrating mind, body, spirit and heart.

As humans, we can get used to anything – we have conditioned tendencies that can make even the most bizarre or horrible circumstances seem normal after a time. This keeps us sane in a crazy world, but it also means that we carry and we absorb the stress in our bodies... till the point of breakdown, overload, dysfunction. We pride ourselves on how hard we work, how uncomfortable we become. Most people don't take action or see change as positive and possible, until there is a breakdown. Only a small percentage work out of possibilities, not breakdowns.

Yvonne had been through a traumatic couple of years that had involved several deaths, bankruptcy, and challenges with teenage children. Finally, a space in all the chaos seemed to emerge, and the opportunity to go off to a summer camp for a week with her daughter beckoned. Despite not looking forward to tenting, or to being with younger parents and their energy and seeming omniscience, Yvonne went off....and signed up for a week-long massage training course. It seemed a simple, relaxing and undemanding way to spend the time. In it, she would both give and get massages. She discovered to her delight and surprise, in this week-long course, the wonderful potential of massage to reconnect to her own body and to ground and center in her life. And while the turbulence has continued around her, massage has helped her stay the course and remain true to her essential values. In fact, through massage she has experienced the connection between the body and the spirit and the message that we are not four separate entities but one unified interdependent system. In the same way, the Leader Coach's style with colleagues, customers, and the environment is interdependent.

Head towards friction, towards challenge, with an open heart...friction provides compost for our own growth. As we come into greater awareness of our growth edges, we connect to our spirit - reminding us of who we really are, from our soul's perspective. How am I going to be fully, finally myself, embodying my values **and** in a partnership/relationship with others and the world? How do I grow and honor my truth and others' truth? Make good use of the truth that the friction creates...

Spirit:

And what of the spirit ... that connection we have to the divine, to the universal and timeless energy? For much of the twentieth century, it seemed that conversations about spirit were unusual – heard at wakes and the funerals of colleagues, the brief chats about especially moving moments, perhaps including events at church or synagogue if you were the rare one who attended. For much as we may try to deny we live in bodies, we deny we even **have** spirits, that we are spiritual beings in human form and that these spirits are an essential part of who we are, and why we are here.

> My spirit is, in fact, the well-spring from which my values come, and my optimism and enthusiasm (literally, the indwelling presence of spirit)... I **do** have a spirit and it is – or perhaps she is – an essential component of my leadership coaching essence[1].

With the 'workquake' of the early nineties and the abandonment of so many of the apparent 'sacred cows' of lifetime employment, employee loyalty, corporate inviolability, and work providing the meaning to life, suddenly there seemed to be a recognition, a resurgence of interest and awareness, in the territory of the spirit. "Spirit in the Workplace" conferences, books, articles, websites and chat groups have erupted. As we described in Chapter 1, this dawning awareness has broadened and deepened the understanding and experience of leadership and therefore also informs and affects leadership coaching.

Going within as into the domain of the sacred – with the use of metaphors, the language of imagery, of poetry[2]... is entering a realm with an awkward language, with myriad assumptions. Some of us have had experiences that taint our notions of belief, faith, divinity. In the workplace, we tread gently to avoid disrespecting cultural and ethnic differences, competing world views and value sets. The Leader Coach's awareness of diversity includes a curiosity about different traditions that speak to the territory of the spirit. Prayer, meditation, even journaling can be an excursion of the spirit, for the spirit. Incorporation of the spiritual realm makes the Leader Coach a whole adult, who acknowledges the mystery and is comfortable in her "un-knowingness". Also, the Leader Coach lives in and holds out the possibility of hope - hope attached to the imagination, the imagination of a brighter tomorrow, the possibility of greater vitality, deeper meaning, **vital** – vita, life!! The Leader Coach is manifesting in her own life, in her interactions, the belief and experience that there is always the choice for hope.

Here is an allegorical tale about the denial of the mystery, and the hope of transformation.

Once upon a time in a not-so-far-away land, there was a kingdom of acorns nestled at the foot of a grand, old oak tree. Since the citizens of this kingdom were modern, fully-westernized acorns, they went about their business with purposeful energy and since they were midlife, baby-boomer acorns, they engaged in a lot of self-help courses. There were seminars called "Getting all you can out of your shell". There were woundedness and recovery groups for acorns who had been bruised in their original fall from the tree. There were spas for oiling and polishing those shells and various acornopathic therapies to enhance longevity and wellbeing.

One day, in the midst of this kingdom there suddenly appeared a knotty little stranger, apparently dropped "out of the blue" by a passing bird. He was capless and dirty, creating an immediate negative impression upon his fellow acorns. And huddled beneath the oak tree, he stammered out a wild tale. Pointing upward he said, "We….are…..that!"

Delusional thinking, obviously, the other acorns concluded. But one of them continued to engage him in conversation. "So tell us, how would we become that tree?" "Well," said he, pointing downwards, "it has something to do with going into the ground…and cracking open the shell". "Insane", they responded, "totally morbid! Why, then we wouldn't be acorns any more."

Humor aside, the point is obvious – at least when it comes to acorns. An acorn is only a seed; its nature and destiny is to become an oak tree. Everyone knows this. What's much more difficult is to apply this parable to ourselves. …This "I" whom I take to be myself, this individual who moves about on the planet making choices and doing her thing, is not who I am at all. It's only the acorn. Coiled within this acorn is a vastly more majestic destiny and a true self who lives it. But this oak tree of myself can only come into being if it loses its acorn. [3] The questions of purpose and meaning, of contribution and legacy, which the Leader Coach asks herself continually and explores with others may help the acorn to see its oak-tree destiny. The Leader Coach, living a life of authenticity true to her core values, sees in her contribution to her organization one avenue through which she can explore this majestic destiny…it is not that work is the only way in which the oak tree grows, nor is work **not** the place where it grows….it is simply part of the ground.

Heart:

The heart is considered our emotional center, the host of our hopes and fears, our courage, caring and love as well as our anger, hatred and despair. When we are 'whole hearted' or 'open hearted', we connect to all others, all life, with an honest personal authenticity. When we are 'cold hearted', we are separate from ourselves and others, denoting a kind of living death. The heart, then, is the seat of our emotions and we must know what is in our hearts and how we can best reveal our true character to others in our relationships.

Daniel Goleman[4] has done much in the past few years to shed light on the emotions as a whole field of 'intelligence' that is central to leadership coaching. His four categories of self and social skills, and self and social awareness make up the emotional intelligence competencies needed for effective interpersonal functioning. Goleman has found that the emotions – the heart - are the starting point for our behavior, not the mind. In other words, our heart tells our mind what to do, for better or worse…

Cynthia Bourgeault reflects this reality when she talks about the connection of the heart and the emotions:

"In the language of sacred tradition, the emotional center carries the "reconciling" force. It serves as a bridge between the mind and the body, and also between our usual physical world and {an} invisible other realm. When properly attuned, the emotional center's most striking capacity, lacking in the mind alone, is the ability to comprehend the language of paradox. Logical inconsistencies which the mind must reduce into a simple "either/or" can be held by the heart in "both/and" - and more importantly - felt that way, without the need to resolve, to close down, or protect oneself from the pain that ambiguity always brings."[5]

And why might we be interested and concerned about the sense of balance, in which the heart is the reconciling force between the mind and the body? Clearly, an effective Leader Coach, a person poised in all four contexts, balanced and alert, seems to come from a deeper, steadier and quieter place. We are "present" ...fully occupying the "now" in which we find ourselves.

Mind:

Perhaps to reinforce this interconnection and interdependence, we need to come back to the mind, to acknowledge that it too plays a part, shares the space, helps to create the Leader Coach in the world. What we also need to do is remind ourselves of what the mind cannot do...that there are aspects of life that are not rational and will not be understood. They can be experienced in the body, the heart, the spirit and can be observed by the mind...but we may not find explanation. The mysterious, the inaccessible, the synchronistic, the magical...the alchemy may be at its furthest point unknowable...and we need to resist the temptation to judge that it is therefore suspect or less valid or somehow lacking. Attributes of courage, imagination, optimism....and the generative ability to integrate, see patterns, take learning to a higher level that includes all these different sources of discovery...these are the terrain or domain of the Leader Coach with a fully integrated embodiment of heart, mind, body and spirit.

Embodying Leadership

What does this notion of embodiment mean? How does the whole system of self that is comprised of body, mind, heart and spirit operate? How does the body lead? How does the spirit coach? Are they in fact separate? In one sense, of course, they aren't – we are one complex and interconnected system, with our mind interpreting and analyzing the data our bodies generate. For the purposes of this exploration, however, we will consider them as separate. Another *both/and* discipline will be for you, the reader, to hold the wholeness, the interconnection and the interdependencies, as we explore each one.

How does the body lead? Is there a way in which a body leads or does not lead? Coaches or does not coach? This goes beyond a simple awareness of, and attention to, body language in coaching and leading situations. It is wise to remember the degree to which the messages sent even inadvertently by body language can speak volumes, can aid immeasurably in the creation of a trust-based relationship. At a deeper level, however, the nature of embodiment is about a kind of transparency, about allowing that which is inner - your core values, your beliefs about yourself in the world - to be reflected out into the world. It is not simply having a high regard for health but about ensuring that choices in every context are towards health and away from dis-ease. It is about a sense of physical fitness that is a manifestation of your values around resilience, preparedness, vitality and energy. It is about acknowledging that there is a body, a frame for this mind and heart and spirit, which has needs, which gets tired, which needs refreshment, which wears clothes, and portrays not only our physical but also our sexual and sensual selves. Certain fabrics, certain fragrances, certain colors, certain styles of dress and costume….these choices we make are all in the light of our sense of our bodies…and the essential interconnection of the body, mind, heart and spirit. The body leads in how you walk, how you talk, the tone of voice, the vibrancy of your intonation, the intensity and focus with which you listen, the gentleness in your eyes when you make eye contact to encourage, the challenge in your eye contact when you hold a colleague to account.

The body also leads by what it does not do – the degree to which the body can be self-abused is an indication of the degree to which the self is out of tune. Alcohol, tobacco, caffeine, drugs, food, inactivity, long days and weeks without natural light or fresh air or the physical nourishment of contact with nature. A self out of tune is not a self truly credible as the embodiment of leadership coaching values. There are certainly times when the choices we make, sometimes for the short term, sometimes for expediency's sake, seem wise and inevitable. However, if they persist over any length of time, they become choices we are taking, rather than changes we are making.

And does the heart lead? Is there a way in which the heart leads? In the world of business, there's been an uneasy truce between the apparent rationality that plays out in meetings, memos and most days' interactions and the undercurrent of emotions and more primal expressions that runs beneath all of that. Goleman's research and writing has more recently brought the two domains of head and heart together in a new way, suggesting that in fact the heart does lead… we develop self awareness and self mastery so that we can interact effectively through building strong relationships with others. Perhaps it's even more appropriate to ask in what ways does the heart coach? For coming from a certain place of self-awareness and self-esteem, the heart can empathize with others in a way that is respectful …that may do nothing more than acknowledge and stand in the paradox, the ambiguity that is the current reality.

As Leader Coaches, we need to model the integration of mind, body, spirit, and heart, in all aspects of our lives. And we model or embody integration not only in terms of this sacred foursome; we also embody other kinds of balance. We cannot state, to our team colleagues, "Yes, I support you in your attempts to lead a balanced, blended life", and be working on Sunday morning, sending out emails at midnight from home, and sacrificing my daughter's story time for another client dinner. The demand to 'walk the talk' involves a holistic approach …it's hard, it's complex, it's going to provoke some difficult choices. The alternative, to be a terrific leader at work at the expense of your health, your relationships, your spiritual development, your 'play quotient', is to be not yet a fully evolved Leader Coach. So the question becomes not why, but what and how. Let's have a look at the competencies that follow from this discussion and how they fit into the four basic elements of the self, the inner alchemy.

The Competencies of the Leader Coach

The traditional concept of a job competency as defined by Boyatzis[6] is an underlying characteristic of a person. It may be a motive, trait, skill, aspects of one's self image or social role, or a body of knowledge. Competencies are causally related to effective and/or superior performance in a job, meaning that the characteristics must precede the performance. Now, twenty years on, we can take this notion of competencies from the narrower scope of a single causal relationship in a single job to the larger contexts of the whole self. We are indeed talking about the underlying characteristics of a person… leading not only to superior job performance but to a richer, more authentic life.

In addition to expanding the definition of a competency beyond the confines of a job, we want to propose that the notion of an 'alchemic' competency requires two additional attributes. The first is that a competency is in the service of transformation, that we are talking about change, growth, development. The second is that a competency is both complete in itself and a reflection of the whole. It is holographic, constantly intermingling with all the others. We are therefore presenting not a full set of leadership or coaching competencies but a full representation of transformative elements, perhaps best viewed as a prism, a kaleidoscope.

Rather than traditional competencies that can be described as mutually exclusive behavioral statements, we invite you to experience these feelings, thinkings, doings, beings, as a whole – turn the kaleidoscope just a little or change the light on the prism a bit and you have the same elements put together in a slightly different way, another opportunity for discovery.

Alchemic Competencies	Core Competencies "Being" in Spirit	Emotional Competencies "Feeling" with Heart	Cognitive Competencies "Thinking" with the Mind	Practical Competencies "Doing" from the Body
Co-creation of Futures	Experience: Mutuality Passionate intent Appreciation Creativity and vision	Center in: Courage Conviction Ambiguity Paradox Influence Humor	Recognize: Assumptions Patterns Strategic options Intellect	Build: Communities Dialogue Processes for engagement
Holographic Perspective	Exude: Purpose & values Authenticity Self-awareness Understanding others	Commit to: Empathy Purposeful Congruence Composure Patience	See: Whole systems Self in system Business insights Human natures	Choose: In the moment Based on integrity "Collaboraction" Embodiment
Leadership Through Heterarchy	Embrace: Diversity Wholeness Power of self Connection	Feel: In service Energy Excitement Vitality Emboldened Humbled	Express: Communication Imagination Capability Responsibility Willingness	Facilitate: Synergy Alignment Active listening Multiple voices Team development
Inter-dependence and Meaning	Seek: Relationships Common ground Honesty & integrity Personal learning	Integrate: Hopes Fears Experiences Yearnings	Reflect: Adaptability Discovery Transformation Reinvention	Model: Co-action learning Personal change Boundary spanning Alliances Networks

Chart 11: A Framework of the Self as a Leader Coach

Chart 11 outlines the territory of the 'ideal' Leader Coach, understanding that we cannot necessarily attain all of this or sustain it all over time but that we can strive to be our best in every situation and to learn as we go and grow. Let's have a look at how these interconnected domains contribute to our sense of being whole and present in our work and life.

The Co-creation of Futures:

The Leader Coach co-creates futures in which all stakeholders have a valuable voice and play a meaningful role. There are several components involved.

By **embodying courage in ambiguity**, the Leader Coach manifests authenticity - challenging assumptions, articulating fears and doubts while also holding true to values and convictions, knowing how to let go and lose control without losing direction.

By **building community**, the Leader Coach creates organizations which constantly reinvent themselves, through learning about and using innovative ways to participate, through engaging in individual and group dialogue, through searching for patterns that lead to new strategic options, through pulling with others toward a vision of a fuller future.

By **leading with passionate intent**, she uses creativity to envision the world as a better place and striving to make it happen, in appreciation of the part that others can play in the co-creative process, in a spirit of mutuality rather than self aggrandizement.

And by **holding the paradoxes**, she knows that contradictions are a part of changing times and that holding both sides of the polarity at once is critical to developing futures that are meaningful to and inclusive of all stakeholders.

A Holographic Perspective:

The Leader Coach uses the co-creative process to develop a holographic perspective for herself and others that embeds the vision and values in the community so that dispersed decisions and actions are aligned with the whole.

By **being authentic**, starting with herself and with building her own self awareness, the Leader Coach lives 'on purpose', from her values. She shows up consistently in all roles, in all contexts, no matter how challenging – she **is** her values. From this place, she seeks to understand others, not only on the surface but in their full human natures.

By **integrating the whole and the parts**, seeing the whole system and its components, the Leader Coach can herself embody the values of the community. As each member of the team carries the cultural code, at the cell level, in every analysis, in every moment of truth, in every decision, in every interaction, the whole is reflected in each of the parts. As a result, each person is willing to stand for, in the face of conflict and challenge, not only her own values, but the values of the entity she is part of creating,

By **acknowledging the limitations** as well as strengths of her own self as a system, she can relate to others in integrity, feeling empathy, and knowing that her patience and caring will encourage their own purposeful behavior. She admits her mistakes openly; she is a perpetual learner, and expects the same of others.

And by **acting in the moment**, based on the values imprint, reflecting the community, she is confident that others will do the same – a "collaboraction" that creates the hologram over and over again as each member of the system does their part. There is a constancy and consistency in the holographic perspective that is magnetized and aligned by values.

Leadership through Heterarchy:

The Leader Coach models heterarchy where each person has a right and a responsibility to lead in their turn according to their capabilities and the needs of the community.

By **embracing diversity**, the Leader Coach models wholeness and encourages the breadth of opinion and perspective necessary to encompass complexity. She listens to and connects with others in all their diversity, understanding the power to achieve results that comes from being all of who you are in what you do, including the alignment of spirit, heart, mind and body.

By **generating energy and excitement** through shared leadership, the Leader Coach supports the growth and vitality of others and builds their commitment to their own preferred futures. She emboldens new leaders to take their rightful place in co-creation and is humbled by their magnificent contributions.

By **being a willing communicator,** creating, participating in and sustaining true feedback-based communication, using imagination to deal with resistance, she is capable of confronting and resolving conflict without damaging relationships.

By **facilitating the development of heterarchical teams,** the Leader Coach fosters willingness to share power, to step forward, to feel and know the sense of competence and responsibility to lead, to create and enact their best destiny.

Generating Meaning through Interdependence:

The Leader Coach recognizes the importance of interdependent relationships both in the world around us and the world within us – the 720° view – in generating our meaning in life and work.

By **thriving in change**, the Leader Coach models learning and discovery - the natural process of adaptation and renewal through the adult life cycle - and the ability to undertake personal transformation in relation to new insights and experiments. She is constantly experimenting, learning, getting energized by change, being and becoming more fluid and flexible. She seeks out and exploits the transformative potential in the energy that change creates.

By **choosing interdependence**, the Leader Coach recognizes that her boundaries have expanded, that she is both independent in the sense of being a fully functioning adult and that she is also interdependent with others who are both contributors to and generators of her fulfillment and success. She values her relationships as mirrors of her self.

By **creating meaning**, the Leader Coach connects others to meaning in their own lives and also prompts the realization that meaning is the glue, the web silk that binds us together and gives us our common ground. She bases her own life, and her leadership of others, on the pursuit of meaning. She has moved beyond ego and self interest to a life of integrity and fulfillment with and through others.

By **being a continuous learner**, the Leader Coach understands deep change and is committed to personal exploration. She models co-action learning, reflecting on her actions and their consequences in community with others, and in the context of our global village. She examines her hopes and fears, her yearnings for a better world, and then crosses boundaries and builds networks and alliances to make them happen. She is a searcher and creator of opportunities to learn. She is alert to the possibility that learning occurs more in the heart, the spirit and the body than in the mind.

Our hope is that from this discussion you have a sense of the competencies of the Leader Coach, their density, their challenge, their interrelationships. These are the elements of the alchemic leader – we invite you to consider your own "inside out" journey to develop your inner self with the potential for your own transmutation from the leader you are today to the alchemic leader you can become tomorrow.

Here is a poem from a friend of Carol's to start you on your way.

I can find no better words to convey this sense of balance and presence in all four centers of the self – spirit, heart, body and mind – than those of Jane Hooper, a wise woman who died in June 2000, not quite 51, after a three-year journey with brain cancer. The following poem, written just before that journey began, and shared with her friends at the annual summer Long Dance on Whidbey Island, Washington, captures the "soul" of leading from the inside out.

<u>Coming Home</u>[7]

Please come home. Please come home.
Find the place where your feet know where to walk
And follow your own trail home.

Please come home. Please come home into your own body,
Your own vessel, your own earth.

Please come home into each and every cell,
And fully into the space that surrounds you.

Please come home. Please come home to trusting yourself,
And your instincts and your ways and your knowings,
And even the particular quirks of your personality.

Please come home. Please come home.
For you belong here now. You belong among us.
Please inhabit your place fully so we can learn from you,
From your voice and your ways and your presence.

Please come home. Please come home.
And when you feel yourself home, please welcome us too.
For we too forget that we belong and are welcome,
And that we are called to express fully who we are.

Please come home. Please come home.
Thank you, Earth, for welcoming us.
And thank you touch of eyes and ears and skin,
Touch of love for welcoming us.

May we wake up and remember who we truly are.
Please come home. Please come home. Please come home.

A Personal Reflection:

Body/Mind/Spirit/Heart. While there are many ways to experiment with the interconnections of body, mind, spirit and heart, we want to encourage you to begin to engage with a more integrated and interdependent reality and existence. Here are a few things to think about, play with, meditate on, feel…

Body. A colleague who was quite overweight and couldn't see his feet, commented that he had been so disconnected from his body, for so many years, that he couldn't remember any other way of being. Try getting connected to your senses….to temperature, to the breezes on your skin, to the sensation of your clothes on the backs of your knees, to the various levels of sound that you tend to 'tune out' in your immediate environment – the hum of the computer, perhaps, the vibration of the lights, the rumble of distant traffic, the voices, the telephones, the bustle of life around you…and have you truly enjoyed the taste of something fresh, and wonderful today? How are your senses? Do they need to be enlivened? Awakened? Can you do something to connect to your sensory system right now? Have you had a massage lately? Given a massage lately? Have you exercised today? This week?

Spirit. Have you sometimes sensed the presence of the divine? Can you remember the situation? Have you sometimes been in the presence of what you sense is a miracle, or something impossible to believe, actually happening? Can you meditate on that sensation of awe and wonder? For some, it's a matter for allowing themselves to surrender to a sense of serenity, calm, quiet, and peace. Here is a meditation to help you experience a sense of stillness. [8]

Imagine finding an inner space that allows you to feel…whether the darkness of night is descending or the dawn of a new morning is rising in your life, imagine a natural scene at the transition of night and day. See a lake, imagine a bird flying over head, a fish jumping, or a shooting star skimming through the sky. Given the stillness of this scene you'd be sure to catch the movement and be able to share in the sheer beauty of the moment. Perhaps you'd even find meaning in that particular event happening at that exact moment. The free spirit of the bird's flight might inspire you. You might recall a treasured memory of a family outing. You might take one of the signs as a "hello" from a loved one who recently passed away. Or you might find yourself marveling at the exquisite beauty of nature that is always around us.

•

When you are in a state of stillness, you also become more attuned to your own process. You are better able to pick up the subtle cues in your daily life that bring you hope, perspective, and inspiration. Your mind is more open than usual to making new connections that can lead you out of the dark and into the light.

Take time to be still in the coming weeks and months. Return to this imagined scene if it helps or find a picture you can keep in your home or office that evokes this sense of peaceful stillness. Don't expect yourself to live in this state all of the time – our lives are just to busy for that - but consciously create pockets of time when you can be alone and at peace.

While you are at peace you can think or not, listen to music or not, contemplate a quote or not. Experiment to see what style works best for you.

An Exercise to Share:

Choose one of the four aspects of self – body, mind, heart or spirit – perhaps the one you feel least connected to, or the one that has stirred something in your self reflection. Refer to the Alchemic Competencies chart in the chapter and make some notes about how you could connect to or develop your competency in this aspect. How would you **be**? How would you **feel**? How would you **think**? What would you **do**?

For example, if you choose the Emotional Competencies: "Feeling" with the Heart, how could you be more courageous in expressing your convictions? How would it feel to have more empathy for others? How do you experience paradox in your life and work and what do you think about these contradictions? And finally, what could you do to integrate your feelings – hopes, fears, yearnings – into your relationships with others?

When you have your notes, share them with someone you trust and who knows you well enough to discuss them with you and offer feedback and suggestions. Perhaps they will be willing to consider similar questions for themselves and share them with you as well. Talk about what you have learned from the exercise and how you can support each other in moving forward with your plans.

A Self-Assessment:

Alchemic Competencies	Core Competencies "Being" in Spirit	Emotional Competencies "Feeling" with Heart	Cognitive Competencies "Thinking" with the Mind	Practical Competencies "Doing" from the Body
Co-creation of Futures	Experience: Mutuality Passionate intent Appreciation Creativity and vision	Center in: Courage Conviction Ambiguity Paradox Influence Humor	Recognize: Assumptions Patterns Strategic options Intellect	Build: Communities Dialogue Processes for engagement
Holographic Perspective	Exude: Purpose & values Authenticity Self-awareness Understanding others	Commit to: Empathy Purposeful Congruence Composure Patience	See: Whole systems Self in system Business insights Human natures	Choose: In the moment Based on integrity "Collaboraction" Embodiment
Leadership Through Heterarchy	Embrace: Diversity Wholeness Power of self Connection	Feel: In service Energy Excitement Vitality Emboldened Humbled	Express: Communication Imagination Capability Responsibility Willingness	Facilitate: Synergy Alignment Active listening Multiple voices Team development
Inter-dependence and Meaning	Seek: Relationships Common ground Honesty & integrity Personal learning	Integrate: Hopes Fears Experiences Yearnings	Reflect: Adaptability Discovery Transformation Reinvention	Model: Co-action learning Personal change Boundary spanning Alliances Networks

Chart 12: As Assessment of the Self as a Leader Coach

Here is the Alchemic Competencies chart again. Spend some time thinking about yourself and your experiences in relation to some of the words. Then give yourself a rating on each of the four aspects of the self and each of the competency themes. Rate yourself High (H), Medium (M) or Low (L) on each dimension.

− Which aspects of your self are you most comfortable with, most connected to?
− How does this connection, this comfort, play out in your life and work roles? Your leadership coaching?
− Which of the words are descriptive of your experience? Which are not? What can you do to find out more about those?
− What aspects of your self are you least comfortable with, least connected to?
− Which of the words are strange to you? Perhaps don't fit your values? How are your words, your values, different?
− How does this lack of connection, this discomfort, play out in your life and work roles? Does it have an impact on your ability to be a Leader Coach?

Where are your highest and lowest scores on the four competency themes? Compare these to your ratings in the self-assessment you did in Chapter 3 – have your scores changed based on your reading of this chapter? Do you understand the competencies differently now? What specific words in the cells of the chart are important to these scores, compared to your former scores, do you think? Are there development areas that are reinforced in this reassessment? Are there areas that you need to learn more about? What are one or two action steps that you can take?

A Team Exercise:

One of the best ways to learn about something that may feel foreign is to unleash the team's creativity. Divide up the four aspects of the self – spirit, heart, body and mind – and have members of the team divide into pairs or triads and choose one of the aspects to work on. Do the same with the four competency themes – co-creation, holograms, heterarchy and meaning/interdependence - if your team is large enough, or have two sessions.

Give the pairs or triads a couple of weeks to do their creative work. They can create a skit for the rest of the team that expresses how the team would incorporate or improve upon this dimension, they can sign a song, write a poem, create a work of art... You can either specify what the final product should look like, or leave it up to the pairs/triads to decide. The ground rule is that it must creatively express the benefit to the team, and be no more than five minutes in length. When the team reconvenes, the team leader can emcee the proceedings. After the presentations, team members can discuss what they have learned from this and how they can build the team based on the suggestions – have fun!

Although not so much fun to do, an alternative is to give the pairs/triads the task of coming up with a statement of team principles or 'rules of the tribe' for the dimension they have selected. These are presented back to the team, discussed and compared. The end result is a new statement of team principles based on the suggestions.

If you have completed the team exercise at the end of Chapter 3, you can build on it with this exercise, perhaps doing both at a team retreat.

EndNotes:

[1] Mary Beth O'Neill, in *Executive Coaching with Backbone and Heart*, calls this essence 'signature presence'.

[2] David Whyte has written extensively (*The Heart Aroused*) about bringing spirit, through his poetry, into organizations worldwide.

[3] Bourgeault, Cynthia. *A Short Course on Wisdom*, Praxis, 2002.

[4] Daniel Goleman has written *Emotional Intelligence, Emotional Intelligence at Work*, and lately *Primal Leadership*, all building on his brain research about how the emotions are at the core of our behavior.

[5] Bourgeault, Cynthia. ibid.

[6] Boyatzis, R. *The Competent Manager: A Model of Effective Performance.* Wiley-Interscience, 1982.

[7] Published in "Branches of Light", a quarterly publication of Banyan Books, Vancouver, January 2002. Quoted here by permission of the publishers (and Jane's husband Kolin Lymworth).

[8] Extracted from a website which has images and exercises to prompt personal reflection: http://www.getrollingagain.com/product/stuckbooklet.html

Chapter 5
Inside Out: What's in the Shadows?

The Existence of Shadow Side Incompetencies

We have been discussing the importance of the self – the honest expression of who we are in all we do - as the starting point for Coach Leaders building the authentic relationships that are at the core of leadership in turbulent times. Part of this exploration of the self includes that part of us that may be denied because it is less acceptable and less good. Carl Jung[1], who wrote extensively about this shadow side of the personality, thought that one of the goals in life was to get to know ourselves fully, to understand our "other side", not to suppress or repress it, but to express and control the whole range of human capabilities. In other words, to be fully human.

We want to turn now to this aspect of leadership and to draw it into our awareness, for it is also part of becoming a Leader Coach. The shadow has to do with what happens when leaders can't handle the complexity, or can't act in the uncertainty of rapid change. What happens when leaders don't have a strong value base, or their only value is an unrelenting drive for perfection and success? What happens when leaders are threatened by others and see the exercise of power over others as their only means of control? What happens when leaders don't have the time or inclination to be reflective, to learn, and instead become brittle and arrogant? If leaders are continuously learning and changing, they can't be perfect or always right; they must recognize their fallibility and their mistakes, and see room for improvement. What if that isn't the case?

Turbulent times bring out both the best and the worst in leaders. We hear many stories of heroism in unexpected tragedy – the rescue workers and firefighters who gave their lives in the aftermath of the collapse of the World Trade towers. And we hear of fraud and deceit – the leaders at Enron and WorldCom who took advantage of their investors and employees. Both the light and the shadow are at play in the complexity and uncertainty of global hyper-turbulence[2].

For those whose sense of self is incomplete, it becomes especially difficult to admit that they are inadequate or incompetent or wrong. In fact, they may not be able to see it at all. The 'elevation' of the leadership role inhibits self-reflection or recognition of limitations. Leaders' power, isolation and autonomy can create immunity to negative feedback. The leadership job rewards constant high-paced activity leading to bottom-line performance, not personal reflection. And leaders are socialized to wear a mask of optimism, of competence, and not to let their true feelings show, in order to meet their own strong ego needs and the expectations of those around them. They are paid to do, not to feel, not to be.

As followers, we are often culpable too, if our own self esteem is not strong. We tend to invest in our leaders a confidence that they know what we don't. They provide the sense of stability we need in a chaotic world by seeming to be on a clear path and giving us the means to follow. Dee Hock in an article on leader-follower relations says that if we want to ensure that leaders are ethical, open and honest, we must "follow those who will behave in that manner. It comes down to both the individual and collective sense of where and how people choose to be led. In a very real sense, followers lead by choosing where to be led. Where a community will be led is inseparable from the conscious, shared values and beliefs of the individuals of which it is composed."[3]

Time magazine's "Persons of the Year"[4] in 2002 were Cynthia Cooper of WorldCom, Coleen Rowley of the FBI, and Sherron Watkins of Enron, three women who chose to expose their leaders to the separation between their values and their behavior. These three "whistleblowers" believed in their organizations and wanted them to live up to their potential. The Time article ends with a quote from Ibsen's *An Enemy of the People*, a classic in unwelcome truth telling. They quote, "A community is like a ship – everyone ought to be prepared to take the helm." These women demonstrated true leadership - one might argue heterarchical leadership - by acting in accordance with their values and ideals.

By denying our own self-leadership, we can create dependence by assuming that only senior leaders can guide us, that without them we are powerless. To respond to these assumptions in us, they feel they must not let us down by showing weakness or uncertainty. It can be a vicious circle. So, over time, leaders can come to believe their own rhetoric, to live in their constructed realities, and be reinforced by those around them.

This is not a single choice at a single point in time; it is a series of many small steps and seemingly minor decision points. Rather than admit their fallibility, leaders can deny it, ignore it, suppress it, cover it up, through a series of choices and behaviors over an extended period of time. And with each step along this road, it becomes increasingly difficult to admit that they **are** on the wrong road, often only because they have to admit that they must go back to the first wrong turn, and must accept the fact that they have wasted energy and time along the way.

This sets up a classic double bind – the constant fear of loss of control or exposure of weakness, and the inability to admit to it, especially to oneself. Instead, more and more complex webs of confusion and pretense are created; leaders split themselves off from others and from their true selves, and perhaps worse, use their power to make scapegoats of others to protect their self-deception. This is certainly not to say that all leaders find themselves in these double binds but that there is a significant potential in the underdeveloped self for the shadow side to emerge – we must recognize and name the danger for what it is.

WorldCom CEO Bernard Ebbers is just one recent example. Mr. Ebbers not only built WorldCom on a mountain of debt from acquisitions but he also built a huge personal empire by borrowing from a host of banks who courted him as a customer because of his WorldCom connection. He bought for his private holdings timberland, farming, trucking, lumber and boat building concerns on a massive scale. He paid some loans with others and when he needed more, borrowed almost half a billion dollars from his WorldCom Board who were afraid that if he sold his shares as a way to repay the loans, the stock would drop dramatically. As of the end of 2002, Mr. Ebbers still owed this money to the company, although they have seized collateral assets, and owed another half a billion to the bank[5]. In addition to the company's $9 billion accounting scandal, the CEO, in his own acquisition spree, had run up a billion dollar bill! This is fraud of inconceivable proportions... it is obsession without regard for consequences. What of the employees of WorldCom? What of the investors? What kind of leadership does this represent? And what of the ethics of the banks who underwrote these schemes? It would be terrible if this was a unique example but it is not. The scandal created by the leaders at Enron and Anderson is even more staggering. And there are many others.

Have we created leadership jobs that are impossible to carry out because the demands are superhuman? Many leaders give up any semblance of a balanced or complete life in order to devote themselves to their work. Do they feel as payment, like Bernard Ebbers, that they deserve to be omnipotent kings with unlimited financial rewards? The trouble is, even with this level of personal investment in the role, the range of required competencies to lead at this scale is such that no one can to it alone. We need mutuality. And there is an implicit paradox in the role - it is expected that neither the leader nor others will openly admit that it may be impossible to do the job. For if they do, it is assumed that the whole "house of cards" may come tumbling down, the emperor will have no clothes! So, for leaders to succeed, they must be able not only to accomplish the superhuman in the role but also to transcend the paradox in recognizing that their success depends on their willingness to admit their own imperfections and be humbled by them[6].

So, the shadow side qualities emerge in leaders who do not have the contextual competencies – both inner self-strength and outer change strength – to cope in turbulent times. An important distinction here is that these are 'skilled' incompetencies - they are defensive routines, "fancy footwork" - rather than a lack of knowledge or ability. They are the harm that is done both to the individuals themselves and, more importantly, to those around them when, in the name of business competition and superiority, leaders protect their self-image of perfection and control by manipulating others. The use of power to diminish the spirit of others for the purpose of preserving our own illusions is evil. It is these leaders that Scott Peck calls "the people of the lie"[7]. Zimbardo calls it "creative evil" when humans use their intelligence to be destructive and violent toward others[8].

This is obviously difficult territory to consider. We have tended not to want to recognize or discuss this shadow side of the leadership coin. Just as we have tended in organizational life to separate from our higher selves – our spirit and heart – we have, perhaps because of this, also separated from our baser selves as well. Somehow we have assumed that although evil exists in the world, it would not infiltrate our organizations. Again, those thick walls, those boundaries between organizations and their environments, have been assumed to

protect those within. We believe it is particularly critical to highlight the
dangers in light of what we see in both corporate and political situations around
the world. It is precisely because we live in turbulent times that the potential for
evil in our global organizations and our global leaders is most dangerous. And
as we each take up our rightful leadership roles in our workplaces and in our
lives, in heterarchy, we must also be cognizant of the *both/and* dimensions of
the shadow as well as the light in each of us.

The Link to Turbulent Times

Let's return for a moment to reflect on the links between a world of
chaotic change and the emergence of evildoing. When change is slower, or at
least to some extent predictable, and when problems have solutions, or at least
the possibility of trade-offs, and when leaders can feel at least some sense of
control over their context, there is less likelihood that they will feel incapable
and need to deny, split off, and project their shadow sides onto others. So there
is a greater tendency in turbulent times, where chaos is the order of the day,
problems are unresolvable messes and control is a myth, for leaders to have to
hide their perceived deficits behind a false mask. For this reason, Zimbardo
recommends that we distinguish between "disposition", the evil present in
individuals such as Hitler, and "situations" that facilitate the birth and existence
of evil. When we bring this situational or contextual link into play, it is easier to
understand how basically good people can be involved in evil behavior.

There are more organizations today with more leaders, who have more
power over more people and their lives, than ever before. And these
organizations are fighting for their very survival, amidst unbridled acquisition,
massive restructuring, aggressive cost cutting, and a culture of fear in the
workplace. Those who began their careers with the expectation that they would
have choices and be able to continue to grow, now very often feel they have no
choice but to cling tenuously to their perhaps temporary security or to launch
themselves out into an even more frightening world.

There are a number of factors involved. One factor of significance is
that we tend to reward tough leaders who can generate short-term financial
results. Because there are often long lead times before the costs of this short-
term thinking can be measured, the true costs of poor leadership are sometimes
overlooked. Many of Wall Street's favorites have been decimated or swallowed

up when the consequences of one dimensional leadership became apparent. There are many examples, especially in the boom and bust high-tech sector.

Another factor is that leaders are not closely supervised. They operate with significant autonomy within organizations where they may not be known as in the past and where it is difficult to see downward abuse. Again, "as long as the numbers are right…" With this kind of denial, it may be some time before the complex web of issues can be addressed. Finally, when a leader is incompetent and in denial, employees will sometimes collude in protecting her, covering up the reality, both out of loyalty to the organization and because they may be dependent on the leader for their wellbeing. So, as Peck points out, these people create for those under their dominion a miniature sick society. Such was the case with Ebbers and his Board of directors as well as his stable of competing bankers. None of them could afford to have Ebbers fail so they kept propping him up, knowing that if he failed, they would too.

We must reinforce that we are not suggesting that these shadow qualities have not existed in leaders as long as we can remember, regardless of environmental conditions. The twin shadow and light sides are deeply imbedded in our myths, our religions and our cultures through time. Reflecting back on our history and mythology, there has often been a "twinning" of king and priest, of church and state, to balance these dual forces. The king has represented the external, material, more masculine world, the priest the interior, spiritual, more feminine world. In modern times, we have rejected the priest, or spiritual realm, and followed the material world almost exclusively. We are as a result alienated as individuals and societies from our inner selves. Our organizations exist within a spiritual vacuum and that is now recognized to have serious consequences. It is for this reason we believe that we are in a period where the potential for the emergence of the shadow side of leadership is greater and the recognition of the dangers has just begun to dawn.

The Nature of Leadership Malevolence

Let's have a closer look at the relationship between leaders and followers. Leaders by definition have some power over others, which they can use positively to engender trust and initiative or negatively to engender fear and passivity. We have talked in earlier chapters about power as a limitless resource which, when shared, builds positive energy and commitment. Here, we want to talk about power when it is seen as a limited resource, as power over others, used to bully them and force their compliance.

These behaviors emanate from a deep fear in the leaders themselves that their imperfections, which they cannot acknowledge, will be exposed if they allow any challenge at all to their fragile and false self-images. Some leaders work tirelessly to preserve their sense of control by scapegoating those who dare to dissent. People fear these leaders, quite appropriately. They fear the repercussions of their use of power. These repercussions fall into two types: first, the subtle, indirect and often delayed behaviors, and second, the more immediate, direct abrasive shadow side behaviors.

The direct behaviors are a more immediate response to a situation in which the leader feels threatened or wants to exercise control. They can range from sarcastic innuendo to an aggressive controlling manner to direct verbal assaults on an employee's character, competence or credibility. They include childish temper tantrums with yelling, swearing and shoving. These leaders often use public criticism and embarrassment of another to direct attention away from their sense of threat. They can also set up an abusive work culture, characterized by unrealistic demands, unpredictable requests and arbitrary deadlines. Targets are often subjected to constant detailed scrutiny of their activities.

Listen to this professional employee:

"I got a new boss. She didn't want anybody in the department who had worked there longer than her. She was very insecure. She wanted everybody to learn her way. She would choose a particular part of the department for critiquing. From then on, nothing good could come out of that area. People who had been there for years were suddenly inept, and were let go. They were always let go on Friday night. This happened four times. Then I knew it was my turn."

Another colleague described it this way:

"It was a nightmare. She criticized people openly, made obscene comments to my co-worker, humiliated people. I thought about the situation twenty-four hours a day, playing over the incidents that might happen. In some cases, these things actually did happen."

These workers' stories also speak to the second type of behavior – the subtle, insidious repercussions that are disconnected from the immediate situation but that have a powerful indirect impact on another's reputation and influence. Examples are secretive decision-making that excludes a targeted individual without reason, and selective communication, or lack of it, also designed to exclude and to send a signal of discounted value. Mixed messages and confusion also characterize these indirect behaviors - being a great guy one minute and a monster the next, or saying one thing in private and the opposite in a group - making people feel as it they are at fault and to blame. Leaders can also use subtle references to discredit members of their staff, damaging their reputations, credibility and future careers.

These behaviors are potentially even more damaging because they are covert and difficult for other senior people to accept. One of the employees quoted above, continues:

> "I went to the CEO. He said he couldn't perceive this person doing these things. They take the attitude that if you complain it must be a vendetta. I think he dismissed it as a woman-versus-woman conflict."

A manager in a major corporation who was demoted by his vice-president several months after he challenged a new marketing program comments:

> "He never came to me. He carried out the demotion in the classic large organization way, by assassinating my reputation and career without me knowing where it came from."

Or take the story of Jack, a plant manager who was removed from his job after seven years. One employee wrote a letter which included the following points about Jack:

> "He was a tyrant. He had temper tantrums, shouting and screaming. He was emotionally unstable. One day he would threaten to fire everyone; the next day, we were a great team. Jack was paranoid. At night, he'd search through wastebaskets looking for secret memos. He ruled by edict: 'There shall be no machine breakdowns.' 'Efficiency shall be improved immediately.' He talked about how

things should be but was unable to understand the realities of how things were."

The letter caused a stir at headquarters and Jack's boss arrived about a week later to interview Jack's team members and got essentially the same story from all of them. His final response, after lengthy discussion, was:

"How could I do anything? The bottom line looked good."

This "tough boss" style, in a less dramatic form perhaps, has characterized our North American role models of leadership in the past few decades. The macho management style is portrayed as a bit heroic, something to be emulated, or at least to be expected and tolerated as part of the "creative genius" personality. Times are tough and leaders must be tough too. And tough doesn't only mean endless restructuring, layoffs, iron-fisted cost cutting, and maniacal frugality. It may also mean 'psychological oppression' – bullying, cruelty and mind games designed to diminish and intimidate rather than expand and develop others.

Susan speaks here of a personal experience with this kind of malevolence in a boss.

I was a Director in a large corporation heading an organization change function. I had been working to build credibility and momentum for about two years, with the full support of my boss. Despite lots of resistance, I had made some headway, built some credibility, and things were really starting to pop. A new CEO was appointed, who brought in a new VP of HR as my boss - a woman. I was excited to begin working with her.

Our first meeting was a day long session with all the HR leaders from head office and the field. The new VP asked us each to report on our activities. She listened well and responded positively as we went around the room. When it was my turn, her attitude changed. She became very critical, asked disbelieving questions, frowned rather than smiled, and finally made a joke at my expense. She then continued with the others in her friendly way. I was shocked – her behavior was so pointedly different with me. Several of my colleagues asked what I had done to make her dislike me so quickly.

In our one on one meeting the following week, I asked if there was anything I needed to know or change in what I was doing. I said I wanted to check out what I had perceived to be her uncertainty about my performance. She said everything was fine and quickly moved on.

Things got much worse over the next few months. Her treatment in public seemed designed to single out, belittle and humiliate me. For example, she would ask my peer group for ideas about solving what she saw as the list of shortcomings in my function. Most of my colleagues sympathized but felt they had to play along or it might happen to them. She cancelled programs, moved new projects to a colleague, and planned to cut my staff and budget dramatically. I was feeling completely victimized – out of control, vanishing confidence, anger, confusion, isolation, self doubt, fear of failure – my shadow was clearly also hard at work! It was hell. I was ready to quit but felt I had to protect my staff from her attacks.

One day a person from outside HR came to me with a fantastic story. We met at my home because she didn't dare to be seen talking to me at work. She said she was involved in the budgeting process and had to warn me about what had been going on. The VP wanted me to resign so one of my close colleagues could be given my organization. They had been working together on this plan for some time. They were surprised I hadn't already quit and the VP was prepared to discredit me and downsize my responsibilities until I did. Armed with proof, my "deep throat" approached an influential SVP to tell him about the situation in the hope that he could somehow intervene.

Just at this time, the CEO was fired. His replacement had a mandate to bring about the changes I had been working toward with limited success, and suddenly I was on a special assignment to develop strategies for the change. I no longer reported to the VP. It was like a great weight had been lifted. I hadn't realized just how tense and stressed I had become until I was removed from the situation. Three months later when the change recommendations were presented, both the VP and my colleague left the organization.

And these situations are not limited to leaders and their team members. At the other extreme, in a recent news article[9] on ethics in law, one irate litigator referred to his counterpart on the other side as "Dumbo", and poured coffee on his papers, four times!   And this is among professionals who represent fairness, justice and ethical practice.   These nasty encounters have become so common that Law Societies these days are deeply engaged in monitoring and reprimanding abusive behavior.

As we discussed previously, the scale of abuse has increased dramatically in the last few years. It seems to have become part of the North American corporate culture – a greed game – to "cook the books", to amass personal wealth, to grow at all costs. Leaders have become further removed from their constituents, more personally disconnected, less accountable. The bursting of the Enron bubble was just the beginning as organization after organization, CEO after CEO, have fallen into the morass. The impact on those who have lost income, employment, pensions, pride in their work, and loyalty to their companies is immeasurable.   We have learned the hard way that we must both lead and follow differently in the chaos of hyper-turbulence.

The Challenge of Moral Paradox

So how do we understand what is required of us? What is the moral challenge of leading in turbulent times?

We believe we are dealing here with another paradox, this time a moral paradox – a need to contain two apparently contradictory stances at the same time. First, we must see in the shadow side the potential for evil, for that is the only way to deal with it. Both the shadow and the light must be always in view. Our challenge is to reclaim our own shadow sides, not suppress them, recognizing that we all have the potential for evil – both good and evil exist in each of us as a coincidence of opposites. Evil is not only "out there", but "in here" as well. Rather than projecting our shadow sides onto others, we need to own these parts of our character. What are our own shadows? How are we susceptible to wrongdoing, to moral lapses? What are our assumptions about others that may in fact be a reflection of our own character flaws?

It is in our awareness of this tension between opposites and our subsequent choices that we express our moral character. It is critically important that we *feel* these choices, for it is our ability to *feel* that we have lost; it is our heart and spirit, especially at work, that identify the shadow side for us. It is a paradox of our chaotic world, where the unexpected is the only certainty, that the major threats to our survival come not only from nature without but from our human nature within.

Alchemic Leadership and the Shadow

If this is the challenge, how does the alchemic leader, the Leader Coach, respond to transform these shadow themes? How does alchemic leadership relate to the potential for both good and evil? How do our alchemic leadership competencies deal with moral paradox? The framework below contrasts the shadow side "incompetencies" we have been discussing with our alchemic competencies.

The Leader Coach as an alchemic leader starts with herself, acknowledging the possibility, in fact probability, of failing to see things for what they are. From this base, she seeks out others' opinions to broaden her horizons, to keep her honest, to co-create with her so that she can manage the shadow potential in herself and become part of the community ethic that oversees the whole.

Shadow Side "InCompetencies"	Alchemic Leadership Competencies
Manipulation; cover up; scapegoating; greed	Co-creation; sense of self as whole being; mutuality
False values; mask of goodness and perfection; pretense; fraud; infallibility	Construction of values through dialogue; holographic 'code'; error embracing
Power over; diminishing others for self importance, control	Embracing diversity; shared heterarchical leadership
Inability to deal with uncertainty; no acknowledgement of imperfection; isolation	Recognition of interdependence; meaning through relationship and community

Chart 13: A Framework of Comparative (In)Competencies

Through dialogue, common values are constructed and imbedded as genetic code in the layers of members of the organization who then own them authentically. Masking and pretense are more easily recognized and exposed. Mistakes are expected, not covered up. Humility is a valued trait. Diversity of opinion and belief are embraced. Power and control is dispersed and leadership is everyone's right and responsibility, not concentrated in the hands of a few.

Perhaps the most important distinction of alchemic leadership competencies, as opposed to shadow "incompetencies", is the constant nurturing of a sense of community, of a common set of values and futures, a community that actively discourages denial of the whole self, and the breaking apart of mutuality that leads to isolation. In these communities, people are *expected* to grow and develop – it is imperative if they are to thrive on chaos – including failing and learning from it and trying again, with the support and encouragement of others.

Here is another quote from Dee Hock, speaking about "true leaders".

"True leaders are those who epitomize the general sense of the community – who symbolize, legitimize, and strengthen behavior in accordance with the sense of the community – who enable its conscious, shared values and beliefs to emerge, expand, and be transmitted from generation to generation – who enable that which is trying to happen to come into being. The true leader's behavior is induced by the behavior of every individual who chooses where they will be led."[10]

Before we invite you to a personal reflection about all this, Carol will share her own perspective on the shadow she is now more aware of.

This reflection starts with a quotation from Susan Chance in *Intimacy,* I find very reassuring:

"One day you will wake up and you will feel that a weight has been taken from you. You will understand that you will never forgive yourself, but you will also realize that you are strong enough to live with yourself. This is called grace. It always happens."

When I think of strong emotions that might hint at my shadow side, I recall a meeting that was catalytic to the changes I have made. I had been consulting to an organization for over two years and had become so entrenched in the organization structure and culture that I had begun to forget who I was, who I worked for (myself!) and where the boundaries were between life and work. I was working long hours and was assumed by many employees to be a fulltime member of the executive team. But I was not, and this meeting reinforced that message. I had asked my client contact if we could talk about the plans for the next few months of this long consulting assignment and what my role might be. Her response was vivid and immediate:

"Picture a bucket of water. You put your fist in. You pull your fist out. That's the impact you've had around here. Don't ever forget that."

My first reactions were shock, disbelief and a sense of being almost physically hurt and attacked. I knew I needed to leave the meeting, to sort out my feelings, and get them "under control". Why had her comments provoked such strong reactions in me? I think it was my shadow!

While I could rationalize some of this with comments that perhaps she was jealous of my influence and charisma in the organization, that many employees had asked if they could work with me and recognized the contribution I had made in their own working lives, there was a deeper quake in my spirit. While my first thoughts to myself were outrage...she can't be right, I can't have made that little a difference after two years!! I was also aware of a deep sadness and anger at myself. I was angry that I cared so much about my work and that I had frequently made choices and decisions that had placed my work as so important. My mother was dying at the time, (we thought) and I had put added pressure on my family by being in so many meetings, so late into the evening. Why had I made those choices? Did it really mean nothing?

When I explored the messages that my shadow was prompting in me, I discovered comments like: "You work so hard, so that you will be deemed worthy of respect."....which might translate into "You aren't worthy of respect unless you work hard" or "You're not good enough doing a normal day's work, you have to do an extraordinary amount, extraordinarily well"...How good is good enough? How much is enough? The shadow says, "I am unworthy" or "I'm not good enough" and prompts me to work hard to try to earn someone else's contrary view that I am. I am dependent on the validation of others. I don't know where these messages started. I do know that I am today filled with gratitude that this client was as direct and blunt as she was. The vivid imagery of the bucket of water helped me to realize I wanted to make different choices from now on. I wanted to place work in a different relationship to the other parts of my life. While I'm not perfect, and won't be, I can now experience that sense of Grace that Susan Chance talked about, where a weight is taken off you as you forgive yourself for being human, for not being perfect. And for me, this has had the literal manifestation of losing weight, in a slow, steady and sustainable way, for the first time since I was a child.

Personal Reflection:

The first step in incorporating our shadow side is to begin to recognize its presence in our behavior. Often, our deepest emotions are felt when our shadow is operating. A heightened sense of anger, for instance, or frustration, may signal a situation that evokes our shadow. This happens to everyone – it is part of who we are. The goal is to let it surface rather than deny its existence, to manage our emotions rather than allow them to control us.

Think of a time when you may have been unnecessarily angry at someone else... what were the circumstances? As you imagine the situation, can you see your own role in the unfolding scene? What about and within you contributed to your anger? What triggered it? Was there something in the other person that may have been a reflection of something in yourself? Something that you may not have wanted to recognize at the time? Was your shadow operating in some way?

It is time well spent to quietly contemplate circumstances in our lives that we perhaps regret, where we may have diminished others for our own sakes, or where we felt superior to others and treated them badly. Reflect on these episodes in your own life and what you could have done differently. How did you feel at the time? How would you have felt if you had behaved authentically? Would there have been a different outcome?

An Exercise to Share:

It takes great courage to recognize that our shadow has gained the upper hand in a situation and to admit our mistake. Yet this is what authenticity is about; it's what true leadership means.

In the personal reflection, you may have thought of a situation you regret, and that you could address with the other person. Think about what you could say to express your regret and to repair the relationship. Be sure that you acknowledge your role in the situation, your feelings now, and your wish to make amends.

This may feel very hard to do. But do it anyway! Take the step. If you cannot communicate directly, try writing it down and saying it aloud, as you would if the other person were present. When you have had the conversation, think about how it went, how you feel about it, and what you learned from it.

A Team Exercise:

Shadows operate in community as well as in individual interactions. Often, a team will have its own shadow, a pattern that repeats itself and that goes unnamed and unaddressed. It is an undiscussable, and team members quickly learn either to be passive or to join in so they feel included. It may be that one person's ideas are continually discounted. It may be that a personal conflict is played out in the team. It may be that team rivalry is expressed by making fun of or belittling their members.

What is a shadow pattern in a team that you lead? Can you identify a behavior pattern that inhibits the team's learning and growth? What are the consequences of this pattern, for individuals and for the team as a whole? Can you give it a name? Can you see your own role in the pattern?

What could be done to expose and address this pattern? How could you embody the alchemic leadership competencies in this situation? What would the differences be, do you think? How would it be best to proceed? Could you as the Leader Coach make a difference? How would you behave? Who would be involved? Who might be hurt? Are you willing and able to act? What support would you need and from whom?

A Self Assessment:

One way to assess your ability to incorporate your own shadow is to reflect on how you have felt as you read this chapter.
– What emotions did it engender?
– Did you find yourself stopping and thinking about situations in your own experience that related to the material? Has someone in your work life mistreated you, or have you mistreated someone else? Have you betrayed your own sense of ethics and regretted it?
– Are you having trouble seeing how this relates to you? After all, you're not a greedy corporate CEO or someone who has abused subordinates... What does this have to do with you?
– Or have you been thinking about how you might behave differently in future, perhaps bringing to the surface and exploring situations where you see your own shadow and perhaps others shadows in play?
What can you learn from this assessment? What does it tell you about your sense of self? What more do you need to know in order to meet the challenge of moral paradox in your own life?

Endnotes:
[1] See, for example, "Dream Symbolism in Relation to Alchemy" in *The Portable Jung*, Joseph Campbell Editor, Viking, 1971.

[2] Wright Susan and David Morley. *Learning Works: Searching for Organizational Futures.* ABL Publications, 1998.

[3] Hock, Dee. "The Art of Chaordic Leadership", in *Leader to Leader*, Volume 15, Drucker Foundation and Jossey-Bass, 2000.

[4] *Time Magazine*, "Persons of the Year" cover stories, December 22, 2002.

[5] *Wall Street Journal*, Tuesday, December 31, 2002 – Vol. CCXL No. 128.

[6] Collins, Jim. "Level 5 Leadership: The Triumph of Humility and Fierce Resolve", *Harvard Business Review* #20101D, January 2001.

[7] Peck, Scott. *The People of the Lie: The Hope for Healing Human Evi.,* Touchstone Books, 1983.

[8] Zimbardo, P.G. in an interview with S. Carpenter, *Journal of Counseling and Development,* 2001.

[9] *The Globe and Mail,* Monday, December 30, 2002, Page B10.

[10]Hock, Dee. "The Art of Chaordic Leadership", in *Leader to Leader*, Volume 15, Drucker Foundation and Jossey-Bass, 2000.

Chapter 6
Outside In – Practicing as a
Leadership Coach

In this chapter we look from the outside in, at the settings in which Coach Leaders operate and the way they apply the competencies discussed in Chapter 4 in those settings. What does the practice of leadership coaching look like in an organization? How do you apply the concepts and competencies we have been discussing in your daily practices? We will first review the different scales of impact at which Leader Coaches work – the individual, team, and organization wide levels. We will then examine the different depths of intervention; that is, the degree of personal learning and change desired by the person being coached – adaptation, renewal, and transformation.

Each setting presents a unique context within which to build a relationship. Their fundamental similarity is that they are all embedded in a larger context of change. For each setting, we believe it is important to be clear about the scale and depth of coaching so that we apply the appropriate competencies, tools and approaches to the issues being presented. Although they are all about change in some way, each one requires something different on the part of the Coach Leader and the person being coached.

To maintain our metaphor of alchemy, however, it is also wise to bear in mind that the process of mixing, of experimenting might in fact be catalytic...it might shift what had appeared to be a desire to adapt, into a desire to transform, on the part of the person being coached. There is a magic that emerges in the midst of the coaching process. The Leader Coach is aware of and alert to all possibilities, always ready to be in service to the desire of the individual…at whatever depth and scale.

Remember the four underlying goals:
- **Co-creating** futures that challenge and engage the whole person
- Making the vision **holographic** so that it can be co-acted by everyone
- Sharing leadership in **heterarchy** as a right and a responsibility
- Finding passion and **meaning through interdependent** contribution.

Scale of Leadership Coaching Contexts

Leader Coaches frequently operate simultaneously at the individual, team and organizational levels in their everyday roles. Most often, you will have a direct report team with whom you interact individually and collectively on an ongoing basis, or you will be head of a project team with a change or development goal. You will also be a member of at least one peer team as well as functional or project groups. You may also have responsibility for some aspects of organization-wide change or improvement involving strategy, structure or culture, for example. As a Leader Coach, you will be in a constant state of learning and applying your learnings, so what you experience at an individual level with one person may prompt you to apply something new and different at the group level, or in coaching yourself.

The scale is dependent not entirely on the number of people involved in the actual coaching but on the size of the system being affected. You may be part of a team of three or four whose mandate has an organization-wide impact. Or you may be working with an individual leader to develop her effectiveness with building her team. It is important to ask not only how many are being coached but what is the boundary around the issues being discussed – the context - and what will be the impact of the conclusions. Let us look at each of these scales.

At the **Individual** level, leader coaching is one-on-one, focused on the individual's[1] need for personal learning and development within her role. The Coach Leader must understand something of the talents and aspirations of the person and challenge them to express that in their work – to bring all of who they are to what they do – building over time a mutually open and supportive relationship.

At the **Team** level, leader coaching is done with intact groups working toward common goals. These can be ongoing workgroups, standing committees, peer groups or temporary project groups. The goal is to encourage the team to create a compelling shared vision that each member can uniquely contribute to. Working at the individual and team levels together reinforces the principles and powers positive results.

At the **Organization** level, leader coaching builds community across a broader population, up to the level of the whole organization. It may involve participating in a strategic review, leading a culture change process, or managing a merger or acquisition. The goal here is to involve all stakeholders in the co-creation of futures that can be encoded and enacted across a wide range of situations and interactions, providing leadership opportunities for many and generating excitement and drive to overcome obstacles and see the vision realized.

When these three scales are operating simultaneously, a leadership coaching culture is born. Each leader IS a coach, and each leader HAS a coach in her own leader. Teams are learning entities, moving as needed in the organization to address change and development goals. And the organization as a whole is a socio-ecological community, made up of interdependent relationships creating meaning for its members and results for its investors and customers.

Depth of Leadership Coaching Contexts

There are three depths of leadership coaching issues also to be considered, each dependent on the extent to which a change in fundamental purpose is desired. Does the person seek to re-examine her inner values and passions? This implies a fundamental reassessment of purpose and how that purpose is expressed in goals and roles. Or does she simply want to enhance her skills to stay current in her present role and perhaps to prepare for the future? This implies that her purpose is sound and that she is seeking to adapt to changes around her rather than to take on a personal transformation.

Similarly, when dealing with teams, is the goal to create a new team from scratch where the purpose and goals are not yet clear? Or is it to integrate a new member with her values and approaches, which will require the whole team not to start over again but to step back to bring her up to speed and incorporate her unique contributions? And at the organizational level, is the desire to create a leadership coaching culture to manage rapid growth, affecting all members of the system in rethinking their roles and contributions? Or is it to address a talent shortage in technical areas by team representatives from across the organization undertaking aggressive recruitment and development changes?

Each of these depths, as you can see, requires of the Coach Leader a different focus, different competencies, a different level of interior exploration with the person. The deeper the issues being discussed, the more the inner world of the person being coached is evoked and must be met with the full presence of the Leader Coach – listening and engaging with the information, in the moment, with full embodiment of heart, mind, body and spirit. This is the challenge of 21st century leadership – not just outmaneuvering the competition externally but engaging with the internal transformative potential in individuals. This is the playing field of the leadership coach and the domain from which external success will be generated.

You might be wondering where the alchemy is in all of this. The alchemic leader is aware that she is operating at all these levels at the same time. She is the same person holding the same values in all contexts and is profoundly aware of the holographic nature of her leadership – her interactions, her choices, her words and her actions. All are congruent and in alignment, one with the other and all with the higher goals to which she is aspiring. Her approach is always heterarchical… as much when she is a member of a team herself as when she is leading or sponsoring teams. She is always on the lookout for meaning and for contribution…and she is asking the questions of herself that will allow and encourage others to do the same. And through all this, she is continually co-creating futures. She is never defaulting to an oligarchic or narrow point of view but always seeking to learn and grow. She is fully present as a complete and complex person herself and she acknowledges that trait in others around her. The continually emerging interplay of these principles is **how** she is, in one-on-one coaching, in teams, in her organization. And it's **who** she is, how she shows up, whether it's a performance review with a direct report, or whole scale organizational and cultural change.

A Map of the Territory

Chart 14 uses the dimensions outlined to map a leadership coaching territory at various scales and depths of context. The examples given are indicative of the kinds of issues that may be presented. Let's examine each of the cells in the matrix to note some of the distinctions for the Leader Coach.

Individual Adaptation involves fine-tuning an individual's skills or behaviors in order to achieve desired results in the midst of changing circumstances. In regular one-on-one meetings, the Coach Leader reviews expectations and results, gets feedback and input on problems and opportunities, ensures that the individual is both supported and challenged, and addresses any issues that arise. The discussions may also involve creating a learning plan to acquire new or underdeveloped competencies to suit the individual's aspirations and the organization's future needs. A review of plans and priorities may be part of the leadership coaching where an individual's role is evolving and efforts need to be focused on the transition.

Depth of Intervention	Scale of Impact		
	Individual	Team	Organization
Adaptation	Fine-tuning: Skill/behavior Development need Plans & priorities	Enhancing: Goal/role clarity Accountability Work processes Inter/intra-team dynamics	Improving: Climate Customer focus Leadership Succession systems
Renewal	Orienting to: New role/level New company New career stage	Integrating: New team members New demands Multiple systems	Incorporating: New leadership New structure Stakeholder needs
Transformation	Redefining: Career/field Competency set Work passion and purpose	Creating: New team Clear vision and agenda Sponsorship Resources	Radical Change to: Strategy/Positioning Structure Culture Revitalization

Chart 14: A Framework of Leadership Coaching Issues in Different Contexts

Individual Renewal is concerned with adjusting to new circumstances where a greater level of change is required. An individual may be assuming a new job and need help to create a comprehensive transition plan including building new relationships, learning about the new business, and making plans to grow into the role. Or a move to a new level in the hierarchy may be involved, where the individual is seeking a better appreciation of the interpersonal dynamics in her peer team. The Coach Leader may also be helpful to an individual joining a new company and needing to orient to the new culture, or entering a late career stage and needing to adjust to a changing level of influence.

Individual Transformation involves a rethinking of the meaning of work and its role in the individual's life based on a fundamental misfit with the existing situation. Here, adjustments are insufficient and wholesale changes are required. An individual may decide, or be forced, to consider a new career path or a new field of endeavor. A move from internal management to external consulting, requiring the development of a new competency set, is an example. Or the decision to leave a senior technical or scientific stream to assume executive duties. It may also be that a new stage of life reduces the meaning derived from current work and a new life and work course must be charted.

In each of these settings, the Leader Coach brings her full presence to the conversation, without judgment, with empathy and understanding. It is not so much to solve the problem or find the answer as to 'lead from behind' by asking exploratory questions and allowing the individual to find their own path. Once that commitment to a future is made, then the leader can play more diverse roles in planning how to get there. The Coach Leader challenges, supports, guides the process and, when appropriate, broadens the perspective with ideas, options and experience.

Working with individuals over a period of time usually involves a deepening trust that engenders deeper conversations and raises more transformative issues. A direct report, for example, might be coached by her leader on skills and networking issues for the first year in the job, then move to more developmental coaching as she prepares for her future, and in the third year move to a new role where transition coaching is sought. In the fourth year, the individual may decide she wants a better work and family balance and may discuss working part-time as a senior professional rather than as a manager while her children are young.

Team Adaptation centers on enhancing an intact team's ability to achieve its mandate while circumstances around it may be changing. This may mean ensuring that the goals and roles are clear so energy is focused on the tasks at hand. It may include coaching on working together well as a team - generating a common vision, deciding on a plan for realizing it, and holding members accountable for their commitments to the results. Attending to regular team development may involve periodic assessments of team effectiveness, revisiting the team's purpose statement when differences arise and ensuring that each member has some leadership responsibility according to her talents and interests. Teams often need coaching on the underlying dynamics that inhibit performance or the relationships beyond the team itself that are barriers to accomplishment of objectives. Whatever the issues, the Leader Coach's goal is to build a strong community, a sense of shared leadership and responsibility for results, and to instill meaning through the common effort to realize the vision.

Team Renewal focuses on the inevitable adjustments required to accommodate changes in membership or mandate as the team moves forward. Teams need to step back temporarily, for example, to integrate new members or evolving demands. Using a mini co-creative process is critical. The views of a new member or the challenge of a new requirement are incorporated into the team's overall vision so that each member has the renewed code and is able to utilize it in their leadership within and beyond the team. Often, as teams implement new ideas, they are faced with resistance from the surrounding organizational systems and must work through these barriers to reconcile their actions with larger concerns. This is another opportunity for stepping back and incorporating the diversity of the larger system into the team's thinking and actions.

Team Transformation centers on the creation of common purpose and direction when the mandate is ambiguous and the stakes are high. Team members often have different interests, backgrounds and perspectives, and may not have worked together before. An executive taskforce charged with developing a merger strategy is an example. In such situations, it is critical that the team co-create futures that they can all participate in, or the strategy will fail. The abysmal record of mergers has less to do with the economics of particular cases and much more to do with the relationships between conflicting parties. Too little time and effort is spent at the outset to create a common vision that each member can carry back to their respective organizations and replicate through their own leadership. The team must form a clear purpose and agenda, working through individual differences and sponsorship issues in the larger system, and ensuring that resources inside and outside the team are maximized. Again, it is community building as a model for others to follow and must be authentic or it will not work.

Intact teams, that is, groups with a common mandate that meet regularly over an extended period of time, will work at all three levels of adaptation, renewal and transformation. There is a natural deepening of the relationships that occurs in high performing teams as they face challenges and overcome them. Often, peer members of the team will begin to coach each other, usually with good natured humor, as they **adapt** to the demands of their mandate. New members are coached as they integrate into the team, and the whole team is **renewed** in the process. As the team experience matures, it can take on changing and uncertain challenges with greater resilience, and **transform** more quickly and effectively as required. The team will recycle through the different **Depths of Intervention** and learn how to move among them according to the needs of the moment.

Organization Adaptation seeks to align some of the organization's components within its current strategy, structure and culture. For example, a COO may want to improve the working climate to better leverage current resources, or better focus the work of the organization on a current customer service plan. Looking ahead, an executive may see the need for leadership development and succession systems to be revamped as part of an emerging retention issue. At this scale, there are necessarily many more people involved, each with their perspectives and agendas, and often including outside experts. All these stakeholders will need to be part of the planning, design and implementation of the changes. Many Coach Leaders undertaking these kinds of projects use their own coaches, usually a trusted insider or an experienced external coach, to assist in the preliminary planning and ongoing implementation. The coach may also backstop the leader by rehearsing important events, giving ongoing feedback on her presence and impact on others, and generally providing a second pair of eyes on the process.

Organization Renewal is concerned with working through the issues involved in incorporating new components into the organization's overall direction. A Board encourages a CEO to develop an acquisition plan, forcing a rethinking of the company's current strategy. A recently acquired business or change in business unit structure requires an adjustment in organization design and reporting relationships. A newly promoted executive has significantly changed the leadership group and needs their commitment to a new vision and their help in its implementation. This is not wholesale change but it is sufficient to create perceived winners and losers, inevitably raising resistance to the changes and challenges to implementing them. Again, with many more stakeholders involved, the Coach Leader must have the competence, confidence and credibility to open the process to diverse views and engage those affected in determining the outcomes. This is not to say that everyone will have their way and be happy; it is to say that everyone will understand the issue and have a voice and a role in resolving it. In the end, this is often enough.

Organization Transformation involves the most complex, high-risk, long-term organizational learning and change process. The conditions are usually "sink or swim" for the company and may affect thousands of people. Managing this kind of turbulent change requires a fundamental rethinking of the organization's purpose, leading to changes in strategy, structure and culture, based on a new vision of desirable futures. The Leader Coach will necessarily be part of a team of people who are primarily responsible for making the changes and will be in the spotlight of customers, investors, suppliers, local communities as well as employees and management. The full range of alchemic leadership will be required here, from designing co-creative processes to determine the direction, to embedding the vision as code in the management and employees through all kinds of communication and participation. As stakeholders in pulling the organization into its waiting future, each individual and group will then take the lead in implementing their parts and managing the hurdles with outside groups such as suppliers, customers and community interests. Progress will be celebrated, setbacks will be examined and learned from, and a new culture will evolve. This is not to imply that it will be painless or easy. It will require each individual to make the choice to be part of the new vision, or to leave. It will require the company to make that choice clear and to support the decisions either way. The greater the scale and depth of the challenge, the greater the need for leadership – in our view, leadership alchemy, that blends together the inner and outer contexts of turbulent change.

Implications of the Leadership Coaching Map

There are a few important observations to be made from looking at leadership coaching in this way. First, it is easy to see how one Leader Coach role can evolve into another over a period of time. For example, coaching a number of direct reports individually and extending that into their team setting - an evolution of scale from Individual Adaptation to Team Adaptation. As an example of evolving depth, a Leader Coach may be working with a direct report team and extend that to integrating a couple of new team members, requiring a team renewal process – from Team Adaptation to Team Renewal. She might be sharing the Leader Coach role in a peer team in her division when it is decided that the divisional structure should be redesigned and she then takes on the leadership of the process - another example of moving from Team Adaptation to Team Renewal.

There are many examples of each of these cells in our business life. See if you can identify which ones you are currently involved in and which you have experienced recently. You may not see yourself as a leadership coach but you will have been in many settings where you have had the opportunity to be one. As you reflect on these examples, think about whether applying the principles of *both/and* leadership coaching would have made a difference in the outcomes from both a results and relationships point of view. How would you characterize your own leadership in these examples? Were you an alchemic leader?

High	Dissociated Leader	Alchemic Leader
RESULTS		
	Failed Leader	'Political' Leader
Low		

| **Low** | **RELATIONSHIPS** | **High** |

Figure 14: A Model Relating Results and Relationships

A second implication of the Leadership coaching Map is that the Leader Coach is in a unique position to see the larger systems when working with an individual or team reporting to her. An outsider, even within staff functions like Human Resources, will not have the business perspective of the leader herself. This is important because the depth of coaching may need to be matched to circumstances in the wider setting. Sometimes, of course, the presenting issues are just what they are – a need for performance improvement, a renewal or a more fundamental transformation arising from the individual's own learning requirements. However, it is often the case that changes in the larger organizational system have a significant impact on individual behavior that needs to be reflected in the coaching approach. When, for example, a team member is being coached on fine-tuning a skill while at the same time the team itself is about to undertake a major transition, then it is wise to consider a more comprehensive development plan for the team member as well. The Coach Leader can help the individual to anticipate emerging needs and take proactive steps in line with a deeper examination of purpose and goals.

Another important implication of this territory mapping is that the Leader Coach remain fully available to each individual or team when working with them, maintaining integrity and confidentiality, and aware of crossing contextual boundaries. Each time a Leader Coach moves from one cell to another, the context has shifted. An obvious example is that the Coach Leader does not betray confidences when working with different members of the team or with the team as a whole. As trust builds in these relationships, the Coach Leader will have more information, and more sensitive information, than before and it is critical that confidences not be shared. Also, it is important that the Leader Coach is aware and makes explicit when she is crossing a boundary between cells, because it will involve a change in focus, interaction and skills. Asking permission to coach is a powerful invocation that puts control in the hands of the individual and notes the boundary change. For example, the leader may simply say, in the midst of a budget review with a direct report, "Can I give you some feedback on the way you introduced those numbers in the presentation the other day?"

This brings us to a fourth implication. As well as shifting between these settings, the Leader Coach may also shift roles within the overall coaching relationship. For example, in coaching an individual transformation where the person is choosing between a technical and managerial career, roles may include simply listening and probing with questions as the person talks about their aspirations, providing lessons from the leader's own experience, giving background information on career tracks in the company, and suggesting books and other resources for understanding how the changes may impact the individual's training, work/life balance, promotions, and so on.

These roles are all undertaken within the context of the coaching relationship and are difficult to separate. The Coach Leader may be an expert, a manager, a teacher, or a consultant, but the important point is that these roles are all secondary to the primary coaching relationship. Once the relationship between coach and individual is cemented, role boundaries naturally become more permeable. However, it is up to the Leader Coach to ensure that they remain secondary to the coaching role. For example, if a leader has been coaching a direct report on improving her writing skills but always edits her drafts with masses of red ink and sends them back to her, the individual is getting mixed messages about whether she is being coached or not. The leader needs to review suggested changes with her, understanding that some may be grammatical rules she must adopt (expert role) and some may be style points she can choose to express herself (coach role).

A final implication of the map is that it assists the Leader Coach in assessing where her skills lie and in determining the areas in which she will be competent and confident to coach. Very few Leader Coaches will be skilled in all these cells; many will not be in a position to undertake organizational changes and some may not even be comfortable with team coaching. What is important is that Coach Leaders are aware of their skill sets and apply them appropriately. With practice and further development, competency will grow and a natural evolution to cover more of the map will take place. It's grow as you go! We believe that the principles discussed in Part One and the process discussed in the next chapter are the same no matter where the leadership coach practices. It is the contexts that are different – both outer and inner – and must be matched to the Leader Coach.

It will be clear by now that at each of the scales, the Leader Coach will need an understanding of a larger outer context – organization systems, team dynamics, politics, large scale changes, etc. And at each of the depths, the leader coach will need an understanding of a deeper inner context – life purpose, personal change, adult development, resistance, etc. And so, we return to the blend of inner and outer contexts that are the practice domains of the alchemic leader.

In the next section we tell some stories that further elucidate the map of the territory we have proposed. Three stories, one at each scale and depth, provide a composite of our experience with clients and their organizations. A reminder – we are using 'loaded' language here that you may associate with more traditional ways of doing things. Using the term 'manager' for instance may raise assumptions about control and supervision. We encourage you to hold your judgments – when you hear your little voice saying, "That's not going to work!" try to imagine how it could, in the context we are discussing. Try reframing your own assumptions about what some of these words mean.

An Individual Adaptation Story – Identifying Potential

Here's the situation. In a fast-paced, dramatically growing and incredibly successful organization, the Human Resource team had historically been relegated to the role of personnel administration. Indeed, the founder's mother was the HR head and had only the "school of hard knocks" as her education in what would work in this organization.

She retired, and a new HR Head was hired - Grant, whose prior experience and philosophy conceived Human Resources as a professional discipline and a strategic contributor to the business. He also had a belief that the people within the HR team might well thrive under a different approach to management, one that encouraged and challenged rather than punished and limited them. He was eager and enthusiastic to try this with the team and also to model it himself. He was also a little nervous about whether the larger organizational culture would allow him the room to experiment with this approach.

One of the people reporting to him, Mae, had been hired to do a very straightforward administrative and primarily data entry job, which she did brilliantly. The performance review interview was a bit one-sided, given her excellence. She was very accurate and quick in her work. However, Grant knew that in improving HR processes, many aspects of her job would likely disappear, as it was comprised largely of repetitive steps to ensure that managers hadn't erred (or cheated!) in relation to strict company guidelines. Mae was also of South Asian extraction and had been raised in a culture where "the boss" was invariably right, and the subordinate's primary role was to obey. She had not previously been encouraged to grow or think about what more she could take on. She'd been in the role for more than four years when Grant arrived and he soon began to think about some changes in roles, structures and systems, based on client needs.

Grant chose to involve Mae very early on in the discussions about what changes the clients in the organization wanted to see in the HR function as well as what process improvements the new HR Information System might offer. Grant was also aware of the need to not appear too directive with Mae, as she might simply 'obey' him. He tried to be patient as he initiated conversations with her, though he was aware that he sometimes had "the solution" leaping quickly to his mind. When Mae first heard of the proposed changes for the HR system and began to think about her own role, she confided, after some encouragement, that she felt threatened and frightened that she wouldn't have a job or that the job she would have she wouldn't be able to fulfill successfully. She seemed to cry a lot and to express reasons why various suggestions and improvements wouldn't work. She didn't seem able to imagine any changes that would be positive. She seemed overwhelmed by the notion of change. She knew the systems and processes so well, she could immediately anticipate the problems with any proposals to change things. She seemed negative, skeptical, and some began to wonder if she could adjust to the changes in the company. Grant asked Mae if she'd be interested and willing to talk about this more with him, in a one-on-one coaching relationship.

Grant's first task was to build trust with Mae, to ensure that they had a relationship within which some coaching could occur. He believed that there was in Mae great potential. So he began his conversations with Mae, with lots of encouragement and enthusiasm, describing to her his own career and the confidence that an earlier boss had shown in him. He described in more detail the vision he had of how the HR department could become a real partner to line managers and employees, rather than a police department. He suggested that Mae look at her immediate tasks and see if there were changes and improvements she could make, while the job was in transition. And finally, over a period of several weeks, he began to encourage Mae to think about where she wanted to take her career and how she could imagine her skills contributing to the team in a new way. Grant was aware that he was at an important stage of his relationship with Mae, and deliberately practiced "unconditional positive regard" with her as he worked to control his impatience.

Mae began to realize that her strengths, which included an extraordinary accuracy and attention to detail, a wonderful sense of commitment – if she said something would be done, and by when, it would! – and lots of energy to try new things, could serve her in good stead with her new boss, and perhaps in a new role. She began to suggest how her work could be streamlined, some steps that should be removed completely, and she offered to be the member of the team who learned EVERYTHING about the new HR automated system that was about to be introduced. She learned about new features that could further streamline her own job as well as those of other HR specialists, line managers and employees. Grant knew that he could now step back and allow Mae to take more of a leadership role herself - he could let go and celebrate.

While Mae was adjusting, she sometimes worked some very long hours, and in fact, so did many of the team. There were certainly some days 'out of balance' but on the whole the team was performing to a high standard. There was a sense of fun and adventure as people began to realize that the goal of the team Grant was leading was not to enforce rules but to find ways to do work more simply, to do work that moved the business forward, and to put more and more discretion into the managers' and employees' hands.

As a result of a team meeting to prepare for the new year's goals, two team members proposed a new position in the team: HR Business Partner. This would require a fairly seasoned HR professional, working inside the various operating teams, to understand the business issues and provide a 'people perspective' at an early stage of strategic planning. There were several members who could easily become Business Partners on the team, but Mae was not one of them. As a result of observing both how line managers valued the role and the kinds of skills and talents that the "BP's" displayed and needed, Mae took the bold step of proposing to Grant that that she, too, become an HR Business Partner one day. She described how she wanted to shadow one of the more seasoned HR business partners, when that was appropriate. She described the programs at community colleges and universities that she had researched and asked her team for suggestions on which program they thought might be most beneficial for her to take. She also described a small administrative unit, which had not had a Business Partner assigned, where she thought she might be able to add value.

The relationship between Grant and Mae was now such that he could challenge her about her motives for wanting the BP role. Was she clear about what the new role would entail? Was she prepared for the level of development she would need? Did she have the strategic thinking ability to succeed? Grant and Mae worked through these questions until they were both confident of Mae's success and how Grant could support her. She then presented her proposal to the entire team. She committed to the team that she would also continue to do her "day job" with the HR system. The team applauded and encouraged her, and required only one concession from her…that she make a commitment to her own health and well-being, by managing her work/life balance and not fulfilling her new responsibilities by working longer hours.

Grant realized that he needed only stay in touch with Mae as she continued to grow. She had understood where the line managers and employees needed HR to serve, she had worked to understand both her own strengths and a value-added role she could play. As a result, the whole team again examined processes for further improvements and time-saving steps, and took more and more advantage of the capacity and capabilities of their new HR system. And when Mae was ready to negotiate the role of a quasi-business partner to support the administrative unit. Grant made the first call to ensure that there was some receptivity to the notion, and worked with Mae to coach her on how to make the offer. The offer was, of course, accepted and Mae began her path into a more professional HR role.

Mae has thrived in this role, which accesses her deep desire to be of real value and service to her clients, to make their work lives better, to feel as if she's helping to make a difference. She has surprised herself with her new-found confidence most days. When she slips back into feeling fearful, she talks about it with Grant and other members of the HR team, often practicing or role-playing what she might say. The HR team has recently been challenged with a complex merger of two entities with very different cultures, and Mae has been asked to be one of the HR reps on the Merger team. Her concern, given the time demands of the merger, is whether she'll still be able to go bicycling in Vietnam this spring as she'd planned. Her colleagues, both in HR and in the line, are frequently commenting to Grant that they can't believe the difference in Mae.

Questions to Think About:

Grant was coaching Mae on her performance, in addition to working with her on her new role.
-   What might Grant have done differently here, to ensure that he had an authentic and open relationship with Mae?
-   How different might this story have been, if had Mae not been a strong performer?
-   Do you think Grant was pushing Mae too hard? Had he forgotten that in the end it is Mae who is 'driving the change' in her life and career?

A Team Renewal Story – Changing Team Norms

The Property Management, Investment and Consulting team of ten included several senior consultants who had specific areas of expertise that were highly sought after in the business community. Working with them on projects were more junior consultants who were deepening their technical skills. In addition, the team included two support people whose roles were primarily document preparation and the maintenance of the office. The team was very strong, dominating the market due to its commitment to client service and quality.

Leading the consulting team had been Marcia, who had belonged to the firm for many years. She had suffered a severe health crisis, which appeared to be at least exacerbated if not caused by overwork. Bob, recruited from across the country, filled her role, at first on a temporary basis. He had extensive consulting and work experience that allowed him to consult in most disciplines that the team practiced in. There was a significant skill gap in one discipline, Property Development, however, that neither he nor the other senior consultants could fill. There was a new graduate in the team, Chris, who had the brainpower and determination to be a Property Development consultant some day but her development plan was ambitious and her learning curve steep. The other more senior consultants - Hans, Dean, Georgina and Rosie - were involved in Chris' training plan as it related to their disciplines.

The firm had a strong reputation, and was famous for its demanding, grueling and internally competitive culture. Bob had already experienced in another consulting firm that it was possible for consulting teams to operate differently, despite the high demands for client service and the traditional compensation structures which encouraged individual rather than group effort. Soon after he arrived, he held the first team gathering, which was a shock to some consultants trained to value nothing that was not billable. And indeed, it was a challenge at first to convince these hard-driving, high performing consultants that a day spent in learning more about each other's communications and working preferences, would build a stronger team and would in the end serve both the clients and the individual consultants better. Bob was feeling a bit worried but decided to try the experiment of being very open and honest in his communications, within his own team and in other firm meetings.

In the first team "offsite" the agenda included several things:
- The team spent time using a simple tool called "True Colors", a scaled down version of Myers-Briggs[2], to help the team members learn more about their own working styles and the preferences and strengths of those around them. The approach encouraged with True Colors is a very appreciative one, seeking to celebrate the strengths and diversity of the team.

- Simply eating together, chatting about personal stories, memories, funny incidents on projects, began to create a bond of trust that was different and deeper than that created by simply working together on client assignments. Bob set the tone by telling a story about an earlier client assignment in which he was able to laugh at himself and encouraged the others to do so too.
- They examined a recent client project, looking for what went well and what could have gone better, not just from a technical and data point of view but from the perspective of team dynamics and processes. This was such a rich discussion that the team agreed to look at this topic each time they gathered.
- They also looked out beyond the team to both the national and international firm and the market locally and nationally. The gap of expertise in Property Development became clearer and more pressing.
- The team learned more about the possibilities of working more cooperatively and collaboratively but was still quite skeptical. However, they decided to try to articulate the team norms and values that they held to be important and to which they aspired. These values would become the barometer for team morale and would counter or complement the firm's measuring stick of productivity based on billable hours.

Bob knew that the next few days would be really important – had this day been a waste of time, or just some R&R, or had these commitments really signaled a desire to change? Bob noticed that a number of the team members had posted both the List of Team Values, "How we want to treat each other and be treated", and the "Who we want to be" lists from the retreat on their own bulletin boards, along with pictures of the day...

Completely by surprise, a Property Development consultant who was based in New York walked into the Toronto office of the team and asked if there were any openings. He was originally a Canadian and wanted to move home to be nearer his aging parents. His skill set was a complete fit with the already identified gap in terms of technical expertise. In fact, the team had been scanning the Canadian labor market without success for exactly the combination that Duncan brought with him. He was energetic, creative, articulate, dynamic and clearly the master of his body of knowledge. After a series of interviews with many senior firm members, Duncan was offered the role in the Toronto team. His very strengths, however, were a caution to some - he was so driven to succeed that there was concern that the fledgling team norms and morale might be jeopardized. Bob knew there were some risks with introducing someone of Duncan's dynamism into the team, and also knew that it was a risk worth taking.

A second team retreat day was scheduled soon after Duncan arrived, to ensure that his start with the team was a successful and positive experience both for him and for the team. The team again referred to True Colors, as it had proven to be a helpful tool, providing a language that permitted the team to address potentially 'sticky' issues of interpersonal conflict. From this process, it was clear that Duncan had a very different style than most of the rest of the team; and while this style was no doubt part of why he was so successful in his field, it was also a challenge to some team norms. And the person he was going to work most closely with, Chris, was a very different type. Chris liked work that was orderly, scheduled, predictable, and checked several times for errors. Duncan liked letting his creativity wrestle with the client's issues, often till moments before the presentation to the Board. He'd sometimes work through the night in a burst of creative fervor. He seemed to like working right to the edge of boundaries and deadlines.

The team was immediately aware of the potential disruptions and challenges that the inclusion of this new and powerful member of the team might bring. Bob met individually with some team members who were particularly anxious, encouraging them to raise the issues in team gatherings, addressing the specific people with whom they were challenged, rather than turning to the 'boss' to fix things. In some cases, the conversations become a three-way one, with Bob acting as a kind of mediator and facilitator as the team members struggled both to express themselves clearly and to find solutions that worked.

In the second team gathering, there were moments of clear tension as the team struggled to both celebrate and include what Duncan brought, and to preserve what was working of the team values and the new operating processes of cooperation and mutual support. Hans, one of the other consultants, found himself playing a bit of a clown in this meeting, perhaps due to his own discomfort with the tension. The humor, however, helped everyone to remember what was important and to recommit to the team as a whole, to its values and how the team was choosing to work together. The team members spoke passionately about the kind of team they were creating and how important it was to them that Duncan find a way to both be himself and be in line with these values. Duncan agreed to support the values, though he also acknowledged that this was going to be particularly challenging for him, as he had been "raised" in and had been so successful in, such a different corporate culture. The team established several mechanisms to encourage the maintenance of these new team norms, and Duncan was excited to be a part of a team stretching to practice open, direct and honest communications with each other.

Bob too was nervous and excited. He met with each team member as part of their development planning process and worked with each one to ensure that whatever 'learning edges' had been identified in the team processes were captured in the learning plans for the next year. This varied from team member to team member, and included getting specific coaching on how to express opinions in team meetings, how to hold to a point of view when others were in disagreement, how to resist the corporate emphasis on billable time at the expense of family time, and other individual challenges. Clearly, the team members also had billable time targets that integrated with the larger practice and the firm's goals, and they had to find a harmony between these "soft" goals that the team valued and the "hard" goals that the firm required. At first, the team tended to 'keep below the radar', talking openly only about the 'hard goals' of billable time, client satisfaction and market share. However, their success emboldened them.

The time taken for these offsite meetings was at first greeted with puzzlement within the firm. How could not working on billable work possibly improve team results? However, the skeptics were soon to acknowledge that something was working! The team went on to become the highest performing team in the global firm, achieving new levels of client satisfaction, overall productivity, and team member morale. Team members were cited for their creativity, their generous support and contribution to others' ideas and projects... and were the team of choice to work with. While there were still some upsets, particularly between Duncan and Chris, who worked most closely together, they were both committed to trying to work out as quickly as possible what had gone off the rails, and to trying to learn from those experiences to improve their relationship. Bob realized he need no longer be the initiator of ideas and suggestions...in fact, he could hardly keep up with the suggestions the team was now making!

Questions to Think About:

- Once the team had incorporated Duncan into their dynamics, what role should Bob have played to ensure that these values continue to be monitored and maintained?
- What else could he have done?

- What else might the team and particularly the Leader Coach have done both to sustain their core values and to welcome the newcomer and all that he would bring into the team?

An Organization Transformation Story – Building a Coaching Culture

Background on Alchem:

This is the case of a large national company – we'll call it Alchem - an independent subsidiary of a global enterprise in a technical business requiring specialized skills. The company is a known and successful brand in its markets. It has a tradition of strong leadership, clear values and a focus on talent development. The company has drawn its leadership primarily from the ranks of the senior technical professionals who have broader strategic interests and has given them opportunities to learn through experience on the job and from mentors. There has been a dual career ladder for many years. The culture is collaborative, results-oriented and there is pride in the innovative spirit.

About three years ago, Alchem began to focus on its leadership succession and development system that was installed across the company. Despite a good deal of effort, retention remained a critical issue. The company was growing rapidly in some business units and there was insufficient leadership talent to sustain the success. Good people were being lost to the competition and new recruits were often isolated and not integrating quickly enough into the culture. After 18 months, a climate survey reported that employees felt driven to produce results and their managers didn't spend enough time on communications and development. The senior team members shook their heads, not sure why they had failed.

Alchem had some coaching at senior levels, mostly from outsiders who had been hired to coach high potentials for accelerated promotion to fill more senior slots, and a few successful sales executives who had poor interpersonal skills that needed to be addressed. In most of the business units, there had been 360° feedback processes with short-term follow-up coaching as part of the succession and development efforts. In two of the more innovative business units, executive coaches had been hired to work with each member of the senior team, including its leader. It was difficult to judge the effectiveness of these initiatives but because of the retention issue, and with some skepticism, expenditures were approved.

A year ago, a new President, Jim Smith, was announced, rotated from one of the other companies in the parent's portfolio. Jim is not flashy or fancy. He comes across as caring as much about people as about results. He's curious, likes to know something about people, what makes them tick. He's also known as tough and decisive in business. He had been coached for more than two years before his appointment and had adopted a coaching style in his leadership. He felt confident that this was the key to his leadership success and had found a great deal of satisfaction in the meaningful relationships he had built with colleagues and customers. He came to Alchem with a mandate to solve the talent management issue and decided that the way to do it was to build a coaching culture.

The First Ninety Days:

Jim continued to work with his coach on his own integration into the new company as well as on the coaching culture process. He introduced the coach to his senior team and said she would be helping them in the effective transition of leadership and culture change. He suggested that each senior team member have an external coach for at least six months, to give them the experience of being coached and to support them in becoming coaches with their own teams. He added that he would also be coaching them in his ongoing coach leadership role.

Several members of the senior team received this news with great skepticism, perhaps even disbelief. Who was this guy? There were pressing business issues to be dealt with and he was spending time and money on a coaching culture! However, they had learned over the years to go along and so, in the first 90 days, the VPs spent six half-days learning about Jim's vision and why he thought it was critical to growing the business. A number of high potential directors were also included in these meetings. They had many opportunities to shape the thinking and planning to fit the current circumstances. They learned how other companies had approached culture change and they learned about leadership coaching from outside experts. Jim was open about the fact that he didn't know how this was going to work but he believed in the concept and needed their help to bring it about. Some rose to the occasion and took leadership responsibility for different aspects of the transition; others felt this reinforced his unwillingness to give strong direction and withdrew from active participation.

Jim used this period to do a number of things. First, he wanted to model his own coach leadership style with each of his team members and to coach them as a team. He wanted to know them as individual leaders and see them in action in a variety of settings. He also wanted not only to get a solid appreciation of the business but to assess his senior leadership group and their ability to move into the kind of future he envisioned. At the end of three months, Jim had a career review with each member of the senior team to talk about his or her competence, commitment and ongoing roles in the organization. As a result, two of the five business unit heads stepped down, two functional leaders were replaced and a new head of Talent Management and Development was named for a two-year term. To fill the vacancies, Jim promoted three directors to vice president and recruited a financial VP externally, someone he had worked with previously. He now felt he had a competent, committed team, one that could move forward with a single voice. They would continue to work on improving, of course, but they were beginning to take the shape of the future.

The Second Ninety Days:

During this period, each of the VPs replicated the President's model with their own teams – they coached each individual and worked with their direct report teams as well, they used their external coaches to support their teams' development, they held several sessions with their leadership groups to co-create the way they would implement the coaching culture. Jim supported these efforts through his ongoing coaching and also began to communicate broadly about the initiative and its importance to the business. He made speeches, sent emails, was interviewed in the company newsletter, and had open sessions for any of his leaders to attend. His theme was "Leadership and Partnership".

Toward the end of the first six months, Jim invited the VPs and Directors as well as a number of high performing and high potential managers and senior professionals to meet for three days on the "Leadership and Partnership" theme. The first day was a coaching culture workshop. The next two days were spent in "open space" where anyone could put forward a topic of interest or challenge to discuss with others. Leadership roles were assigned according to interest, need and ability. The energy was high as people moved to and fro, joining groups to express an opinion and hear from others, then taking their insights into the next group, and so on. For many, the ideas gained breadth and depth, the challenges became clearer, the vision gelled. For others, it was a chaotic, unproductive waste of time. The action plans at the end of the day were still quite vague – very counter culture for Alchem! The outcome was a deeper understanding and experience of the coaching culture, of creating the future, taking responsibility for leading in it, and seeing it happen at the organizational level, to add to their experience in individual and team settings. It was either highly motivating or a strong message about moving on. After the event, several of the directors stepped forward and asked to lead project groups to plan cross-company initiatives. A few gave notice.

The Second Six Months:

During the second half of his first year, Jim felt like an orchestra conductor – waving his arms, sending messages, coaching and coaxing, practicing and sometimes succeeding and often failing but starting again - slowly seeing his musicians come together and begin to play their own unique instruments in harmony. There were several business crises that had to be managed. There was a 30 percent turnover in the top four layers of management as the implementation moved forward. He never doubted his path but often wondered if he could do more to support others.

Several cultural principles emerged in this time, not because he dictated them but because they arose from the discussions and experiences and became the foundation points for the "early adopter" business units. A few of them were:
-    Coaching is the leadership style for success at Alchem.
-    Every leader IS a coach and HAS a coach in her own leader.
-    Leadership is a right and a responsibility at every level.
-    Development is a part of every leader's role in every situation, not just with her own team.
-    Every Alchem employee has a development plan and a career goal.

Jim was very proud of his senior leadership team. He made one more staff change during this time but could see his direct reports modeling the principles, each in their own way to suit their particular piece of the business, taking on the concepts and applying them in their areas of responsibility. Succession and development discussions were now much more than lip service. They brought the business leaders together to share in the development of the leadership group as a whole, to plan the best experiences based on the individuals' expressed interests and the opportunities in the business. Some senior professionals moved into leadership roles and vice versa. New recruits were given mentors, usually high performing mid-career leaders, to speed their orientation into the company.

To reinforce these roles, Jim adopted a new performance assessment model. He gave equal weight to both results and leadership, and the compensation system was adjusted accordingly. He wanted to ensure that simply making the numbers was not enough; leaders had to be developing their teams and themselves as well. Jim also gave his direct reports straight feedback on their performance, as much in the moment as he could, and using behavioral examples. He challenged them to set stretch goals and supported and rewarded them for their efforts.

A second "open space" event was held during this period. It included all of the management and senior technical staff of the company and it focused on the future of the business – How are we doing? Where do we go from here? What do you need to be successful? Again, it was a high energy event, still with some skepticism particularly on the part of the technical professionals. For most, though, it was a golden opportunity for networking, sharing views and plans, raising issues and ideas, getting to know people in new ways, and learning about their areas of interest. One of the most common themes was how the new style of leadership was opening up the culture and making people feel part of something exciting, in their own work and careers and in the business as a whole. They felt they were growing with the business and were proud to be part of it. It was out of this second open space that a number of peer teams emerged, not with a mandated task from above, but to continue the dialogue, to build community, to share challenges and solutions.

If this all sounds too good to be true, it is important to say there were also some hurdles. The businesses implemented the changes in their own ways and in their own time. The President gave them the freedom to fit the culture to their own style and issues within broad guidelines. So some jumped in and others struggled along. Jim's view was that 'pulling' toward a vision was more effective than 'pushing' from behind, so he continued to reinforce the direction through his own leadership modeling and support but the magnetic pull was met with more resistance and inertia in some cases than in others. In the second and third quarters, the business results worsened and the naysayers assumed the whole 'culture change thing' was over. Then, in the fourth quarter, results rallied and they continue to grow beyond previous levels.

There were also many innovations. One of the businesses undertook a "whole-scale redesign" involving most of the employees, in a quality improvement initiative that refocused the business on customers and produced a number of dramatic positive results. Turnover is down; satisfaction is up. It remains to be seen whether the new leadership style becomes a sustainable coaching culture. Jim is counting on a couple more years to embed the new way of doing things. Outsiders have remarked on his 'transformation' of the company and his corporate bosses are confident in its future. Jim, himself, sees that he has lifted the lid and let the natural leadership emerge by building a sense of community with common purpose.

Questions to Think About:

Jim is now planning his strategy for his second year in his position.
- What do you think he should be doing to grow the coaching culture in Alchem?
- What would your priorities be if you were in his role?
- How can he continue the transformation by extending the principles and embedding them in the culture?
- What would you recommend for Jim's own development if you were his coach?

Creating Your Own Map

We encourage your to create your own map of your leadership coaching territory. At what scales and depths do you work? Where are you most effective? Here's an example.

Depth of Intervention	Individual	Scale of Impact Team	Organization
Adaptation	Fine-tuning: Financial skills to better assess impacts of new projects	Enhancing: Effectiveness in providing team direction/vision	Improving: Employee satisfaction ratings to "Excellent"
Renewal	Orienting to: Next move - get a coach to help with preparation	Integrating: New customer relationship rep into team meetings	Incorporating: Nothing here right now
Transformation	Re-establishing: Longer term career goal – where to from here?	Creating: New business model with field teams – co-creative!	Radical Change to: Culture - much more leadership coaching oriented – start with an open space???

Chart 15: An Assessment of Leadership Coaching Experience in Different Contexts

It is equally powerful to apply the map to other areas of your life. You might want to map your family system, starting with scales of Self, Couple, Immediate Family, Relatives, and so on. You might call the depths something like Maintaining Relationships, Building Stronger Bonds, and Making Major Changes. When you think about your family life, how much time do you take to maintain a healthy self? Do you maintain relationships with relatives or have you let those connections slip? Do you build stronger bonds with your children by spending regular time with them and taking regular vacations? What is your leadership role in each of these family settings? Are you doing and being the kind of person you want to be? Are you really investing your energy and presence in these relationships or are you just going through the motions?

Another possibility for a map is your community - your family, neighborhood and local community, for example, and how you lead at these scales and at different depths of energy and commitment. Take some time to think about this system as well, and your leadership in it. As we've said before, the Leader Coach is not a job, not a role you adopt, just at work. It is who you are, in your life, in your skin. To that end, these contexts all touch, all influence each other. This mixing, this blending, is a critical expression of the alchemy, the magic of leadership coaching.

So we come to the end of Part Two and our look at inner and outer contexts. We hope you have gained a better sense of yourself in relation to these two domains - your preferences, your blind spots and your areas for improvement in your coach leadership competency.

A Personal Reflection:

Now that you have read three of our cases, try writing a case from your own experience.
- What situations that you have been in were triggered as you read through the examples in the chapter?
- How would you tell the story of your role as a Leader Coach in one of the cells of the matrix?
- What leadership principles did you use to make changes?
- How did you coach others to enroll in your vision?
- What did you learn from the experience?
- Would you do things differently now?
- How would you coach yourself in applying the principles of inner and outer context we have been describing here?

A Reflection to Share:

You may want to share your case history with a trusted colleague who is familiar with the situation you have described. Ask for reaction, perspective, other perceptions, and have a discussion of strategic leadership. If you are working with someone who is also interested in alchemic leadership, perhaps you will each write a case and compare them to see what you can learn.

You might also use a current project or change issue you are working on. Map out the kind of context in which your project is set, using scale and depth, the key elements of your leadership and coaching role. Then apply the alchemic principles at the beginning of the chapter to your plans and see what different results you might achieve. Select someone you trust and whose input you will value. Discuss the issue and your strategies with them. If you want to try out your suggestions, try actually role playing a key interaction – have your colleague play one of the critical roles you want to influence and try out your leadership coaching skills. The feedback you get will contribute to your effectiveness.

A Team Exercise:

Assign one of the cases in the chapter and have each member of the team prepare ahead using these questions:
- What are the pivot points in the case, the decisions that made the biggest difference?

- What competencies did the leader coach exhibit that were particularly effective in this case?
- What elements of the inner and outer contexts helped or hindered the achievement of goals?
- What leadership lessons do you draw from the case?

Discuss each question, adding diversity to the views and richness to the story. There is no right answer, but there may be a number of useful discoveries. When you end the case discussion, compare some of the points raised to your own team and organization culture.

- Is there a likeness? What are the differences you see?
- How do these similarities and differences affect your team's performance?
- What are one or two steps your team could take based on this discussion?

A Self-Assessment:

Here is the outer contextual map introduced earlier in the chapter. Plot yourself into each of the cells of the map using the rating scale below. Think about the extent to which you feel comfortable at each scale or depth, how often you have found yourself in these kinds of situations, and your level of confidence and competence. Include any feedback you have received that might contribute to an understanding of your effectiveness. It is not necessary to be a trained Leader Coach or to have been in the same situations we describe. Just think about your experience, your sense of yourself as you rate each of the nine cells.

Outstanding, one of the best	5
Talented, better than most	4
Skilled, about average	3
Developing, need improvement	2
Undeveloped, untried, novice	1

Once you have finished your ratings, look for patterns or themes in the chart. You can add down the columns to see your scores on the Individual, Team and Organization scales of impact. You can add across the rows to see your scores on the Adaptation, Renewal and Transformation depths of intervention.

Depth of Intervention	Scale of Impact			Total
	Individual	Team	Organization	
Adaptation	Fine-tuning:	Enhancing:	Improving:	
Renewal	Orienting to:	Integrating:	Incorporating:	
Transformation	Redefining:	Creating:	Radical Change to:	
Total				

Chart 16: An Assessment of Development Opportunities in Different Contexts

Here are some questions to reflect on:
- Are there one or two scales and/or depths at which you prefer to work, or at which you have most of your experience?
- Where are your highest and lowest scores?
- Do you work at transformative levels with individuals or teams?
- Have you played a leadership role in making radical changes?
- Are there projects or processes that you could initiate or participate in that would broaden your experience of these contexts?
- How do you feel about your leadership from what you see?
- Are there areas where you would like to see higher numbers?
- What can you do in the next six months to a year that would raise your ratings?
- Are there major changes needed in your family system, a career change to reduce your stress and its effect on your family, a dedication to an aging parent?
- What are your learning edges? What development steps would you take to become a more alchemic leader?

EndNotes:

[1] We are using the term 'individual' here, or person, rather than client or coachee to reinforce the organization structure reality – that you are likely working in a coaching relationship with someone who reports to you…and that some of the attributes of a pure coach/client relationship may get tested or even strained by the reality of hierarchy and the power relationships in it.

[2] See, for example, Katherine C. Briggs and Isabel Briggs-Myers. *An Introduction to Type.* Consulting Psychologists Press, 1987, and Mary Miscisin. *Showing Your True Color.* True Colors Inc., 2001.

Part Three – Processes

The Invitation

The next part of the book will look at leadership coaching processes. We have talked about the concepts, then applied them to different contexts, and now we want to discuss how all this plays out in stages and cycles, in conversations, in interactions between the leader and the person(s) being coached. Because it is the subject of many other coaching books, we will devote only one chapter to the actual leadership coaching process. Our three-stage process is similar to other models[1]. However, there are two points worth drawing attention to at the outset.

The first is to frame the coaching process as a method of building self-awareness in the person being coached such that she is inspired to take action to change the issue or problem being discussed. Figure 14 below looks at the role of feedback in coaching - what we know and don't know about ourselves that others may or may not know as well. It is patterned after the Johari Window[2]. The coaching goals are also highlighted.

What the Leader Coach seeks through the coaching relationship is to guide those being coached to become authentic leaders who see themselves essentially as others see them, so they are congruent in all roles, and can leverage that authenticity to model the way for others. Often, though, we mask our true selves, assuming that we must fit a certain mold - Leader Coaches work to understand and reveal the whole person so we bring all of who we are to what we do. Many times, others see strengths and weaknesses in us that we ourselves don't see – the Leader Coach helps to integrate these disconnected parts of our behavior so that we can take full advantage of our strengths and develop blind spots that may inhibit our effectiveness. And finally, there is all the potential that neither we nor others have discovered in us that the Leader Coach can help the person being coached to unearth and apply.

	Know	OTHERS	Don't Know
Don't Know	Hidden Strengths, Blind Spots *Develop*		Potential Self *Discover*
SELF			
Know	Authentic Self *Leverage*		Masked Self *Reveal*

Figure 15: A Model Relating Self Awareness and Coaching Goals

The second point to mention as we begin is that we want to highlight, as we describe each of the stages in the Leader Coaching process, the particular distinctions we see as a result of applying our concepts and contexts to the process. How are the alchemic leadership competencies demonstrated in each of the stages? What does the co-creative process look like with a team? How is the process like a hologram? How does 'leading from behind' promote heterarchy?

In Chapter 8, we present a case study of a company dealing with change, both predictable and unpredictable. We use the case as a learning tool for thinking about large-scale transformation and the ways in which our concepts, contexts and processes have been applied to make effective change. How did leadership see its role in the process? What did Leadership Coaching contribute to positive outcomes? This is not an ideal case; it is a real one. It is neither a success nor a failure; it is both. It is full of random events, surprises, and choices in the moment that are the complex arena in which the preparation and practice of the Leadership Coach are tested.

Our goal in this part of the book is to give sufficient structure and guidance to your coach leading that you can begin to practice the process everywhere. It can be applied to any relationships in your work and life - your colleagues, team members, boss, teenagers, parents, and so on. It is best not to get into a formal coaching relationship with someone personally close to you because you will not be able to maintain the objective distance necessary, but as a way of attending to others, of bringing yourself to the encounter, the process can be used anywhere. At its simplest, it is dialogue. As it deepens, it is connection, community, meaning. At its best, it is transformation, it is magic.

Leadership Coaching Themes/Principles

Before beginning, let's review the eight key principles of leadership coaching from Chapter 2 and keep them in mind through these next two chapters:

Deepening Context. Coaching deals with both our personal context - our frames of reference, our perceptions - and with our leadership context - our work cultures, our interpersonal relationships. Coaches link these two to help align our personal development and leadership development with our goals.

Working through Stuckness. Coaching is centrally about being stuck in a rut, usually beyond our awareness, that inhibits us from living and working fully. It is a natural state. Coaches bring resistance to the surface, confront it, and allow us to reframe our perceptions so that we can act effectively.

Living on Purpose. In a world of change, purpose is the central reference point, the inner compass that directs our intentions, our expression, in our life and work. Coaches focus on purpose as a way to integrate the whole person – mind, body, heart, spirit - providing the fuel for driving change.

Being in Service. Coaching is in service to the person being coached, who is in control, who shapes the agenda, who commits to action. Coaches serve in partnership, in shared leadership or heterarchy, to develop individuals, teams and organizations.

Using Conversations. Dialogue is the medium of leadership coaching. Language is our means of expressing who we are and enacting who we want to become. Coaches help us see the mismatches in our feelings and actions so we can address them.

Sustaining Diversity. The broadest possible perspectives are required to match the variety and complexity we find in everyday problems. A narrow view is simply not going to afford the range of alternatives necessary; when creativity and innovation are the order of the day, diversity of every kind is the best strategy.

Modeling Change. Coaching emerges as the leadership style in hyper-turbulence because most people need support in responding to the challenges of constant change. Change is a way of life and a way of being. Coaching elicits faster, better, deeper change.

Continuous Learning. Learning is the antidote to change. Coaching promotes adaptability and renewal through fundamental learning, in both the leader and the person being coached. It deepens awareness about our circumstances and our reactions, accelerating transitions.

Reframing Paradox. Self awareness about our 'stuck' points allows us to look at our situation in new ways and often to grasp the paradoxes that have limited our choices. Coaches provide tools and support for positive reframing, for new perspectives and possibilities.

A closing caveat on being in service to others as a Leader Coach: it is very challenging for most of us to hand over control either to a person or to a process. As anyone who works in process environments will tell you, there is an oft-repeated saying when, in the midst of progress and for no apparent reason, things fall apart…it is, "Trust the Process." It is well known and well used by facilitators, consultants, trainers, and adult educators, because it is so difficult to do. And for Coach Leaders, it may be that there isn't time to let it happen "just this once", or your bonus is on the line and you can't afford to fail. The need to get the right answer, to step in and solve the problem, is so overwhelming and so ingrained that we have to hold ourselves back, repeat the mantra, and wait in full confidence and belief that the individual or the team will find their own way. So beware – this need will crawl up from within you and threaten to spoil everything, long before the time has come for you to actually intervene, if intervention is indeed necessary at all.

Change is itself a process. It takes its own time and moves in sometimes mysterious ways. Your authentic presence and your belief in others finding their own answers is the most powerful invocation. Beyond that, trust the process!

EndNotes:

[1] Seem for example, Thomas Crane, *The Heart of Coaching*; Mary Beth O'Neill, *Executive Coaching with Backbone and Heart;* James Hunt and Joseph Weintraub, *The Coaching Manager*, Sage, 2002.

[2] Luft, Joseph and Harry Ingham. *Of Human Interaction.* University of California Western Training Laboratory. National Press, 1969 (originally published in 1955).

Chapter 7
Stages in the Leadership Coaching Process

The Coaching Process as a Hologram

We want to start by talking about our coaching process as a whole, and then move to discussing each of the stages in more depth. It is a deceptively simple process – three stages, as shown in the graphic below, each with its own steps, tools, behaviors and issues.

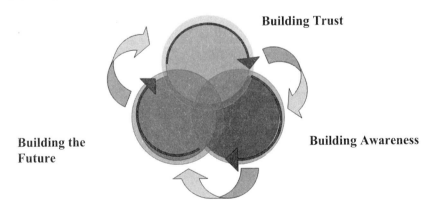

Building Trust

Building the Future

Building Awareness

Figure 16: A Model of the Leadership Coaching Process

The process provides the structure, the "container" if you like, within which the interaction between the Coach Leader and person(s) being coached takes place. It "contains" the relationship, providing boundaries around what is attended to without constraining the conversation too much. In this chapter, we will focus on the individual and group levels of the coaching process and in the next chapter, look at its application in the larger organizational system.

The process begins by **Building Trust**. Without a trusting foundation, there is little chance for mutual learning and positive outcomes. Trust is based on the Leader Coach listening attentively to the individual's "story", the need they are expressing, and demonstrating that she has been fully heard by mirroring back in her own language what has been said, validating her experience, empathizing with her problems and concerns. The Leader Coach ensures understanding by asking clarifying questions, reflecting on her experience, searching for underlying causes, patterns, and themes.

Based on a foundation of trust, the next phase is concerned with **Building Awareness** of the gap between the individual's goal or expectations and what has actually taken place. Often, the Leader Coach is first to see this gap, either in skill, behavior, or breadth of perspective, because being somewhat removed from the action, she is able to observe it more objectively. She provides feedback on her hunches about the situation, allowing awareness to grow and learning to take place through ongoing questions and conversation. The individual may resist this new information, in which case they must surface the block, the coach challenging the individual to move beyond self-imposed limitations in order to progress. Once the individual can incorporate the insights, then together they reframe the previous perceptions and create a new vision of how to move forward.

With this new vision, **Building the Future** involves creating alternatives for addressing the gap and finally making plans with clear accountabilities, "what by when's", that will structure the individual's commitment to action. The Leader Coach encourages and supports implementation of the plans and provides continuing feedback on improvement, especially when new skills or behaviors are attempted and the inevitable setbacks are encountered. When goals are met, the coach recognizes achievements and helps celebrate accomplishments.

This process provides the roadmap for the leader in coaching situations of any scope and duration. It is equally as applicable to an "in the moment" coaching opportunity in a hallway as it is to coaching a direct report over a period of years. The issues will come and go, of course, but the structure for dealing with each one is the same. And often, it is not completely step-wise; there will be times when cycling back is critical, for example, when trust is lost and must be rebuilt before moving into more challenging territory. Or when the cycle is complete and a new issue or learning goal is to be chosen. The process can be equally effective with individuals and teams – the tools may be different, the dynamics more complex, and the Leader Coach competency greater – but the process, the container, is much the same.

You might think of the process as a dance between the parties. The steps provide the structure so that the dancers know how to proceed without stepping on each other's toes. The dance floor contains them so they don't dance off into the adjoining kitchen. Depending on the music and the skill of the dancers, one might lead and the other(s) follow or they might share the leading at different times. The dance involves their bodies moving together in unison, their emotions as the music stirs them, their minds as they remember the steps, and their spirits as they enjoy the dance. It might be a waltz for two, or a line dance, or a macarena for a whole room of people. It can be wooden and stilted, like following big footprints on the floor, or it can be like floating on air, transported to a different realm. It can be just one dance or a whole evening of dancing to a variety of music, with different moves and emotions and reactions.

The coaching process is similar. It is a dance using the individual's own music as the story and the coach's steps as the structure. In partnership, they co-create the kind of dance it will be, how fast or slowly they will move, where on the dance floor they will explore, and how they will feel as a result. If it is a single circumstance, like coaching a team member in the moment, it is just one interaction, one dance. If it is an ongoing relationship between a leader and direct report over a period of time, then the coaching moves over a variety of issues, some easy, some more difficult, engendering different emotions and improving the dance between them based on their growing skill and experience with each other. Once they trust the process of the dance, and each other, they can stop thinking about their feet and be 'in flow', with enough challenge to hold their attention and enough creativity to take the dance wherever it goes.

You get the picture…but before we get to the dance hall, we need to learn how to dance, and to coach, in the first place. Perhaps the most important point in this analogy is that the coaching process is like the holograms we have been discussing. The whole is contained in the parts; the smallest fraction has the same elements as the whole number. Similarly, the whole coaching process is contained in any one interaction. A single coaching moment contains the same elements as the whole coaching process. Here is an example.

The Customer Presentation: A Coachable Moment

Sally and her direct report, John, have been at a customer meeting where John has presented to a key customer. Later, Sally meets John in the corridor and asks him how he thought the meeting went. Sally says she thought it went very well, better than they had both expected (*Building Trust*). John comments that he was nervous beforehand but once into it, felt that he had done a reasonable job, and appreciates the rehearsal with Sally last evening (*Building Trust*).

Sally wholeheartedly agrees with John's assessment. She says she is especially pleased that they had rehearsed the probable questions and his answers because these went much better than previously. Sally asks John how it might have gone even better. John isn't sure and asks Sally for her comments. She says she still sees some room for improvement in the responses to financial questions and John's fluency with the figures in the customer proposal, and wonders if he agrees (*Building Awareness*). John responds that this is still the most difficult part for him and, although he feels he is doing better, he is aware that this is definitely his learning edge (*Building Awareness*).

Sally asks John how he sees himself improving in this area and if there is anything she can do to support his learning (*Building the Future*). John comments that he would like to accelerate his learning plan by seeing his tutor twice rather than once a week and enrolling in the Finance for Non-Financial Managers program in the next month rather than waiting for next quarter (*Building the Future*). Sally asks John to send her an email with the time and cost commitments so they can finalize the plans at their one-on-one next week. As she continues down the corridor, she congratulates John on a job well done (*Building the Future*).

Here, we have an example of a chance meeting, one that Sally takes advantage of to both congratulate John on his presentation and give him some feedback about his financial skills. Obviously, this is a moment in the flow of their continuing conversations about John's presentations to customers and particularly his financial skills. He is working on his development and isn't surprised at Sally's feedback. They trust one another and have discussed these issues before. In that sense the whole conversation takes place in Stage Three – Building the Future. Sally is encouraging and supporting his development plan, which we get the sense they have been working on together, and giving him ongoing feedback about his progress, so that he can continue to refine his plans and actions.

You notice, however, that the conversation includes all three stages. Sally opens the conversation with a trust building comment and question, listens to John's reply and builds on it by asking about his awareness of his financial performance. When John agrees it's a learning edge, Sally moves him to a future action step by asking how he intends to address the gap. This conversation has taken less than a minute or two but mirrors the three stages and, in so doing, ensures that the trust, awareness and future commitments continue to build.

Before we move into the detail of each of the stages, here is a summary of the stages, their focus, and the steps involved.

Stage	Focus	Steps
One	Building Trust "What's So?"	1. Create the appreciative connection 2. Understand the issue/goal/story 3. Use active listening, empathy, clarifying questions 4. Reflect on themes, hunches, causes
Two	Building Awareness "So What?"	5. Agree on the coachable gap 6. Offer feedback as a learning tool 7. Use dialogue to search, explore, gain insight, understand resistance 8. Challenge discontinuities 9. Reframe issue to create new direction
Three	Building the Future "What's Next?"	10. Develop alternative goals/futures 11. Seek commitment to accountable action plans 12. Encourage, support, evaluate, celebrate, recycle

Chart 17: A Framework of the Three-Stage Coaching Process

Stage One – Building Trust

There are four steps in Stage One that are used to build a trusting environment in which the coaching can occur. The objective is to understand the issue or agenda for the interaction – to "get" the story. The key question is: "What's So?" What is the full reality of events, issues, and emotions in the situation? The critical process aspects are that the leader establishes the credibility and competence to coach, and that the individual being coached feels heard, acknowledged and safe to continue into the more difficult part of the journey to follow.

Create the Appreciative Connection:

The attitude of the leader is central in beginning a new coaching relationship or preparing for a coaching meeting. The presence of the leader as a coach, the way the leader connects and establishes rapport, will be the main factor in building the trust needed. Those being coached may initially feel uncomfortable and it is up to the Leader Coach to put them at ease. To do this, the coach must be self aware - conscious of her own mood, assumptions, pre-conceived ideas, and able to put them aside, to center herself in the other person, to be authentically present.

Psychologist Carl Rogers[1] introduced the concept of "unconditional positive regard", the holding of another individual in a positive frame, setting aside any 'conditions' or presumptions, being open to hearing whatever is said with a positive curiosity. This doesn't mean you have to agree but you hold the perspective, you contain the issue, until trust is built and it can be further explored. In other words, you begin each conversation, each interaction in appreciation of the paradox, the complexity, the diversity, that characterizes individuals and their lives – you engage in the relationship with a learner's mind, without judgment or power over them.

This is a significant discipline for the Leader Coach: to become aware of the biases, judgments, interpretations and irritations that another person might prompt in you. Does his first name remind you of an irritating co-worker you once had and are you looking for evidence that he's the same way? Does her laugh prompt you to think she's flighty and irresponsible? Peter Senge describes this as the 'ladder of inference' where you take data presented to you (her laugh) and ascribe meaning to it (she's irresponsible). The danger in coaching of course is that this meaning might begin to influence the authenticity of the relationship and have nothing to do with HER at all.[2] So prior to and early in the check-in process, the Leader Coach reminds herself of the unconditional positive regard in which she holds her clients.

These "check ins" happen each time you meet. Often, it takes just a minute to step into this appreciative connection, once the relationship is established, but it is critical to return to build the trust each time. If it is a group setting, allowing people a sentence or two to bring themselves into full presence in the group builds trust in the community for the work to be undertaken.

Powerful Comments and Questions:
–   How are you? How are you feeling? Let's take a minute to check in…
–   What's up with you? What's going on in your world?

Understand the Issue/Goal/Story:

With an open mind, the leader listens to the individual's issue, concern or need. The objective is to hear the individual's point of view, to step into their shoes, even though the content may be familiar territory to the leader. As the issue unfolds, the leader can clarify the coaching goal – does the person have an expectation from the meeting or interaction? Is this something that needs attention right now, or is it a future-focused goal? Is it something that is part of an ongoing coaching relationship, or is it a new issue? The Leader Coach is looking to identify the questions, the challenges being presented so that once the issue is clear, the focus of the coaching will also be clear. It will be possible to establish a 'contract' to focus on some goal, some improvement, some change, at least initially, that will frame the subsequent interactions.

Listening to understand is easier if you imagine you are listening to an unfolding story, a mystery that you must unravel. You want to know the key elements of the plot, who is involved in the story, what they are doing and feeling, what has happened so far and what is anticipated. Like a good detective, you investigate everything that you can think of so you have as much information as possible to use in your analysis. You put yourself in her position and see the story through her eyes.

Powerful Comments and Questions:
–   Tell me something about the situation…
–   What did you do? How did you feel? What happened next?
–   Who else is involved? What role did they play? How did they react?

- Where does it stand now? What will happen next?
- I think I understand… Would it be helpful if we focused on… ?

Use Active Listening, Empathy, Clarifying Questions:

One of the key elements of trust building is the Coach Leader's language. It is best to use the language of the person being coached as much as possible at this stage, reflecting back to them what you have heard, in their words, to be sure you have correctly understood. The goal is to make the person feel heard and acknowledged. Using empathy validates people's experiences, reinforces the connection and demonstrates that you appreciate their position. As you mirror their story back to them, they also understand it better and begin to learn from its telling.

If it is a group setting, you must ensure that equal time is given to hearing each person and all sides of the issue so that each person is validated and the story is told in its full complexity and diversity. It is critically important at this stage that you as the Coach Leader and others participating do not judge or analyze what is being said. That will come later. Your questions must be for clarification only, to better understand the story, not to judge its rightness or wrongness. This is not the time to confront the issues or offer your own interpretations of the events or emotions. As the coach, you must be sure that individuals do not assign blame or get into conflict but simply state their own perspectives and allow the contradictions to stand for the moment.

Powerful Comments and Questions:
- That sounds like quite a challenge/an experience…
- I hear you say it was (frustrating, fearful, joyous, wonderful…etc.) Tell me more about that…
- Was that very difficult (or stressful or emotional…)?
- I hear some anger in your voice… Is that how you're feeling?

Reflect on Themes, Hunches, Causes:

Once the issue has been aired and understood, and some focus has been achieved on what is required in terms of the follow-on coaching, there will be sufficient trust in the relationship to end this first phase and move on. Usually, the signs that trust has been established include a relaxed positive atmosphere where the individual is able to communicate openly about strengths and weaknesses and where there is a mutual understanding of the direction in which the conversation is headed. Trust is a fragile bridge, though, and must be attended to throughout the relationship. Often, with ease comes some laughter, some lightness, perhaps some tears.

This final step in Stage One is for the leader alone, following the interaction(s) with the person or team being coached. The purpose is to reflect on the story in order to formulate some theories, hunches, themes that form the preliminary subtext of the investigation. The Coach Leader mines the data in the issue for possible assumptions, perceptions, meanings, that need to be explored with the individual(s) in the next phase. These are tentative assessments, open to reinterpretation, but worthy of further discussion to uncover any blocks to learning and change that may be holding the individual(s) back.

Powerful Comments and Questions for the Coach:
–   What did I observe in the individual's behavior?
–   I wonder if there is another meaning to…
–   What did the person mean when she said… ?
–   What do I need to know in order to fully understand?
–   What is preventing her from dealing with this situation?

Stage One may take place over several sessions if the person being coached is a new team member or does not have an established relationship with the Coach Leader. In this case, during each of the first three or four sessions there will be an overall emphasis on trust building, within which the individual will also gain greater awareness from telling her story, understanding it and clarifying it with the coach. The coach can suggest an action step after each session, such as further reflection on some aspect of the issue, undertaking some exploration or looking for themes or learnings in the story that have not yet been discussed. In a new team situation, the same will be true – the first three or four sessions may be just getting to know each other and clarifying the issues to be addressed. If it is an ongoing relationship, then Stage One may take only one meeting where the individual or team presents the leader with a coaching issue to be clarified and focuses on some action step that moves its resolution forward.

Building Trust Case – The New Recruit

Gary had been coaching his team for about eighteen months and was very pleased with the way the individuals had matured in their roles and the way the team had come together. They were all, including Gary, getting results and stretching their leadership abilities. Then, because of a reorganization in another group, Gary inherited Dan, a loner who had a reputation for being smart but difficult to work with.

Gary prepared for their first meeting by outlining the role expectations and accountabilities in Dan's new job and included a sheet on the elements of the work group culture that had been generated by the team. Although he had some misgivings, he centered on appreciating getting to know Dan as a new member of his team and learning about the strengths he could bring.

At the first meeting, Gary encouraged Dan to talk about his career to this point, what he had liked and disliked about his previous roles and what he saw in his future. Dan needed the gentle prodding – it was clear that he didn't like to talk about himself and hadn't reflected much on his career. Gary mirrored back his words and then asked if he'd got it right, which seemed to encourage Dan to expand on the points. When Gary said the meeting was just to get to know each other, Dan seemed to relax a bit. He talked a lot about his successes and a little about some of his disappointments when Gary asked him directly. Gary gave Dan some information about his leadership style and how he liked to interact with his staff individually and as a team. Gary also shared with Dan how his own coaching process was going and the fact that he had recently learned how important it was to practice the honoring and expression of feelings, both his own and others, as part of his evolution to a more effective leader. Gary then shared his own excitement at Dan's arrival and his apprehension about the change in team dynamics that always occurs when a new member arrives or someone leaves.

At the end of the session, Gary gave Dan the material he had prepared and asked him to think about how he could leverage his strengths and what support he would need to meet any challenges. Gary also assigned one of the other team members, June, to work with Dan on his orientation to the team and the larger organization.

At the next three sessions, Gary and Dan went through the job responsibilities in detail, with Dan talking about how he would fulfill each one and where he thought he might need help. After each session, Dan refined the accountabilities and created a development plan based on their discussion. Gary concentrated on clarifying Dan's perception of his strengths and weaknesses, rather than evaluating them. He continued to ask about Dan's experience and gradually got a fuller picture of the ups and downs of his career. In most of his technical roles, he had not had much management or leadership of any kind. Gary asked Dan to complete a Career Experience questionnaire on his own and then reviewed the responses with him. It seemed to help Dan to prepare ahead; his conversation became more open and his energy higher when he had the prepared notes in front of him.

During this time, with June's help, Dan had met with each of his team colleagues using a structured interview format where he had gathered information from them on their roles and goals and had shared similar information about himself. He had attended a team meeting where he had presented what he had learned in the interviews with the team members and discussed his tentative plans for contributing to team goals.

This was all new to Dan and he was finding it both frightening and exhilarating. He had never belonged to a group with so much focus on understanding each other and working together. He had never been asked to communicate so much about himself and his perspectives on things. It was stressful because he wanted to do well here; he liked his boss and his colleagues and wanted them to like him. He was certainly feeling that they were interested in him and his success, and were giving him every opportunity to show his stuff and fit in. He was beginning to relax a bit as the weeks went by. He decided to give it a shot, to trust that they were who they said they were and that he too could be more like himself than he had been for a long time. He was even able to express some of this sentiment to Gary in their next meeting, saying he was glad to be part of the group and looking forward to the work ahead.

Gary had been observing Dan and reflecting on his history and personality since their first meeting. He thought he could see Dan's strengths – his intellectual talent, his problem solving ability, his sound decision-making. He also had a hunch that Dan had pretty low self esteem, was an introvert who needed to be on his own to reflect and prepare ahead, and probably hadn't been given much opportunity to lead except by getting in someone else's way. He hadn't discussed this with Dan other than to reinforce his own developmental thinking but could see that he might help Dan by giving him some new challenges and supporting him in stretching his capability. He decided the time was right at their next meeting to ask Dan if he might offer some development suggestions.

In this example, we see the process of building trust taking place over a month or more as Dan and Gary get to know one another and understand each other's goals and expectations. Gary has created an appreciative connection with Dan, mostly listening and clarifying to be sure he gathers as much background on Dan as possible. He also gives Dan an idea of what it is like to work in his new role, with his new peers, and for Gary as his new boss. Dan doesn't yet feel part of the team but he sees the potential for it to happen. So Gary answers the question, "What's So?" both for himself and for Dan. He also has some hunches that he can explore with Dan in their ongoing coaching sessions as they move into Stage Two. You may have noticed some of the references that indicate Gary has built trust, motivated some new awareness through the discussion, and requested a future action step in each of their meetings, further reinforcing the consistency of the process so that Dan learns to trust it.

Stage Two – Building Awareness

There are five steps in Stage Two having to do with building a deeper awareness in the individual being coached so that new possibilities for action emerge. This is the heart of the coaching process and the stage that most coaches feel least confident and competent about. This is perhaps because it involves digging into the information that has been gathered in Stage One, working with it, confronting the resistance to change, and learning through a process of joint enquiry how to use the information to help the individual close an identified gap in performance, development or potential. It answers the question, "So What?" What is the underlying meaning in the data, in the stories, that can inform individuals about some aspect of their behavior they would like to be different? What feedback can be added to provide perspective? What barriers, perhaps out of awareness right now might be holding them back from becoming who they want to be? This is not something that most leaders have been schooled in or have been encouraged to practice in their roles. In rankings of leadership competencies of North American managers, developing and confronting direct reports are at the bottom of the list.[3] So this stage may feel less comfortable and require the coach, too, to dig into her own resistance so that she learns through appreciation and inquiry something about herself as well as others.

Agree on the Coachable Gap:

At the beginning of Stage Two, it is important that the individual, not the leader, choose the focus for the coaching. This usually evolves naturally from discussions about what's required in the job, what the leader expects, and how the individual can deliver. It is still a tentative agreement, subject to change based on the continuing dialogue but it establishes a boundary, a 'container' so that the individual knows what is included in the coaching and, more importantly, what is not. The leader doesn't just coach on anything – the individual must own the responsibility for what is to be discussed and acted on and must be motivated to close a gap through the coaching. Although the Leader Coach can certainly play a role in determining what the focus is, if it is the leader's agenda alone, the co-creative process is lost.

Agreeing on the coachable gap usually involves some conversation where the leader asks questions about her hunches from Stage One, raising one or two themes she has seen so far or suggesting a possible new interpretation of some experience. This is done gently, in a spirit of curiosity, and using neutral rather than judgmental language. A good way to start the enquiry is with the words, "I wonder…" or "I am curious about…" The leader needs to monitor the response carefully and back up to rebuild trust if the process has moved too quickly for the individual, perhaps returning to it again later or letting the individual raise it again after having time to reflect. Or it may not be meaningful to the client and the coach then moves on.

This process is similar in a team setting where the Coach Leader may offer a point of view about an issue the team is working on. If the team has built trust, the leader may offer an interpretive perspective on the story the group has been telling, a kind of meta-story. It is helpful to think of this as a kind of investigative report, the result of taking a broad view, including all sides, standing back to reflect on the whole picture. The group can then engage in discussion of the perspective, shaping it and taking ownership of it until it is clear enough to frame a gap that can be explored. A note of caution: in the team, the leader does not evaluate individual members' performance, nor are others allowed to do so. The discussion is about the team's issue and actions and must not be focused on blaming or embarrassing individuals, or trust will be lost and honest participation will evaporate. If individuals step into the dialogue with interpretations of their own role or behaviors, then this data becomes part of the learning and shaping of the issue but it is focused on clarifying the gap, not evaluating or improving the person. Members must own their own part in the team issue and discussion and not direct or suggest to others. Again, this is where the delicate dance steps of the Leader Coach are so critical: she must be ready to intervene, to protect the fragile bridges being built, while still practicing Unconditional Positive Regard, to guide the process but not direct the outcomes.

The objective at the end of this step is to have a stated gap between current and desired performance, capability or potential that forms the 'contract' for the coaching to follow.

Powerful Comments and Questions:
—   I wonder what you think about… How does that fit for you?
—   A different interpretation of the issue might be… How do you feel about that?
—   How could we think about that as something we could work on?
—   Is this a gap that you are interested in exploring?
—   What is the nature of the gap you are referring to, do you think?

Offer Feedback as a Learning Tool:

With the coachable gap in mind, the leader and person being coached move into the enquiry to build greater awareness of the issue. Although it is usually unnecessary in a trusting relationship, it is a powerful signal when the Leader Coach asks the individual for permission to give feedback. This clearly invests the ownership and control of the process with the person being coached. The coach only offers feedback that she feels will be helpful in the context of the gap, based on observation, discussion and reflection. This feedback is crucial to the individual because the leader is in the best position to see where skill, attitude and behavior are exemplary and where they can be improved. And it is important to focus both on strengths and development areas, balancing reinforcement of what is going well with attention to what can be better.

The Leader Coach may also suggest using feedback tools to gather additional information. Many such tools are readily available to use independently or through a professional facilitator. Instruments can be chosen for self assessment or to enlist others in a broader comparative analysis. The "360°" leadership competency survey, including self, boss, peers, direct reports and often customers, is one of the most common feedback tools used in organizations today, and is particularly helpful where the individual can compare ratings against the set standards for the job. The important point here is that the assessments are used to inform learning and not to evaluate performance. Reports can be generated for both individuals and groups for most feedback tools. If a professional is hired to administer the feedback assessment, then the leader's role is to provide the benchmarks of success, to reinforce the importance of engaging with the data, to welcome any and all information that the individual is willing to share as part of closing the coachable gap, to offer comment and perspective on it if asked, and to require a broader development plan based on what has been learned from the feedback as a whole. It will be important for the feedback coach, if one is used, to understand the values and philosophy the Leader Coach and her team believe in and practice in their everyday leadership moments of truth.

Feedback is difficult to give, which is why most leaders don't do much of it, and it is difficult to receive, which is why it usually causes some degree of resistance in the person receiving it. This is to be expected. We don't like to hear that we have weaknesses and often shy away from or discount our strengths as well. So coaching moves out of most people's comfort zone when it gets into feedback but this is precisely the way that awareness grows and informs us about what to do next. Feedback uncovers both hidden strengths – capabilities we have that others see in us but we don't – and blind spots – weaknesses others see in us but we're not aware of. Both hidden strengths and blind spots require acknowledgement because strengths are wasted if we don't use them and weaknesses may be inadvertently causing us great harm (See Figure 15 in The Invitation to Part Three on page 184.)

If you as the Leader Coach sense that an individual is becoming tense, withdrawn, angry or unable to engage in a learning conversation, it is best to step back, name what your hunch is, and discuss the situation before moving on. Just acknowledging the discomfort and encouraging the individual to give it voice can often diffuse the anxiety and allow the conversation to continue. It may be necessary to end the meeting and continue after the individual has had time to digest the information or regain composure. This may happen in the early stages of a coaching relationship and can reoccur at times throughout the process when new insights occur. Offering feedback is not something that the leader does once. It becomes part of the ongoing coaching as the leader observes the individual and can offer positive support and guidance on progress, both in the moment and in the longer term coaching conversations. The coach may also become aware, on reflection, of her own resistance: "I noticed I got all red in the face when she reported that people label her a workaholic…did I avoid talking about that? Should I have pursued that? Should I be alert to those non-verbal cues?"

Powerful Comments and Questions:
-   Could I offer you some feedback on that?
-   What I see as a strength is... What I see as a learning edge is...
-   What did you learn from your assessment in relation to the gap?
-   What were your surprises?
-   How does this information fit with what we've already discussed?
-   How might you leverage those hidden strengths? How might you compensate for or develop those blind spots?
-   Your body language tells me you are feeling uncomfortable... Is that the case? What can we learn from this? Would you like some time to reflect and we'll meet again tomorrow?

Use Dialogue to Search, Explore, Gain Insight, Understand Resistance:

Using feedback from the Leader Coach and any other sources, this step involves engaging in conversation to gain mutual insight into the issue or gap being addressed. It is the exploration of new territory together, as adventurers, being aware of everything pertinent and searching for new meaning by putting the pieces of the puzzle together in a new and more complete way. The coach uses similar methods as in Stage One – active listening, mirroring back what has been said, using engaging and challenging questions - but now is working in partnership with the individual in deeper interaction where both can bring all of who they are to the dialogue. The Coach Leader makes observations, gives feedback, offers perspective. The person being coached sifts and sorts, reacting to the information and generating other options. They search for the answer to "So What?" – what do the data tell them, are there other meanings, what are the recurring themes, the patterns of behavior that are relevant to the issue?

For some people, this is an exciting adventure of discovery, a learning journey. But for most, dealing with the resistance that arises is a significant part of the dialogue. It is, in fact, the signal for both parties that the individual has embodied the gap and is now feeling it viscerally as a pull toward something different and potentially frightening. The natural tendency is to resist the pull. We often stay stuck in our outmoded behaviors and attitudes long after they are productive simply because we can't get past the wall of resistance. It is important when the individual gets into "Yes but..." reactions that the coach identifies the 'stuckness' and tries to reveal what's behind it. Dealing with resistance is about coming to know and understand our fears, our shadows, and feeling that we can incorporate them, get through in spite of them, perhaps even in concert with them. Each time we succeed, we are that much stronger and more able to recognize and resolve them the next time. As a Coach Leader, it is often useful to focus the individual on the goal, to paint the picture of the benefits of overcoming resistance – keep your eyes on the prize! – rather than dwelling in the negative possibilities.

In groups, dealing with resistance can be even more daunting and can tempt the leader to step out of the coaching role and back into more traditional power and control. The good news is that not everyone will resist the same things at the same times, so some members will usually take the lead, show the way, and encourage others to come along. The bad news is that the dynamics, the interplay of connections and conflicts in any group makes it that much more difficult to locate the underlying issues or to work through them. In teams that have built a trusting environment, if all voices are heard and opinions considered before the decision is made, then members feel validated and can usually accept the outcome. Sometimes the team establishes a process to deal with resistance. Working to air and dissolve dissent before a decision is made is one avenue. Being willing to accommodate other views for the benefit of the team is another. Peers often coach each other when they are feeling reluctant about a direction. Or the team will return to its charter, credo or first principles to settle a conflict. In a team setting, it is often the case that the individual who raises a barrier is actually speaking on behalf of others who have the same feelings but not the courage to express them. Allowing the resistance to surface and be voiced is also a test of the principle of diversity where all opinions are valid and considered. The Leader Coach needs to reinforce taking the time, within reason, to debate different points of view and create a consensus.

Powerful Comments and Questions:
- So what does all this tell us? What do you think it means?
- What's your best guess about why that is so?
- How does this relate to that? And that? How does it all fit together?
- I hear your reluctance to discuss this... What are the voices in your head saying to you? Can you identify them?
- Can you rephrase the statement using "I" instead of "They"?
- What strengths do you have that would balance that perceived weakness?
- Would you review the goal you are seeking and why it is important to you now? Are you willing to let go of that goal? What will the consequences be?

Challenge Discontinuities:

One of the things that happens at this stage is that the Coach Leader and sometimes also the person being coached, become aware of discontinuities in their perceptions. There are holes in their story, things that don't add up. These discontinuities need to be confronted. For example, an individual feels he is organized and timely in making decisions. His own self-analysis as well as feedback from others may say he is disorganized and takes too long to ponder his actions. And he is usually late for the coaching meetings! These perceptions may be blind spots that, once revealed, can be relatively easily improved. Sometimes the gap is between thinking and feeling – a person's results are good but they feel they are not doing well in the job. Again, these feelings can be explored and better aligned. These differences between perception and reality are what Flaherty calls our "structure of interpretation"[4], the ways we interpret events that then change the way we behave or feel about things. He argues that these structures must be changed to align with our highest potential, and with practice our behavior will follow.

Another area of discontinuity is the gap between what is hidden and what is revealed – the undiscussables we hold on to because we fear the consequences of revealing them. The Leader Coach usually has some hunches about what these might be and can float them with an individual or in a group to learn what is behind behaviors that may be inhibiting high performance. Again, the trust level with the individual or within the group will determine how far this discussion can be taken but some gentle encouragement usually goes a long way.

Powerful Comments and Questions:
–   I notice you said "x" today and "y" last week…can you explain?
–   You say you're not good at strategy and yet I see you leading the team in this area – how do these two views fit for you?
–   I have a hunch we are avoiding the issue of work/life balance – how can you do this within a reasonable work day?

Reframe Issues to Create New Directions:

This final step in Stage Two focuses on using the insights gained through feedback and dialogue to recast the original coaching goal in light of the new awareness. This begins the transition to Stage Three where action planning takes place, but first the leader and person being coached reframe the issues to take account of what has been learned through the process so far. The objective is to create a new direction from which alternatives can be generated and explored. It may be as simple as learning a new skill that will close a performance gap, or setting a career goal that will form the basis for a development plan. Sometimes, it will go deeper – moving from a managerial to a technical role in order to have time with small children, or rethinking the fundamental purpose of work and its role in the individual's life.

At this point in the coaching relationship, the dialogue is easy and the issues are known – anything within the boundary of the coaching contract can be discussed. The atmosphere lightens and humor grows. The individual may have an emerging sense of exhilaration about what is ahead mixed with some nervousness about how it will be achieved. More and more time is spent looking forward rather than back, trying to get a clear picture of the new goal and how all the pieces of the current reality will fit, or not fit, into it.

Powerful Comments and Questions:
– What alternatives do you see for achieving that goal?
– What would a better option than the current one be for you?
– How could you see that working? Paint me a picture…
– What if we step back and see the bigger picture – what would that look like?

The Time spent in Stage Two varies depending on the depth of the issues, the degree of resistance, and the complexity of the factors involved. It may take several sessions to give and discuss feedback, then work through any resistance to the point of having a clear goal. Or it may take several months to dig into an ambiguous malaise and uncover a misfit with the current role, then decide how to make a major change. In the middle, it may feel like going around in circles, looping back to rebuild trust when the individual feels threatened or returning to previous discussions to challenge discontinuities. There is a tendency to want to move through this messy state as quickly as possible but it is important to sit in the stew long enough for the awareness to grow and insights to emerge. There may even be a greater temptation not to head into this messy state at all, as it's hard and it's been there for a long time. In fact, as the coach you may need to steel yourself, to move into the mess, the ambiguity, the resistance, the confusion, the discomfort zone, and not worry that you will destroy the trust you've taken so long to build. In fact, with a strong foundation of trust, the coach can, and perhaps must, head into the friction, to stand beside the client as he finally confronts what he has been resisting for so long. Again in Stage Two, although the overall emphasis is on awareness building, it is critical to build trust at each encounter and to suggest actions that will move the reflection and integration forward.

Building Awareness Case – The Happy Team

Gary's team of eight managers consisted of divisional sales operations, inside sales, product development and finance. He has led the group for two years. Although the results were good, the team was in disarray when he arrived – there was dysfunctional competition among the divisions, overlap between inside sales and the sales reps in the field, and tension over divisional input into the product development process. Gary realized he had to build an effective team and decided to apply the coaching skills he had learned in a recent leadership program he had attended. He has coached each of the individual team members in their bi-weekly one-on-one meetings and also coached the team as a whole for about eighteen months now. He believes the team has matured and is functioning very effectively – the divisions are pulling together to reach the team's overall goals rather than vying with each other, the responsibilities of inside sales and field reps have been clarified, and there is greater input into product development which has resulted in fewer fixes.

Gary felt that there was a sufficient level of trust in the team that he could suggest they gather some feedback on both individuals and the group as a whole in order to establish their development goals for next year. The team chose a well respected 360° feedback survey and it was administered to peers, direct reports, key contacts and customers. Gary completed a survey for each individual, and an outside facilitator compiled the results. She had booked an appointment with Gary to review the results prior to the team meeting but Gary had been "summoned" to a urgent meeting with the COO regarding a disgruntled customer. As he was confident in the results, the planned group meeting went ahead anyway, without Gary having seen the survey results ahead of time. The group report was a composite of the individual scores. The team met to review the results of the group report. None of them had seen their individual scores yet. When the facilitator began to show the results, Gary was shocked – it wasn't at all what he had expected!

The scores revealed that the team had indeed improved in almost every area of team functioning but that this increased effectiveness had not been translated to direct reports, key colleagues or customers. These groups felt that decision-making was slow, the group was not action or results oriented, and there was a lack of strategic skill. When the presentation was complete, the room was silent. Gary asked for a single reaction from each person and found that most of the team members were as surprised as he was but some had been worried this might be the case. One member was sure it was a poor choice of raters. Another thought there was jealousy because they were such a great team - one of the peer raters had applied for a team job and had not been hired. One disliked and distrusted the survey instrument and process. One team member confessed that he had seen this coming, and one was surprised the results weren't worse. His perception was that "we've spent too much time on our own team building, and not enough on the wider constituencies, who pay the bills."

Gary's own 'single reaction' was both disappointment and clarity; he reinforced the good work they had done as a foundation, and said that this made their goals for the coming year very clear. For the rest of the meeting, the team explored the data: which rater groups were high and low on which dimensions, what the key issues were for each rater group, and where the key gaps or largest gaps existed in their team's performance. He asked each team member where they thought the ratings came from and what situations might have contributed to the results. Individuals shared suggestions of how to explain the data, with examples of their own priorities and choices. Of course, while this group conversation was going on, each team member was also wondering how their data contributed to these results…"Am I pulling us up, pulling us down…?" The meeting ended with the commitment to gather again in a week, after each team member had received his or her own feedback and had a chance to reflect.

The facilitator coached individual team members through their own feedback and helped them create a preliminary development plan to be shared with Gary. Each had some sense of the commitments they would make to improve the overall team's performance by the time of the next meeting.

Gary's initial reaction was that he must have been too lax with the team and needed to get control of things. He thought more about the data during the week and the facilitator gave him some coaching about how he might consider the data differently. His new perspective underscored his belief that the team was mature and ready enough to co-create a positive action plan to close the gaps they'd identified.

The foundation of mutual trust and respect the team members had built held, and they were able to confront the issues, challenge their assumptions and set targets for improvement. They also decided that some of their team members had strengths that could be of service in coaching others. Gary began with his own development plan and goals, and encouraged them to share their individual commitments to change. In doing so, they confirmed the common needs that they could partner in addressing and they also realized that their diversity of strengths could be used in peer coaching to serve customers and direct reports in a more effective manner. Overall, then, they were able to reframe their initial disappointment as learning about the next steps they could take to move their team culture out into the wider organization. They were confident they could replicate it in their own teams and in their relationships with customers.

The team members left the meeting with a preliminary action plan that they would implement over the next couple of weeks. They were clear in their resolve to preserve the sense of community they'd established and, in fact, extend it into this wider set of relationships. During this time, they followed up with key people to explore the data with them. The information slowly came together and in a fortnight they were able to pull together an integrated strategy for how to move forward. The plan included:
- More time for coaching of their direct reports so they could take on greater leadership roles, leaving time for the leadership team to develop the strategic skills they needed.
- Seeing the team not just as themselves, but as including their direct reports, key contacts and customers, so that they would work to expand and build an organizational culture reflecting the values that had worked so well for them.
- Making process improvements to increase timely decision-making, as there was a sense that their consensus processes were taking too long.

Gary's role through this process was to question, clarify, challenge, keep the group on track, and not let the discussions go on too long. He was very aware that they had to move to action quickly, given the feedback. When the themes emerged from the data, he was able with the coach/facilitator's help, to frame a more positive picture of what had been done and how it would help with what came next. He did not submit to the temptation to fall back into more traditional forms of control and problem-solving. Gary's work with the coach helped him to realize that he had been, perhaps, too focused on the co-creative process of team development and had ignored the voices of the team members who had tried to warn them of customer dissatisfaction. While he may have empowered and coached his team members, he may not have truly delegated enough to leave them room to lead. In reviewing the last eighteen months, he also realized that building the *team* was necessary but not sufficient, as real transformation had to happen with *all* the stakeholders and not just the people who reported to him. He realized he had to over-balanced on the team participative processes, at the expense of others in the wider context.

He decided to share these insights with his team, realizing he had to develop a plan to improve his own leadership, in blending the results and relationships aspect of the team's functioning. In his coaching, he encouraged each team member to blend an awareness of and commitment to both performance and development, the *both/and* of external and internal focus. He began this process by inviting a 360° process on himself. He was really happy about the first step he had taken but understood it was just that – a first step. He had learned a lot and still had a long way to go.

Stage Three: Building the Future

Step 10: Develop Alternative Goals/Futures:

Based on the direction for the future set at the end of Stage Two, Stage Three begins with the creative process of generating alternative possibilities for making the future a reality. The coach and the individual co-create as many scenarios with their associated pros and cons, as are needed to flesh out how the vision might be implemented. This is an imaginative journey to generate a new story at a future point in time. The objective is that the new story is compelling enough to pull the individual towards it, despite the counter-pull of any leftover resistance. A caution to the coach here: there may be a temptation to solve the problem, to react enthusiastically to one proposed scenario…any indication of favoritism at this point begins to make this your scenario and not the client's.

It is expected that the scenarios will compete with each other; there are some things in each one that don't add up, and there will certainly be aspects of each that are appealing. The idea is not to choose one scenario, but to develop several fully enough that the individual can choose the best possible option from among them. The co-creative process requires that all the possibilities be arrayed and that the individual is encouraged to put them together, 'composing a life' as Bateson[5] says, that includes as many of the most appealing elements as possible. It is part of the paralysis of change, the stuckness that we talked about earlier, that people cannot envision living the life of their dreams, doing the work of their dreams. So, part of the development of alternatives here is, almost at play and in humor and the easiness of the relationship, to get into options that might seem unattainable, naively optimistic, or just plain silly. From this array, the person being coached can often put together a creative composition of many of the desired elements, often beyond what she could have imagined at the start. At the end of this step, the individual will have pulled the pieces of her plan together and is ready to move on.

Powerful Comments and Questions:
-   Let's make these scenarios real – can you describe your perfect day in your new life?
-   Do you feel yourself being pulled toward the future? Is it compelling? Does it draw you forward and inspire you? What are the benefits and consequences of moving in this direction?
-   Of all the scenarios, which are the pieces that appeal to you most? How could you put those together?
-   How do you as the coach control your own internal critic that judges the silly options?

Step 11: Seek Commitment to Accountable Action Plans:

This is the step in the process where the individual commits to specific actions, that is "what by when's". The coach's role here may differ, depending on the quality or state of the relationship with the client and the nature of the results or changes to be achieved. For example, is it to correct a performance problem or to develop a new competency for a future role? Is there a pattern of success or failure in meeting previous commitments that would shape the interactions and the coach's role in supporting the individual? At this stage of the relationship, the Leader Coach can be clear about the hurdles in implementing the plan and the person being coached can ask for what they need.

If a direct report, for instance, has repeatedly failed to meet commitments, the leader must continue to coach, rather than default to tight supervision, unless or until it is clear that the client is no longer intending to commit to a coaching relationship. At this stage, action and change MUST take place… it is not appropriate for the coach to enable inaction. Sometimes positive support alone doesn't work, the individual needs more direction for making change, and needs to understand the consequences and the timeframes of not doing so. This is the most complex situation for a leader coaching an individual because of the potential for role conflict, ambiguity, contradictory cultural signals, and a potential erosion of trust.

In Figure 17, we highlight some of the options for the Leader Coach in supporting and realizing the commitments the individual has made. The coach's role will differ depending on the quality of their current relationship and the experience of success in meeting previous commitments. The Leader Coach begins with the appreciative, positive view and only after evidence that there is not a willingness to change, do the coach's options narrow to requirements and negative consequences.

Acknowledge. If the relationship is good and the person has previously met most, not necessarily all of her commitments, the coach's role may simply be to guide, encourage and support the ongoing successful performance. The coach may recognize accomplishments and hold a mirror up to the individual to help her celebrate her achievements.

High	*Challenge:* "We need to see this by then. How would you like to proceed?	*Acknowledge:* "Keep up the good work. How can I support you?"
RELATIONSHIP	*Require:* "I need to see this by then. If not, you will be removed from your role."	*Appreciate:* "I appreciate your good performance. Is there anything getting in the way of our coaching ?"
Low		
	Low **PERFORMANCE** **High**	

Figure 17: A Model Relating Performance and Relationship

Appreciate. If most of the commitments have been met but an easy relationship has never developed, the Leader Coach's role may be to invite a discussion of what can be done to support the individual's progress and to improve the relationship. This might include offering suggestions of other coaches with whom a higher rapport might be established. Not every coaching relationship results in close bonds, nor does it need to. The individual may in fact be satisfied with the relationship as it stands. But if not, the Leader Coach may initiate a discussion about the chemistry in coaching relationships and options when it is missing.

Challenge. If the relationship is good but commitments have been missed and this issue has been previously understood, the leader's role is to give more structure and more direction within the coaching relationship. The temptation for the Leader Coach here may be to be too soft, to avoid damaging the rapport. Remember that the Leader Coach and the individual can choose to go back and rebuild trust, if the original foundation has been laid. The *both/and* requirement is to nurture the relationship and be clear about the results required. It is not the Leader Coach's role to demand anything of the person being coached. It is the coach's role to be clear about what the requirements are, and to leave it to the individual to commit to meeting them. Otherwise, the coach has destroyed the power balance and assumed responsibility for the required results.

Require. If there is neither rapport nor results… what IS a coach to do? The Leader Coach's role is to state clearly the situation, the requirements, the timelines, and the consequences. Even here, the leader does not take responsibility for the individual's commitment to making change. She can only frame the situation and allow the individual to choose to change. In fact, it may be even more important for the Leader Coach to be true to the coaching process in these situations of failed commitments, in order to reinforce the accountability of the individual for her own performance. However, the reality is that the leader IS accountable for the results of others, and must either work with the individual to effect change, remove the individual from the role, or introduce some other consequence. Sometimes playing the coaching role through to the end still doesn't produce the change required. The leader must have a strategy and the skill to follow through on the consequences. It is not acceptable to leave it unattended – the Leader Coach must, when all else fails, take final action. She may need, for instance, to get coaching herself, from a Human Resources expert, or someone who understands the organization's processes and can advise on the best approach.

Coaching others, especially direct reports, about their performance may also prompt you, the Leader Coach, to reflect on what that performance has to do with you. Is there something about your own leadership style that you can observe here, patterns you can see, a bigger systems perspective you can bring, that allows you to see what part you might be playing in helping or hindering your direct reports in achieving high levels of effectiveness. This reflection on the part of the Leader Coach is an essential part of the learning journey.

Powerful Questions and Comments:
- You're doing a great job! Let's think about your next career move and what you might need to learn next? How can I support you?
- You're doing a great job! Does this relationship serve you in meeting your longer-term goals? How else might we do that?
- You've missed another deadline. I'd recommend you do this by then. Can you make that commitment and deliver on it?
- You've missed another deadline. I need to see this by then, or else you will lose that account. Do you understand this? How can I help you?

Step 12: Encourage, Support, Evaluate, Celebrate, Recycle:

The Leader Coach's role in this final step is to support the individual in implementing her plans. When the inevitable setbacks occur, the coach reminds the individual of the compelling goal, provides ongoing feedback, and helps refine the action steps.

The objective is to be there when the individual feels threatened or insecure, as she tries out new behaviors, practices new skills, takes risks. The Leader Coach provides the ground, the touch point, true north. Not much challenge or resistance coaching is needed at this stage, if things are going well. The individual is self-motivating. She has become a learner, and has gained some momentum from the small wins and achievements. Setbacks may require a return to trust building and new awareness, which the coach can support, because the original plan will never turn out exactly as it was imagined, even in the best of circumstances. This isn't easy; it takes time and the Leader Coach reassures, stands by, persists and celebrates along the way.

When a significant change is being made, the coach 'contains' what may be volatile swings of excitement and depression about the changes and progress. The individual is truly in the middle of something; she has left her old ways and knows she can't go back, and yet the way forward is not clear enough or compelling enough to grab hold of. The individual is not the same person who began the coaching relationship – she has been transformed by her new awareness and needs time and safety to grow into her new self. This is where the consistency of the process so far really pays off. The high trust, the open relationship… these provide the safety for continuing learning, experimentation and risk-taking.

If things are not going well, the Leader Coach may be tempted to give up at this point. There are several steps she can take. She can make clear that there is a need to recycle to Stage Two, to challenge the resistance. She can reinforce the need to redefine a plan that the individual can commit to. And she can examine the relationship for barriers that are impeding results. In the relationship, are you as the Leader Coach the stumbling block? Usually, the Leader Coach knows, and the individual may know, too, that an insurmountable barrier between the two of you can eliminate the possibility of continuing the coaching relationship, in which case other avenues need to be explored. The avenues will depend on the strength of both the relationship and the results, and may include the involvement of an outside coach, an EAP counselor or a peer leader in the organization.

In most cases, although the process may not be smooth, changes are made, the person progresses and the coach participates enthusiastically in celebrating accomplishments and changes. In an ongoing leader/direct report relationship, when one cycle is complete another is begun, a new issue is determined, and although there is a residual trust remaining, the coach returns to the initial steps to begin the exploration of the new issue or goal and starts the process again. And of course both the coach and the individual really start the process for the first time, as the co-creative process they've shared has changed them both. It's good to acknowledge this as a part of the evaluation of the process, which can range from structured feedback to an informal discussion of what went well, what could be improved, and how they will work together differently as a result in the future.

Powerful Questions and Comments:
- Your progress is exciting! How are you feeling about it?
- What more do you need to know to get over this hurdle?
- In what way do you sense yourself getting closer to your dream?
- What have you learned about yourself and your approach to change? What are your particular strengths?
- What worked best for you in this coaching relationship?
- As you reflect on the process, what patterns of resistance are you now aware of?

Building the Future Case – The "Problem" Employee (June)

One of Gary's direct reports, June, gets great results but has poor interpersonal skills. She's highly competitive and has been involved in conflicts over resources with her teammates. For example, she's been accused of recruiting the highest-performing sales reps to her own team, yet they are dissatisfied and say that she wants results at whatever costs.

She and Gary have been coaching for about a year. They have been through the process and June claimed she was committed to improvement, set some clear goals for herself and did a bit to implement her plan, but then slid back because her sales performance began to slip. She again became driven and started working long hours on her own.

Gary has been working with June on her team skills as part of her improvement plan, because her lack of interpersonal skill was a factor in his team meetings. In fact, Gary understands that his relationship with June has been difficult from the beginning. Gary is a people person and has seen June as disruptive and hostile. It took several months for them to build the trust they needed to really begin the coaching relationship. They had several false starts but eventually began to understand each other's strengths and weaknesses and could move on. What Gary learned during this time was that his initial perceptions and his assumptions about June's behavior were a barrier to his trusting her, and in turn, to her trusting him. When he was able to appreciate June's ability to get results with customers, she was able to begin to trust him. Gary felt June could be a success but her lack of interpersonal skills and relationship building ability was holding her back. So the coaching gap they identified was June's interpersonal skills.

Although June agreed that this was something she was committed to, it was clear to both of them that it was not a compelling vision for her, because she valued the results she got more than the relationships with others. Gary talked to her about the perceptions he was aware of in the team, and the members of her direct report group who had approached him about their concerns with her management style. Gary and June discussed her exceptional sales results but also that she was difficult to work with and perceived as arrogant and unapproachable by others.

June was ambitious and so went through the motions of the coaching process. She said she wanted to become a "whole leader", with both results and interpersonal skills, in order to be promoted to the next level. Through the next several coaching conversations, Gary and June developed a plan. The plan she committed to included appreciating others' points before speaking in Gary's team, journaling to reflect on her own behavior, and having regular one-on-ones with her direct reports. Gary added to her plan by suggesting that she gain increased self-awareness in a coaching skills program that would help her in relationships with her peers and direct reports, and also that she work with Dan, the new recruit, on his orientation as a way of practicing her coaching skills. Gary was more confident on the basis of this plan and June's apparent awareness of the need to change but after the first month, he realized it was still only a plan. She was reluctantly meeting some of her commitments and others she had simply let fall away. Gary was aware that there was powerful resistance at work in June, and knew he needed to find a way to help her see it and work through it.

Then, a couple of months ago, two of June's direct reports came to see Gary, threatening resignation because of June's leadership style. And then, just in time for the annual performance review, the results of the yearly survey of direct reports and colleagues came back. At their coaching meeting, Gary confronted June with her failure to meet her commitments and made clear to her that this was her final opportunity to make some changes before he sought her removal from his team.

The data from her direct reports and colleagues shook June out of her complacency. For June, the results were 'hard', numerical, demonstrating to June on her own terms what Gary had really been talking about. She realized that she would never get ahead unless she changed her style. So, for the last two months, June has dug in, taken responsibility, scheduled meetings with her peers and direct reports to talk about her feedback, and created a comprehensive and realistic development plan. She has done some great work with Dan on his orientation, and her coaching program is coming up in the next few weeks. She has shared with Gary that she realizes the reason she's been so driven is her need to be accepted, and a fear that showing feelings was showing weakness and might make her seem a "soft female". With this realization and Gary's encouragement, June has also allowed herself to lighten up, to laugh more and encourage the others in her direct report and peer teams to gently nudge and joke with her when her old "bad" habits recur.

Gary has been thoroughly pleased with and supportive of June's new direction. In fact, June's individual scores on the team 360° feedback already show improvement, and she had the best feedback in the whole team from her customers because of her results and action orientation. In addition to reinforcing June's new behavior, these strengths, because they were missing in several of her team members, have drawn June into the team in a way that allows her to be a leader and coach of others rather than an arrogant outsider. She's seen as a new person, and one of Gary's possible successors.

The extended story we've worked through in this chapter, with Gary and June and Dan and the team, presents the various stages of the coaching relationship with some concrete examples of how it might go. Through it all, there has been the presence, the alchemic leadership of the coach, manifesting in as many opportunities as possible the blend of:

- The Co-creation of Futures: the team's participation in and creation of the go-forward plan to respond to customer feedback.
- The Holographic Metaphor: the opportunity each team member has, in his or her own dealings with direct reports, peers and customers, to be a Leader Coach.
- Leadership through Heterarchy: the transformation in June when she not only began to coach Dan but to interact with her peers.
- Meaning and Interdependence: Dan's discovery that he could be more himself and contribute to Gary's team.

The coaching process itself - Building Trust, Building Awareness, Building the Future – is fairly simple and straightforward. It is available to the Leader Coach at any moment, and at every moment of interaction with others. It is the moment of the dance.

A Self Reflection:

When you read Gary's story, place yourself in his shoes. Where do you think you would have made his choices, and why? Have you had to make similar choices in the past? What do you now realize about the choices you made...what were the influences? What were the possibilities? What might you do differently today, if you could play the "tape" over again?

An Exercise to Share:

One of the opportunities this model of coaching presents is the blend of personal and leadership development. For example, by increasing my awareness of my need for control in new or unfamiliar situations, I can monitor my behavior in team settings to be sure I don't dominate and try to control the process, thereby improving the group's overall effectiveness. Can you think of an area in your own development plan that addresses both the personal and organizational level? Can you have an honest learning conversation with a trusted partner to explore your own plans, your dreams about how these two interact and what kinds of resistance you have experienced as you work your plans?

A Team Exercise:

One of the challenges Gary faced was in becoming as authentic as he could in his own learning journey, and coaching his direct reports as well. Is there an aspect of this story that would make a good "lunch and learn" discussion with your team? What are the key learning points you might want to probe? What are the aspects of this process and this story that are particularly useful in your context? Can you model the alchemic leader by sharing with your team some aspect of your own learning journey, perhaps about Leadership Alchemy?

Once you've had your team meeting, why not jot down in your journal some of the learnings the team discovered? What surprised you about their interaction with the story? Is there something that they have seen in you, a hidden strength or blind spot that you were not aware of?

A Self-Assessment:

Bearing in mind all twelve steps and three phases of the Coaching process outlined here, think through where you believe you will have the most challenge. Develop specific learning strategies to get better at those phases, as you coach your direct reports, peers and yourself.

Stage and Focus	Steps	My Learning Edge Rating 1 (poor) to 5 (great)
Stage One: Building Trust "What's So?"	1. Create the appreciative connection 2. Understand the issue/goal/story 3. Use active listening, empathy, clarifying questions 4. Reflect on themes, hunches, causes	
Stage Two: Building Awareness "So What?"	5. Agree on the coachable gap 6. Offer feedback as a learning tool 7. Use dialogue to search, explore, gain insight, understand resistance 8. Challenge discontinuities 9. Reframe issue to create new direction	
Stage Three: Building the Future "What's Next?"	10. Develop alternative goals/futures 11. Seek commitment to accountable action plans 12. Encourage, support, evaluate, celebrate, recycle	

Chart 18: An Assessment of Leadership Coaching Process Skills

Here are some questions you might ask yourself in relation to your ratings.

- What are my learning goals based on the stages and steps of the Leadership Coaching Process that cause me particular trouble?
- What support and resources will I need to help me achieve my learning goals?
- What possible saboteurs and resistance might I encounter and how might I work through these obstacles?
- How will I know when I'm successful in achieving this goal?

Endnotes

[1] Rogers, Carl. *On Becoming A Person.* Houghton Mifflin, 1961.

[2] Ross, Rick. "The Ladder of Inference", in Peter Senge et al. *The Fifth Discipline Fieldbook: Strategies and Tools for Building a Learning Organization,* p. 242 – 248. Currency/Doubleday, 1994.

[3] Lombardo, Mike and Bob Eichinger. *The Leadership Machine.* Lominger Inc., 2001.

[4] Flaherty, James. *Coaching: Evoking Excellence in Others.* Butterworth Heinemann, 1999.

[5] Bateson, Mary Catherine. *Composing a Life.* Plume/Penguin, 1990.

Chapter 8
Applying the Leadership Coaching Process to Major Change

The Crowstone Story

This chapter is the story of Crowstone, an organization forced to make major changes because of market conditions and lack of attention to succession issues. It follows the events of Catherine, a young leader who has been very successful in her early career. Her evolving role as a change leader and a Coach Leader shapes the change process and the outcomes. We invite you into the story, to 'play along', and encourage you, as you read, to hold what you have learned in the previous chapters in mind. The story is described in sufficient depth that you can see the various models we've presented. At the end, we will ask you to be Catherine's advisor and coach to help her prepare for what's next in her future.

Background on Crowstone:

Crowstone Publishing is an established and successful firm of 1200 employees that has been in business for seventy years. CEO Damian Crowstone runs the company, the third generation of Crowstones to head the business. Until recently, they were regarded as the epitome of the traditional publishing industry, making lots of cash, built on an "old boys network" culture, with a sales force that embodied this style in a "get an account, any account" approach. The product is high quality and Crowstone is respected, with a great reputation. Its account management staff is known to be well educated and customer oriented, although quite traditional. It has tended to retain its people, with many having long service records. People have grown up through the ranks and are perhaps not as well rounded as if they'd had a broader experience. The culture has reinforced the need for care and quality, resulting in a deliberate pace. The structure has been quite centralized. Although the business units are customer facing, they have not had any P&L responsibility. Instead, the budgeting process has dictated to the divisions what their next year's targets would be, based on corporate sales forecasts and revenue projections. As a result, the business unit heads have had very little discretionary power and are not very financially adept. Until three years ago, Crowstone achieved double-digit earnings each year and a certain complacency has become evident in the culture.

In the last three years, however, there have been serious inroads: online offerings are eating away at margins, taking customers and attracting staff, particularly the very people Crowstone needs and wants to retain - the tech-savvy, younger employees. Earnings have fallen to single digit levels and both the Board and senior management are worried about the future. However, Damian Crowstone is a strong leader who has managed to temper stockholder concerns. With the Board and senior management, Damian has been looking at a young company, E'*CUBED*, that they feel might add a needed e-learning element to the business and bring some new energy as well.

Background on E'*CUBED*:

E'*CUBED* was started seven years ago by three students in an applications programming course - two men and a woman, Catherine. Though it had a rocky start, and one of the co-founders had to leave the partnership early due to the financial risks involved, the company has more recently grown quickly and established a strong reputation in the e-learning business for the production and delivery of web-based e-learning content. It now has 180 employees who are primarily young, diverse and technologically savvy, and who embody a "Jeans" culture: loose, smart, sassy, fast and sometimes a bit arrogant and sloppy. It is a place which feels like "family" for many of its employees, particularly as employees at all levels have an ownership stake in the company. They are encouraged to challenge everything - there are no sacred cows. As a result, there is an organizational pride in staying at the leading edge of innovation. There is a constant review and culling to ensure product lines are profitable. The leadership in the company is immature in management discipline terms, with supervisors/team leads who "shoot off their mouths", speaking before they think. They lead mostly creative employees who typically have very non-traditional work arrangements, with many people working in semi-autonomous project teams.

The Acquisition:

E'*CUBED* is bought by Crowstone on January 1, 1999, in a deal that the young company couldn't refuse. E'*CUBED* becomes a business unit, reporting to Damian Crowstone, with the full support of the Board. Catherine, one of E'*CUBED* 's founders, heads up the unit and is deeply involved in the successful integration of the unit into Crowstone, maintaining both morale and profitability over the next year. The unit remains quite separate from most Crowstone influences, apart from some technology synergies and economies of scale, though there is a sense that more could be done to take advantage of the strengths of both the acquiring and acquired entities. The Board is somewhat surprised and impressed with the success of the acquisition and with Catherine.

In November of 1999, Damian Crowstone is killed in a skiing accident, and the Board, in shock, has to search for a new CEO. Crowstone's core business has continued to lose market share and the Board makes a dramatic choice for CEO. After a search both internally and externally, on April 1, 2000 they choose Catherine to lead the company and challenge her to merge the acquired unit totally into the Crowstone entity, and to pull what is best and most attractive out of the old E'*CUBED* into the rest of the company. Catherine, 36, is passionate about learning and the opportunities the merger brings for quantum growth both for her and for Crowstone.

Catherine's leadership team includes:
- *Tom,* VP Publishing Operations. Tom has been with Crowstone for 32 years, from the age of 20. He worked his way up from the press, is well liked and respected by Crowstone employees. He has contacts because of production issues with most customer accounts. In addition, he is close friends with two Board members, and has often been seen as embodying "the Crowstone way". He has expected, with some encouragement from his Board pals, that he would be selected CEO.
- *Trevor,* VP Business Development, a young Australian and ex-consultant who was hired primarily to determine who Crowstone should acquire. He found E'*CUBED* as the potential acquisition, was very involved in the deal, and in folding the new unit into Crowstone. He is a friend of one of the other E'*CUBED* founders. He is ambitious, smart, energetic, and very political.

- **Kwan,** VP Technology, was promoted to the Crowstone management team in the E'*CUBED* acquisition, and understands the E'*CUBED* culture. He is very excited about expanding the power of technology into more of Crowstone's processes, including supply chain management, HR, account management, and anywhere else it adds value. He already models the new values Catherine believes need to be embedded in the Crowstone culture. Catherine asks Kwan to head up the merger of the E'*CUBED* business unit into Crowstone.
- **Stephen,** VP Finance, has been with Crowstone for fifteen years. He has managed the finances for Crowstone and is highly regarded. His style, though, is one of high control and a high degree of centralization. He is very dedicated, highly ethical, works closely with the Board, and they trust him. More than simply a 'bean counter', he does most of the quantitative analysis and measurement of business processes and has established most of the business systems in the company.
- **Tracey,** VP HR and Communications, from Crowstone, is the other woman on the management team. She immediately bonds with the new President and becomes like an internal coach, filling her in on history and culture. Tracey has lots of change ideas but has not found a sponsor or an opportunity to implement them until now.

The First Year:

For the first few months, Catherine is on a steep learning curve…so much is new and time is critical. She establishes a relationship with each of her senior management team members. She assesses their competence and ability to work with and for her. She begins to understand the business and its drivers, particularly what's behind the loss of market share. She forms a preliminary vision and begins to talk about it in relation to the business issues to gather input and build commitment to change. She tries to get a sense of the Crowstone culture and what changes may be needed – she wants to be sure to honor the old but also build the new culture for the future.

During this time, Catherine has regular individual meetings with members of her team to get to know them, their aspirations and ideas. After two months, she holds a two-day retreat to feed back to them her learning so far and to shape the immediate agenda. All the while, she is observing, forming hunches about the management and leadership style and how the senior team has modeled the traditional Crowstone culture, and how this may need to be different.

Also during her first months as CEO, Catherine, along with many Crowstone employees, customers and Board members, talk openly about their shock and grief over Damian's death. But by the time of her second team retreat, her direct report team seems ready to get into the business strategy and how to shape Crowstone's future. Over the next months, Catherine also holds all-employee briefings so they can get to know her, she can get to know them, and she can talk openly about the business strategy. She is absorbing, learning everything, and talking about her preliminary vision of the business and the kinds of opportunities she sees. She describes her challenge in bringing the E'CUBED innovative working style into the rest of Crowstone, scaring some people and exciting a lot of others, not only the younger ones but also some people who had been feeling stifled in the traditional Crowstone culture. She talks about, and cynics frequently refer to, her intent to "CUBE" the culture. She talks openly about the fact that she was not brought up in the business, and is eager to hear from everyone, from the senior management team on down, about what people know, and what ideas they have. She values the front-line employee's input as much as the management team's. She uses broadcast emails, instant survey techniques, video streaming and web casts to keep the pulse of how people are feeling and to ensure she is both sharing with and learning with employees at all levels.

She spends the summer visiting all Crowstone's major accounts. She is testing her own view, developed during her time in the E'CUBED business unit, and supported by Trevor and his research into Best Practices, that the fundamental Value Discipline of Crowstone going forward has to be moving from an "Operational Excellence" view, with low cost production and streamlined processes, to a "Customer Intimate" discipline, where the unique requirements of each customer will be addressed. She takes Tom, the VP Operations, with her to visit one of their largest customers, to propose a different relationship to them. They are eager to commit to a "sole source provider" arrangement and value added pricing, in exchange for much more customization and customer reps located at the customer site. She comes back from this visit, feeling there is immediate proof the shift in business strategy will work. Hard on the heels of her return, however, the VP Sales walks to the competition taking with him two key sales reps…and several major accounts.

Catherine has had some difficulty with her leadership team, almost from the beginning. Tom (who really wanted and expected to get her job) supports her in public but is disparaging in private, including with his Board pals. Trevor is pushing, challenging her, a little disappointed that Catherine, and not some outsider, got the job. He's always testing her, without committing to her or her efforts to change the Crowstone culture and is always talking about the head hunters calling him. For all that, though, he has worked hard to understand the P&L of every major client, and worked with her on patterns of successful client relationships.

In the midst of all this, her "sloppy" leadership style, in the view of the traditionalists, is not as cautious, not as hierarchical, not as disciplined as it should be. She is viewed by some as making decisions too fast, before she knows the full implications. She's so keen to please the customers that she commits too much without knowing whether the company can deliver. Her team think she's not taking a broad enough strategic view of the business as a whole. She appears not to listen to Stephen, the head of Finance, and seems disinterested in the numbers. She trusts him, of course, as others do, but doesn't have her mind wrapped around the strategic role and the critical nature of the numbers in the business going forward. "That's what we pay you to worry about, Stephen!" He's afraid for the company!

After Catherine's first year in the job, in April 2001, the Board reviews her performance. The stock has flattened and the quarterly earnings are dropping, and Crowstone has continued to lose market share. The accounts lost with the VP Sales still rankle. The Board is getting nervous, especially after hearing from Tom's two cronies that people don't like her and don't think she's got what this business needs. In truth, these were the original dissenters in her selection – "'I told you so" – and feel they have Tom, their original choice, waiting in the wings. The Board impression for the most part seems to be that she's not really acting like a CEO and has not really grown into the job yet. Their view is that she has done a lot of soft things but not really nailed anything down yet. However, on balance they don't think they can give up on her quite yet so they re-examine the metrics and commit to a revised Balanced Score Card on which her own and all executive incentives are based. It has four components: Financial, Operational, Customer and Employee.

The bottom line: "Not terrible, not good enough." They agree her immediate challenges are:
–   To deal with her senior management team dysfunction.
–   To deal with the market slide.
–   To get her head around the numbers – at a deeper level, and with a strategic viewpoint.

Catherine and the Board agree that she will have another formal review in six months, rather than the year outlined in her contract.

The Last Six Months:

Catherine comes back from the Board review, determined to succeed, and learn the lessons from her first year. The Board has provided her with a coach. She immediately begins working with her coach to understand her strengths and weaknesses and how they will apply in this larger context. It is much more complex than the one she's grown up in and has a more diverse and changing business strategy. She begins to examine who she needs to strengthen relationships with, both inside and outside the company, and how she can build her team.

Working with her coach, Catherine realizes that her own leadership style has to change. While she may have been chosen for her embodiment of the E'*CUBED* culture, her coach helps her realize that it's the blend of the cultures and leadership styles that will take the integrated company forward. It must become a culture that is both disciplined and innovative, both customer-responsive and highly participative, both fast paced and leveraging its history. It's a culture that Catherine can comfortably embody and model in all her interactions. She also recognizes she needs to work much harder at her relationships with some of her key direct reports.

For example, Catherine wants very badly to work out her relationship with Tom, the Operations VP, if he is willing to commit. She makes a direct appeal to him to get beyond his disappointment that she was chosen to run the company. "I need you to stay, but more than stay, I need you to stay authentically – with full commitment to the strategy, to my leadership, to the team. You have several choices… you can retire; you can join the VP Sales, or some other organization. But I really want you to stay, recommitted, re-energized, transformed." The invitation is just what Tom has been hoping for – an appeal to really use his strengths, to value his experience, to be part of the company's future. Tom chooses to stay, committed to entering a different phase of his own growth. He starts to learn again for the first time in years. Catherine immediately senses the difference, and is willing to listen and work with him… "We're partners in this…"

One issue she begins to confront with the help of her coach is the issue of understanding the metrics and structure of the business. She knows intuitively that some of the accounts Crowstone has lost are actually not losses, when viewed against their long-term strategy. They were customer accounts that were in fact costing more than they were making. But she has to prepare the business case to prove that. She is delighted when Stephen approaches her. He can support her with an in-depth analysis. She is determined to understand the numbers so she can argue her case with quantitative logic. Stephen understands the strategy and vision of where Crowstone can go…he doesn't see himself as a Leader Coach but in fact takes on the role intuitively with Catherine. She has been trying to hide her discomfort with numbers by not getting too close to Stephen. She now realizes they can work side by side, in different but interconnected roles. She learns enough to understand how to talk confidently to the Board about the steps they have to take, including the message that some of the flagship accounts are not really profitable, and are detracting from the strategy. Crowstone needs to jettison them to move into a different future.

Catherine also starts to better manage the contact with the Board and to educate the Board about what the talent management challenge is all about. She has learned about being a 'Leader Coach' from her own coach and now understands that this is the leadership culture Crowstone needs for the future. While she might not have chosen to lose the three key sales people, the experience does teach Crowstone that it is necessary to develop a leadership development strategy that includes losing some people, especially if they do not fit the new culture, replacing them with those who do, promoting some unusual choices as they did with her, taking some risks, seeding the organization with change agents and Leader Coaches.

To that end, Catherine creates a Leader Coach council, which she continues to support, but does not always chair. People begin to want to get on this council…she selects the change agents and 'fire starters' to be a part of the council based on their past experience with change. With this group she talks about the vision, she hears from them about the barriers to change, and encourages and empowers them to act to change things in their own domains. Over time, the group expands to bring in "like" others, and is challenged to start their own peer networks in their own business units…always in reference to the desired strategy and change.

Employees beyond these councils are invited to be part of an extensive and participative process to explore values at both the personal and organizational levels. In the end, several hundred are involved in a series of open space and participative planning events. Here is one example of the kind of issue the values teams deal with. It becomes apparent that one of the core values of many long-service Crowstone Publishing employees is their dedication to quality which has been a cornerstone of the company's success. However, the new competitive realities and market opportunities prompt the leadership team to realize, "We can't afford the time it takes to get our 100% reliability in the future...our customers expect it, but they won't wait for it and won't pay for it."

While this is a difficult issue for some employees, they are customer-focused and, once they understand the situation, are motivated to find ways to improve. They are deeply involved in a process of dialogue to co-create a common vision of what quality means for the new Crowstone. Clearly, they have a choice....they can tinker with the current quality standards or they can look at work processes at a more fundamental level to make the company a lot more nimble and efficient. In a series of exercises, the employees commit to retaining the highest quality in customer service. Using cross functional teams working with Kwan's technology group, they dig into streamlining their work processes, especially the hand off points where problems have usually arisen. They examine their decision making processes and technical procedures, and decide to invest in an innovative technology that will provide them with faster quality control information at key points to reduce both time and cost. With few modifications, management agrees with the new design. In a final test of this shift, a group of employees meet with some customer representatives to articulate the changes and ensure there is a willingness both to learn and to revisit these processes on an ongoing basis.

Catherine isn't involved in this process or in the other values teams, other than as a sponsor; they are in fact orchestrated by the VP HR who understands the importance of employee engagement strategies and provides training, information, newsletters and other means to ensure the pipeline is always full of what is happening. The VP HR acts as a megaphone for the President, making sure the message gets out consistently in various media. She also works on the infrastructure to ensure that all HR programs and policies are re-aligned as the values shift. These supporting systems are designed to provide additional support to the culture changes Catherine and her leadership team are making (eg. Compensation, Performance Management, Coach Training).

With these changes, Stephen initiates discussions with the business unit heads about the need to decentralize the P&L into each product line. He has realized that it is not appropriate for him to control the finances of the business units. Instead, he recrafts his role to focus on corporate integration as well as sponsoring the training of the businesses in financial planning, forecasting and budgeting, the balanced scorecard and other business and financial planning systems. He has really enjoyed his coaching with Catherine and wants to extend that role to the business heads, coaching and modeling rather than controlling. In addition, now that he's engaged in the businesses rather than in the back room, he is able to support the recrafting of the customer strategy based on a more sophisticated analysis than a simple profitability formula. He is a true strategic partner with the business unit heads and tries to support their differentiation and customization to the greatest extent possible, rather than insisting on corporate control.

While Catherine has been working hard to realign internal structures and help focus the business units on adopting a more flexible culture and style with their customers, she has also realized that it will be some time before Crowstone can undertake any other major acquisition. This has major implications for Trevor, the VP Business Development. She addresses the fact that he's not got the role he thought, anymore, and they agree on terms for Trevor to leave Crowstone. She is practicing her "learning edge" to address and confront tough issues, rather than waiting for him to be headhunted, or a saboteur, doing damage inside the company. Trevor and Catherine part friends.

Giving Catherine confidence just before she returns to the Board for her six-month review is the capture of a major customer, which signals to the Board that she is able to deliver at least one short-term win, a deal with a major customer, and is gaining credibility for oversight of the whole business.

Your Turn – Preparing for the Board Meeting:

So that's the story. Catherine is now preparing for her six-month review with the Board. She's not really sure where they all stand on her performance and she wants to present a powerful case for their trust in her leadership. She feels like "the mess in the middle" – part way there but nowhere near the end. She wants to step back and look at the whirlwind of the last eighteen months since she became CEO and needs your help. Be Catherine's coach and advisor as she prepares for the Board review.

Analysis of Leadership Choice Points:

Catherine decides to look at the leadership choice points that influenced her appointment as CEO and her performance since she has been in the role.

She feels this analysis will help her to see the big picture and understand the impact of her own leadership decisions and those of others around her. As you reflect on the story, what do you think the major leadership choice points are? Use the following questions to structure your analysis.

1. What was the leadership situation leading to the choice?
2. Who was involved in making the choice?
3. What part did relationships play in making the choice?
4. What impact did the choice have?
5. What other options might have been selected?
6. Given your analysis, do you think this was the right leadership choice?

The first choice Catherine notes is that the Board hired a coach for her after her less than stellar initial year in her role. Her relationship with the Board was uneven at best and she had not paid sufficient attention to building their trust in her. Her coach has had a big impact on Catherine, focusing her on strengths and weaknesses that influence her success and helping her grow into her job. The Board might have simply fired her, or let her flounder… Catherine is appreciative of the move and feels a lot more confident that it was the right decision now than she did at the time.

What are some of the other leadership choice points that influenced the outcome of the story? If you were a Board member, what would your choice be about Catherine remaining in the CEO role?

Catherine's Leadership:

Catherine also wants to look at her leadership over the past couple of years with Crowstone. She has been working with her coach on becoming an "alchemic leader" and wants to assess her progress so far, so that she can talk to the Board about her development plans. How would you assess Catherine as an alchemic leader?

1. What are Catherine's strengths and weaknesses?
2. How did she use her strengths successfully?
3. What were the consequences of her weaknesses?
4. How did she change as she learned about her role?
5. What are her development edges now?

Catherine first notes that she is strong on strategy, having started E'CUBED with her two friends and been the strategist of the trio. She feels she has also used this strategic skill well at Crowstone, focusing on customer relationships and creating a more innovative culture. Do you agree? What do you see as Catherine's weaknesses and how did they affect her performance? Was she able to change, to improve? What should she be focusing on now for her development?

What other aspects of Catherine's leadership would you add, in relation to being an alchemic leader, and how would you advise her to concentrate her learning in the next year?

The Change Process:

Catherine also wants to report to the Board on her progress with merging E'*CUBED* into Crowstone, and particularly her attempts to bring the faster, more flexible culture into the traditional publishing company. She is a fan of John Kotter[1] and has decided to use his eight change steps to analyze not only what's happened but also how people have felt about it so far. Here are the eight change steps.

1.   Increasing Urgency
2.   Building the Guiding Team
3.   Getting the Vision Right
4.   Communicating for Buy-In
5.   Empowering Action
6.   Creating Short Term Wins
7.   Don't Let Up!
8.   Make Change Stick

Help Catherine evaluate her progress by identifying:
–   What, if anything, has been done on each step?
–   How have people felt about the actions taken?
–   What would you recommend doing more of, less of, or the same going forward?

Thinking about "Increasing Urgency", Catherine believed that the loss of market share and sharply declining revenue from the traditional Crowstone product lines were a significant factor in the acquisition of E'*CUBED*. The Board was concerned about the future, and employees and management were worried. This situation increased the urgency to make changes. However, under Damian Crowstone not much radical change was possible – it was only after his accidental death that the Board had the opportunity to put Catherine into the role with a mandate to make more dramatic changes in the culture. This both frightened and excited employees, depending on their point of view. Catherine realized from this reflection that she would have to keep the sense of urgency high if she were to complete the culture change process at Crowstone. As soon as complacency began to set in, her plans for a nimble, flexible organization would be lost.

Think about the remaining steps in leading change. Evaluate Catherine's progress using the points above and recommend what she needs to do next.

The Crowstone Story in Relation to Leadership Alchemy

We invite you now to join us in applying the concepts, contexts and processes we have discussed throughout the book to the Crowstone story. We have been building a case for the essential contribution Leader Coaches can make in organizational performance and effectiveness. See if you can use the Crowstone story as a way of grounding your learning, of applying it to a real situation. We've recapped the themes and important concepts from each of the previous chapters, not as a complete analysis but as a beginning that you can add to, agree or disagree with, change as you see fit, so that you will come away with your own alchemic combination, your own magic touch to the story, to our joint co-creation of the concept and experience of the Leader Coach.

Chapter 1 – Leadership Competencies in Turbulent Times:

Strategic Anticipation:
- Trevor, Business Development VP, sees in the E'*CUBED* acquisition the means to renew Crowstone.
- The Board shows courage and foresight in taking the risk of choosing Catherine as CEO.
- Catherine recasts the customer strategy as a way of regaining the lost market and revenue, and proves her point by making the key deal in time for her review with the Board.

Vision and Values:
- Catherine develops a vision of a nimble, flexible customer oriented organization.

- Catherine uses a participative values clarification process to engage employees in developing the future.
- Catherine encourages communication both ways to grow understanding of the vision.
- Catherine is authentic in expressing her emotions about Damian's death.

Empowering Others:
- The Leader Coach Council seeds the vision and values throughout the company.
- Financial analysis and forecasting is moved out to the business units.
- Catherine is clear about her expectations and gives others choices of whether to stay or not.
- There is continuous communication about the ongoing changes – making it a routine occurrence and using various media.

Learning and Change:
- The market share loss requires rethinking and relearning about what makes the business succeed.
- The acquisition and subsequent merger challenges assumptions in the traditional Crowstone – an example of "creative destruction" to rejuvenate and reposition the company.
- Everyone learns things they didn't know about themselves – the changes produced new awareness in Catherine, the VPs, the Board, etc.

Chapter 2 – Coaching Themes:

Deepening Context:
      The cultures of the two companies clash - they have different beliefs and assumptions based on their experiences in their settings; their inner contexts are also different - some see the changes as opportunity, others as threat; it brings out the ambition, blind spots and arrogance in the senior team.

Working through Stuckness:
      Tom, the VP Operations is stuck in the old culture where he has been successful, while knowing that the world has changed; it's very difficult to shake him loose – he needs an appeal from Catherine and a vision of a different kind of contribution to reframe his thinking and allow him to move forward.

Living on Purpose:

The fundamental business purpose has to change in response to a changing market, and each individual's purpose in contributing to the business has to change as well – Catherine has to stretch to get her arms around the whole business; Tom has to recast his role as heading up a customer organization; Stephen has to let go of control in order to see the business units grow.

Being in Service:

Those in power have to see themselves in service to the organization and not their own ambitions – Stephen is loyal to Crowstone in coming forward with his analysis of the customer account losses despite what he thinks of Catherine and her direction; Catherine needs to understand employees' feelings and spend time listening to their ideas and incorporating their values into the future focus for the company.

Using Conversations:

Key conversations are where the choices are made clear and explored – Catherine with members of her team; the Board with Catherine; Catherine with her coach. In the wider setting, Catherine's ongoing dialogues with her team and those in the whole organization also clarify vision, values, expectations and choices about possible futures for the company.

Sustaining Diversity:

Here, diversity is mostly about opinion and belief – what each believes about the 'other' and how that shifts over time and with experience. For example, the Board's expectations versus Catherine's about the way to build customer and employee relationships; the integration of Catherine and Kwan, both minorities, into the traditional male culture at Crowstone and the initial resistance it causes; and Catherine's initial feelings about the VPs of Operations and Finance as traditionalists who have eroded the company's potential with their old-fashioned ways.

Modeling Change:

The acquisition and merger; the competition and loss of market share; the loss of talent; the unexpected death of the CEO – these are all "normal" characteristics of working life in a turbulent world.

Continuous Learning:

The case highlights the need for continuous learning – about the new organization that is acquired, about how to blend the learning styles of the two different cultures, about how others learn best, and change best, according to their capacity for rapid and continuous learning. Catherine is the model – she sees the potential, has the experience of being a learner in a fast paced business, and brings it to Crowstone.

Reframing Paradox:

All members of the Board and senior management gain new self awareness through their failures and setbacks; they are able to reframe their relationships to make positive headway in the business – Catherine and her relationships with Stephen and Tom are an example.

Chapter 3 – Alchemic Competencies:

The Co-creation of Futures:
–   The inclusive values exercise open to all employees who wanted to participate.
–   The customer account deal that is developed out of a joint understanding of needs.
–   The 'learning journey' of each of the individuals in the story as they work with others to figure out how they fit, how they contribute, and what they need to learn from each other.

The Holographic Perspective:
–   The Board's initial mandate to Catherine, having identified her as the leader for the future, is to create a new culture at Crowstone and model it through her own leadership so that others can see, hear and feel its potential.
–   The values challenge and dialogue with employees at Crowstone builds both their understanding of the new culture and organization and also their commitment to it, how they may be part of the future or have to choose to move on.
–   In their performance discussion with Catherine, when they are not seeing the results they want, the Board's imperative is to push the principles, the values, through all the company's systems so that it will be holographic – the balanced score card, for instance, which will reward the right balance of factors.

Leadership through Heterarchy:
- Stephen, the VP Finance, is the leader on the account analysis, helping Catherine to learn about the numbers and their importance to her customer strategy.
- Tracey, the HR VP, takes the lead on many of the employee engagement strategies and carries Catherine's message out into the organization to disseminate the new culture.
- Kwan, the VP Technology, takes the lead on the merger with his passion for integrating the systems and extending them into new service areas.
- The Leader Coach Council that Catherine begins takes the lead in their own areas by talking about the potential and engaging people in being part of it, and for implementing the changes in their own business divisions, acting as models of the new culture.

Interdependence and Meaning:
- Tom, the VP Operations, unexpectedly finds new meaning in his work as the new organization unfolds, and decides to stay on to contribute to it – he is in a sense reborn into the new culture.
- Stephen, the VP Finance, maintains his passion for Crowstone throughout the changes; his loyalty and dedication are tested, but he finds meaning in his role and changes according to needs so that he can continue to play it.
- Tracey, the VP HR, is liberated through the transition. The meaning that she seeks is frustrated in the old Crowstone but set free by Catherine - she is able to stretch into her role and make significant contributions to the success of the turnaround.
- The Senior Management team, beginning as a collection of individuals with very different agendas, is able over time and as each individual gains their own place in the scheme of things, their independence, to then create an interdependent relationship where each relies on the other in their areas of strength, their relationships are solid and equitable, and they begin to model the leadership they expect to achieve throughout Crowstone.

Chapter 4 – Inside Out Competencies:

Alchemic Competencies	Core Competencies "Being" in Spirit	Emotional Competencies "Feeling" with Heart	Cognitive Competencies "Thinking" with the Mind	Practical Competencies "Doing" from the Body
Co-creation of Futures	Catherine's passion for learning Crowstone's business and helping it achieve its potential	The courage of Catherine's convictions in making commitments to customers to serve their needs	Catherine's strategic ability – she sees the way into the future and goes for it	Building the employee engagement processes for defining values and direction
Holographic Perspective	Catherine sticks to her values despite her early failures – she grows more self aware as she learns on the job	Catherine cares deeply about her team and the employees – she wants them to be congruent with her values	Catherine's difficulty seeing herself as part of the Crowstone system – she has to grow into her role	The Board feels Catherine embodies the new values they want to see in Crowstone
Leadership Through Heterarchy	Catherine comes to see how important her connection to her team and their leadership is to her success	Employees feel excited and emboldened to take the new culture into their own work settings	Catherine communicates constantly in various media and seeks employees' ideas and input	The Leader Coach Council develops a new cadre of leaders aligned with the new values and culture
Inter-Dependence and Meaning	Catherine seeks unique relation-ships with members of her team and learns personally from each of them	Employees experience hopes, fears, doubts, worries but work together to co-create the future	Tom and Stephen both find new meaning in work through the changes in their roles	Catherine builds new alliances with customers across the old Crowstone cultural boundaries

Chart 19: An Analysis of Alchemic Competencies in the Crowstone Story

Chapter 6 – Outside In Contexts:

Scale and Depth	Individual	Team	Organization
Adaptation	Fine-tuning: Catherine and Trevor reaching an amicable agreement for him to leave	Enhancing: Catherine and her team – the first 6 months of getting to know each other	Improving: Catherine and Tracey, VP HR, on communication and involvement strategies for employees
Renewal	Orienting: Catherine using her coach to stretch into her role as CEO	Integrating: Catherine and her team - the second 6 months of sorting out working relationships	Incorporating: Disseminating the new directions through the Leader Coach Council
Transformation	Re-establishing: Catherine and Stephen recasting their relationship	Creating: Catherine transforming her relationship with the Board over time	Radical Change: Catherine using the values exercise as a means of changing the culture

Chart 20: An Analysis of Issues in the Crowstone Context

Chapter 7 - The Coaching Process:

Building Trust:
- Catherine holding two retreats with the senior team, first to get to know them and then to work on business strategies.
- Catherine establishing a vision based on dialogue with others.
- Catherine showing open emotion about the sudden death of Damian Crowstone.
- Catherine taking a learning stance to situations for the first several months, showing that she is interested in the views of employees from bottom to top.
- Using customer and employee meetings to learn and listen, Catherine familiarizes herself with the issues and engenders trust.

Building Awareness:

- Catherine discussing the limited role for Trevor, VP Business Development, in the near future and working out arrangements for him to move on.
- Reframing Catherine's relationship with Tom, VP Operations, so that he finds new meaning in his work and decides to stay.
- Catherine coming to new awareness about her disregard for Stephen and his critical role in analysis and planning, and learning to appreciate his contribution.
- Catherine's first Board review, thinking she is doing well, when she is given her "imperatives" and six months to prove herself.

Building the Future:

- Catherine using "co-creating" strategies with members of her senior team to model the new culture.
- Developing a new customer strategy to take account of new competitive realities and go after the truly important accounts.
- Building a sense of the future through the values exercise with all employees where they have a say in the culture and values of the "new" Crowstone.
- Beginning to implement the new culture throughout the systems and policies, on the recommendation of the Board, so that they will be in alignment with values.

So, this is a little of our analysis. We hope you have been able to add your own insights and ideas to the mix. You might now want to try this exercise with your own organization. How does your leadership and the leadership of your organization reflect our alchemic leadership principles? Where are the strengths? Where are the gaps? How can you coach yourself, and the other leaders in your organization, about what needs to be done to build a more robust both/and leadership coaching capability for the turbulent change in your world? Have a go…

Endnotes:

[1] Kotter, John. *Leading Change* and *The Heart of Change*, Harvard Business School Press, 1996 and 2002.

Part Four:
The Rallying Cry

The Invitation

Now you know a little about this metaphor of alchemy...that it's about experimenting, and never giving up, and blending things and trying things, and seeing things from new perspectives....

And you know that our wish is to include you, actively, uniquely, authentically, in the co-creation of the concept. We've put out in this book what we think the notion of a Leader Coach is about – we've described its antecedents in leadership and coaching writing. We've described how it might show up in the world, and how you might find yourself experiencing the world, as a Leader Coach.

So, in closing we have an invitation, or rather two invitations, for you. The first is to 'go in', and the second is to 'go out', and we'll explain what we mean by both of these.

Going In:

Reading a book, reflecting on your own management, leadership and coaching experiences, learning about ours...has, we hope, engaged your mind in an excursion into a new kind of leadership. But we know the entity of a human being is a complex interplay not only of the mind, but also the body, the spirit and the heart. We therefore encourage you to continue to check in with yourself routinely during your day, not only what's on your mind, but what your heart and spirit and body are telling you as well. We hope you will continue to journal or meditate or do whatever suits you to balance your life and work across all four of these dimensions of the self as you continue to learn and grow into your unique Leader Coach style.

Going Out:

Reading a book is also a fairly passive and one-way experience, traditionally. We would like to shift that pattern, and invite you to do two things.

One is to engage in your own development, starting now, with the people you lead, the people you coach, the people with whom you are in relationship in the workplace, the community… to experiment, to practice, to try it out and take a few risks, to see how you feel and what you can learn. We know from our own experience that leadership coaching isn't something you can do by reading or watching others or talking about it – you have to get out there and try it on for size.

And the other, following on from those experiments, is to be a part, with us, of a learning community that continues the exploration of these ideas. We know that dialogue takes at least two, and we've really been dominating the conversation. So now, it truly is your turn. We'd like to hear from you, your stories of how your experiments have gone, your thoughts about the models and proposals we have put forward here, your learnings as you apply some of these concepts in your own roles.

We want to ensure that both we as authors, and this book as our 'nestling', model what we've been saying about co-creation. This idea is no longer ours - it goes out into the world, and is changed! It is changed already by the very act of being sent out, and it is transmuted again as it is encountered through your filters and biases, assumptions and truths.

We have a number of ways in which we want to engage you in this dialogue, this path of discovery we're all on, and we're hoping you will have some ideas of your own.

We have set up a chat room on the **www.thecoachingproject.com** website, facilitated by the authors, at least to start, with blogs and wikis to support various topics to explore. We're hoping that you will want to share your experiences, your reactions, your questions, your learnings, with the rest of this community. We also intend to provide links to both practitioners and organizations who are working to understand leadership coaching.

We at The Coaching Project are preparing a Fieldbook to further make the concepts here ones you can experiment with, and implement, in the workplace. We welcome stories of your experience, both successful and not, to add to our collection. You can also reach us at **info@thecoachingproject.com.**

We are planning a gathering of people of like minds, to be held in 2004 in Niagara-on-the-Lake, Ontario, in conjunction with the Leadership Coaching Development Program, in partnership with the Niagara Institute and the Conference Board in Canada. More information on the program can be found on our website.

We also welcome your additional comments and suggestions on how to share and continue to explore these ideas.

Epilogue

She was ready to begin.

…she put down the book. Her journal was now full of her scribblings, her experiments, her reflections on how she was learning to be a Leader Coach. At one level, she was more familiar now with the magic, the alchemy that was created by the intermingling of leadership and coaching. At a deeper level, it was as mysterious as ever. She knew she was on a lifelong path of discovery. She was filled with a deep humility about the opportunities presented to her, to co-create futures with those she worked with. She knew she would embody at every turn the vision and values that defined who she was and how she added value in her organization and in her community. She could feel in her sense of self a growing strength and determination to live a totally congruent life, one where the alchemic mixture was constantly being stirred.

She knew there were moments when she fell short of her own goal of integrity and congruence. She knew as well that her aim was to model a leader coach learning and growing. The quest would never be over, and much like Isaac Newton, she would both be in the world of commerce and in the world of learning, the rest of her life.

"In the crescent moon furnace, jade flowers grow;
in the cinnabar crucible, quicksilver is level.
Only after harmonization by means of great strength
can you plant the yellow sprout, which gradually develops"…

Appendix I - A Development Plan Template

The clearer you can be about your development need, the better your chances of success. As you review your notes from the reflections and exercises at the end of each chapter, what are the themes, the key learnings that give shape to your development priorities? Don't skip over the first three questions below – take the time to really understand the need and the goal. It is usually best to limit yourself to a maximum of three areas to work on at once, especially if your development involves behavior change. Otherwise, you will lack the concentration needed to accomplish your objectives. Having a written development plan significantly increases your odds of success. Here is a simple template you can use to get you started.

Description of Current Performance or Behavior:
(What is happening now that you want to change?)

a)

b)

c)

Description of Desired Performance or Behavior:
(What would the ideal outcome of your development look like?)

a)

b)

c)

Description of the Gap:
(What is causing the problem? What's missing? What needs to be done?)

a)

b)

c)

Action Steps and Timelines:
(What will you do, by when, to close the gap?)

a)

b)

c)

Description of Required Resources:
(What resources will you use? Who will give you feedback on your progress?)

a)

b)

c)

Bibliography

Argyris, C. and Schon, D. *Organizational Learning: A Theory of Action Perspective.* Addison-Wesley, 1978.

Ashby, W.R. "Self-Regulation and Requisite Variety", in *"Systems Thinking"*. Fred Emery, Ed. Penguin Books, 1978.

Bateson, Mary Catherine. *Composing a Life.* Plume/Penguin, 1990.

Benedict Bunker, Barbara and Billie Alban. *Large Group Interventions: Engaging the Whole System for Rapid Change.* Jossey Bass, 1997.

Blake, R.R. and J.S. Mouton. *The Managerial Grid.* Gulf Publishing, 1964.

Block, Peter. *Stewardship: Choosing Service over Self-Interest.* Berrett-Koehler, 1996.

Bourgeault, Cynthia. *A Short Course on Wisdom.* Praxis, 2002.

Boyatzis, R. *The Competent Manager: A Model of Effective Performance.* Wiley-Interscience, 1982.

Briggs, Katherine C. and Isabel Briggs-Myers. *An Introduction to Type.* Consulting Psychologists Press, 1987.

Byrd, R.E. "Corporate Leadership Skills: A New Synthesis", *Organizational Dynamics,* 34-43, Summer 1987.

Campbell, Joseph. "Dream Symbolism in Relation to Alchemy", in *The Portable Jung*. Joseph Campbell Editor, Viking, 1971.

Collins, Jim. "Level 5 Leadership: The Triumph of Humility and Fierce Resolve", *Harvard Business Review* #20101D, January 2001.

Cashman, Kevin. *Leadership from the Inside Out: Seven Pathways to Mastery.* Executive Excellence, 1998.

Crane, Thomas G. *The Heart of Coaching.* FTA Press, 1998.

Collins, Jim. *Good to Great: Why Some Companies Make the Leap and Others Don't.* Harper Collins, 2001.

Dannemiller, Kathleen. *Whole Scale Change: Unleashing the Magic in Organizations.* Berrett-Koehler, 2000.

Deal, Terrence and Lee Bolman. *Leading with Soul: An Uncommon Journey of the Spirit.* Wiley, 2001.

Dror, Yehezdel. "Planning as Fuzzy Gambling: A Radical Perspective on Coping with Uncertainty", in *Planning in Turbulence*, David Morley and Arie Shachar Eds. The Magnes Press, The Hebrew University, 1986.

Durrell, Lawrence. *The Alexandria Quartet.* Saber, 1958.

Emery, Merrelyn and Ronald Purser. *The Search Conference: A Powerful Method for Planning Organizational Change and Community Action.* Jossey-Bass, 1996.

Fiedler, F.W. "The Contingency Model: New Directions for Leadership Utilization", *Journal of Contemporary Business* 3(4): 65-79, 1974.

Flaherty, James. *Coaching – Evoking Excellence in Others.* Butterworth Heinemann, 1999.

Frankl Viktor. *Man's Search for Meaning.* Beacon, 2000.

Goleman, Daniel. *Emotional Intelligence.* Bantam, 1998.

Goleman, Daniel. *Primal Leadership*. Harvard Business Review Press, 2002.

Greenleaf, Robert K. *Servant Leadership*. Paulist Press, 1983.

Hammond, Sue. *The Thin Book of Appreciative Inquiry*. Thin Book Publishing, 1996.

Harvard Business Review: "Breakthrough Leadership: It's Personal", *Harvard Business Review*, Special Edition, December 2001.

Hersey P. and K.H. Blanchard. "Life Cycle Theory of Leadership", *Training and Development Journal*, May 1969.

Hesselbein, Frances, Marshall Goldsmith, Richard Beckhard Eds. *The Leader of the Future*. The Drucker Foundation. Jossey-Bass, 1997.

Hargrove, Robert. *Masterful Coaching*. Pfeiffer, 1995.

Hock, Dee. "The Art of Chaordic Leadership", in *Leader to Leader*, Volume 15, The Drucker Foundation, Jossey-Bass, 2000.

Hollenbeck George P. "Coaching Executives: Individual Leader Development", in *The 21st Century Executive: Innovative Practices for Building Leadership at the Top*. Jossey-Bass, 2000.

Hudson, Frederic. *The Adult Years*. Jossey-Bass, 1991.

Hunt, James and Joseph Weintraub, *The Coaching Manager*. Sage, 2002.

Jaques. Elliott. *Requisite Organization*. Cason Hall, 1989.

Kotter, John. *The Heart of Change*. Harvard Business School Press, 2002.

Kotter, John. *Leading Change*, Harvard Business School Press, 1996.

Leider, Richard. *Whistle While you Work*. Berrett-Koehler, 2001.

Likert, R. *The Human Organization*. McGraw-Hill, 1961.

Lombardo, Mike and Bob Eichinger. *The Leadership Machine*. Lominger Ltd., 2001.

Luft, Joseph and Harry Ingham. *Of Human Interaction*. University of California Western Training Laboratory. National Press, 1969 (originally published in 1955).

Mandl, Alex and Deepak Sethi. "Either/Or Yields to the Theory of Both", in *The Leader of the Future*. Frances Hesselbein, Marshall Goldsmith, Richard Beckhard (Eds.), The Drucker Foundation, Jossey-Bass, 1997.

Manuel, F.E. *The Religion of Isaac Newton*. Oxford University Press, 1974.

McGregor, D. *The Human Side of Enterprise*. McGraw-Hill, 1960.

Mintzberg, Henry. *The Structuring of Organizations*. Prentice Hall, 1978.

Miscisin, Mary. *Showing Your True Color*. True Colors Inc., 2001.

Morgan, Gareth. *Riding the Waves of Change: Developing Managerial Competencies for a Turbulent World*. Jossey Bass, 1989.

Moss Kanter, Rosabeth. *When Giants Learn to Dance*. Touchstone Books, 1990.

O'Neill, Mary Beth. *Executive Coaching with Backbone and Heart*. Jossey-Bass, 2000.

Owen, Harrison. *Open Space Technology: A User's Guide*. Abbott Publishing, 1992.

Peck, Scott. *The People of the Lie: The Hope for Healing Human Evil*. Touchstone Books, 1983.

Po-tuan, Chang. "Understanding Reality", in *The Taoist Classics*. (tr. Thomas Cleary). Shambhala, 1999.

Quinn, Robert E. *Deep Change: Discovering the Leader Within*. Jossey-Bass, 1996.

Rogers, Carl. *On Becoming a Person*. Houghton Mifflin, 1961.

Ross, Rick. "The Ladder of Inference", in Peter Senge et al. *The Fifth Discipline Fieldbook: Strategies and Tools for Building a Learning Organization.* Currency/Doubleday, 1994.

Rowling, J.K. *Harry Potter and the Sorcerer's Stone.* Scholastic, 1997.

Senge, Peter. *The Firth Discipline: The Art and Practice of the Learning Organization.* Doubleday, 1994.

Silzer, R. (Ed.) *The 21st Century Executive: Innovative Practices for Building Leadership at the Top.* Jossey-Bass, 2000.

Spencer, M. Signe, and M. Lyle. *Competence at Work: Models of Superior Performance.* John Wiley, 1993.

Taylor, S., L. Klein, B.Lewis, T. Gruenewald, R. Gurung, J. Updegraff. "Female Responses to Stress: Tend and Befriend, not Fight or Flight", Psychological Review 107 (3) 41-49, 2000.

Tannenbaum, R. and W.H. Schmidt. "How to Choose a Leadership Pattern", *Harvard Business Review* 36: 95-101, 1958.

Tennyson, Alfred, Lord "Ulysses" in *An Anthology of Verse*: Oxford University Press, 1964.

Trist, Eric and Fred Emery. "The Causal Texture of Organizational Environments", *Human Relations* 13(1): 21-32, 1965.

Weisbord, Marv and Sandra Janoff. *Future Search: An Action Guide to Finding Common Ground in Organizations and Communities.* Berrett-Koehler, 1995.

Whyte, David. *The Heart Aroused: Poetry and the Preservation of the Soul in Corporate America.* Doubleday, 1994.

Wright, Susan and David Morley. *Learning Works: Searching for Organizational Futures.* ABL Publications, 1998.

Zimbardo, P.G. in an interview with S. Carpenter, *Journal of Counseling and Development,* 2001.

Index